The San Francisco Seals,
1946–1957

The San Francisco Seals, 1946–1957

Interviews with 25 Former Baseballers

BRENT KELLEY

McFarland & Company, Inc., Publishers

Jefferson, North Carolina, and London

ISBN 0-7864-1188-0 (softcover : 50# alkaline paper)

Library of Congress Cataloguing data are available

British Library cataloguing data are available

Cover photograph: Ferris Fain *(Author's collection)*

Manufactured in the United States of America

*McFarland & Company, Inc., Publishers
Box 611, Jefferson, North Carolina 28640
www.mcfarlandpub.com*

For Lynn Hutchings
If she was only a baseball fan she'd be perfect

Table of Contents

Introduction

I find it amazing that there are people out there who have never heard of the San Francisco Seals. I shouldn't be surprised at this, yet I always am. I told a friend — a baseball fan — that I was writing a book about the Seals and he said, "I didn't know you liked marine life." I sometimes forget that the team has been gone for nearly half a century now and that some people were not even born when there were Seals.

I was going to play for the Seals. The Seals didn't know this, but I was. I decided that when I was 11 or 12 in the early 1950s.

We lived in Los Altos, about 35 miles south of San Francisco. The highlight of a sunny summer weekend was persuading my stepfather or big brother to take me to a Seals game, or maybe an Oaks game, but Seals was better. For one thing, Seals Stadium was, in my opinion at least, far superior to the Emeryville ballpark in which the Oaks played. (It was warmer in Oakland, though.)

I never got to play for the Seals, though. When I was old enough, the Seals didn't exist anymore. I remember when it was officially announced that the Giants were moving to San Francisco. All of my friends were excited about major league baseball coming west. Heck, the Seals were major league as far as I was concerned. And if the Giants were coming to San Francisco, what would happen to the Seals? My friends didn't care, but I did.

In 1959 I was invited to Seals Stadium to throw for Giants pitching coach Bill Posedel. As I was throwing in the bullpen I thought of Bill Bradford and Adrian Zabala and Windy McCall and all the times I had seen them doing the same thing that I was doing then. Man, I was in *Seals* Stadium! (Posedel asked me about my military obligation. I had just enlisted in the Marine Corps and had to report in two weeks. "Keep in touch," he said, but I figured if I was a prospect the Giants would find me. They didn't.)

1

But even with no Seals, I was still a Seals fan. I followed Frank Malzone and Jack Spring and Bill Werle and Albie Pearson and any other Seals alumnus in the majors or elsewhere in the Coast League. Ted Bowsfield, Eli Grba, Marty Keough. Lou Burdette.

As time passed, thoughts of the Seals lessened but still lingered in the back of my mind. How many were left? I wondered. And I learned the answer: not many. I began looking for them and calling the ones I could find.

And from that grew this book. It will never make any bestseller lists, but I'll be satisfied if everyone who lives in San Francisco buys a copy.

I need to thank several people. First, thanks to all the former players who took the time to talk with me. And thanks to the people who helped me with photographs. Doug McWilliams has helped me before and Robert Zwissig came through with a bunch.

Jim Rebollini researched the stats, digging them out of old baseball annuals. It's a pain, but each time I asked for "Just one more player," he came through without complaint. To me, anyhow; he may well have complained to his wife about the guy in Kentucky who is never satisfied.

And I want to thank the fans who remember the Seals and who shared their memories.

CHAPTER 1

1903–1945:
The Beginning
through World War II

The San Francisco Seals were a charter member of the Pacific Coast League upon its founding in 1903. It was a six-team league then, with other franchises being located in Los Angeles, Sacramento, Seattle, Portland, and Oakland. Franchises came and went and it wasn't until 1919 that it became an eight-team league, which it remained through 1957, although there were some franchise shifts along the way. (The PCL is vastly different in size, cities, and quality today. We end our consideration of it in 1957, the year before major league baseball moved into its two main cities, Los Angeles and San Francisco.)

The Seals won the team's first pennant in 1909. It was a runaway victory, 13½ games over Portland. Frank Browning (32–16) and Cack Henley (31–10) led the pitching staff, and Henry Melchior (.298) led the league in hitting. In 1910, Ping Bodie's 30 home runs led the league and set a new record, and Hunky Shaw led the league in batting with a .281 average, the lowest batting average ever to lead. Henley went 34–19. In 1913, the fourth-place Seals' James Johnston set the PCL record for stolen bases with 124.

The Seals won another pennant in 1915 by five games over Salt Lake City. Harry Heilmann batted .364 on his way to the Hall of Fame. Spider Baum went 30–15. The next pennant came in 1917 by a mere two games over Los Angeles. Eric Erickson won the pitcher's Triple Crown: 31 wins, 1.93 ERA, and 307 strikeouts. Before the next season began Charlie Graham, a former catcher, bought the team.

The 1920s saw the Seals win the championship four times, in 1922, '23, '25, and '28. The 1922 team beat Vernon by four games. From that

Seals Stadium in the 1930s (author's collection).

team, third baseman Willie Kamm (20-124-.342) was sold to the Chicago White Sox for $100,000 and center fielder Jimmy O'Connell (.335) went to the New York Yankees for $75,000. Jim Scott went 25–9 and Willis Mitchell 24–7 to pace the pitchers.

The '23 team beat Sacramento by 11 games. Rookie outfielder Paul Waner batted .369. Robert Geary, who was a 20-game winner for each of the Seals' championship teams in the '20s, and John Shea won 20 games.

Waner batted .401 in 1925 as the Seals ran away by 17½ games over Salt Lake City. There were four 20-game winners: Geary, Mitchell, Doug McWeeney, and Guy Williams. Mitchell, in addition to his pitching, batted .308.

But in 1926 the Seals plummeted to last, 36 games behind champion Los Angeles. The cellar was not to be visited again for 25 years. Debuting in '26 were Earl Averill (.348) and Smead Jolley (.346). Jolley led the PCL in batting (.397) and RBIs (163) in '27, and then in '28 the Seals were on top again by eight games over Hollywood and Jolley won the Triple Crown (45-188-.404). Averill went 36-174-.354. Dutch Ruether (29–7) led the league in wins. Seventeen year old shortstop Frank Crosetti joined the team.

In 1929 second baseman Gus Suhr belted 51 home runs to set a franchise record that was never broken. He did not lead the league, however; Ike Boone hit 55 and won the Triple Crown for Mission that year. Suhr later enjoyed a ten-year major league career as an All-Star first baseman. He remembers the '29 season: "I played in every game, every inning of every game." That durability eventually led him to the National League record for consecutive games. He led the PCL in runs in '29 with 196, the all-time record for the Seals.

Also in 1929, 18 year old Lefty Gomez won 18 games. In 1930 Crosetti (27-113-.334), still only 20, had the best year of his career on his way to a 17-year run with the New York Yankees.

The next pennant was in 1931 when the Seals beat Hollywood by three games. Sam Gibson had 28 victories and struck out 204 with a 2.48 ERA to win the pitching Triple Crown. The team's batting average was .314, tops in the league, and they set a new league record with114 triples. Prince Oana (23-161-.345), the first Hawaiian to play in the major leagues, and Crosetti, in his last year with the Seals, batted .343 with 143 RBIs, led the potent offense.

This was the debut season for Seals Stadium. Before 1931 they had played in Recreation Park. The stadium was the home of the Seals from 1931 through 1957. From 1931 through 1937, it also was the home field for the San Francisco Missions, also of the Pacific Coast League. And it was the home of the Giants for the seasons of 1958 and 1959. The park was built with three clubhouses, one for the Seals, one for the Missions, and one for the visiting team.

The first base line paralleled Bryant Street, right field to center field ran parallel to 16th Street, center field to left field was parallel to Potrero Avenue, and the third base foul line was parallel to Alameda Street. This was the northwestern portion of the Mission district.

Seals Stadium was a single deck concrete and steel ballpark without a roof over any of the seats, which curved around home plate and extended down both foul lines. In 1946, bleachers were added in right field and in 1951 there were bleachers in left field. More left field bleachers were added in 1958 when the Giants moved in.

The dimensions were 365 feet down the lines and 404 to 424 feet to straightaway center field. The left field line was reduced to about 340 feet when bleachers were added in1951. The Seals almost annually were last in the PCL in home runs due to these far away fences. After 1931 there would be no more huge home run totals by Seals players; Gus Suhr's 1929 team record would be forever safe.

Seventeen-year-old Frank Crosetti in 1928 (author's collection).

Vince DiMaggio played for the '32 Seals and he asked the team to give a tryout to his 17-year-old little brother Joe. As a rookie in '33, Joe set a PCL record with a 61-game hitting streak and he led the league in RBIs with 169 (with 28 home runs and a .340 average).

In 1935 the Seals won another pennant in Lefty O'Doul's first season as manager. They beat Los Angels by 5½ games. Joe DiMaggio led the PCL

Lefty O'Doul in his playing days (author's collection).

Joe DiMaggio scoring a run in the mid–1930s (author's collection).

in RBIs (154) and runs (173), and batted .398 (second to Mission's Ox Eck-hardt, who batted .399) with 34 home runs, the all-time Seals Stadium record. Gibson won 22 games and lost only 4. In his 12 years as a Seal he won 210 games, lost only 123, and had six 20-win seasons.

The third DiMaggio brother, Dominic, joined the Seals in 1937 and batted .306. In 1939, his .360 average was second in the league to San Diego's Dom Dallessandro (.368) and the next year he became a fixture in the Boston Red Sox outfield.

Another pennant would not come until 1946, but the team won the Governor's Cup in 1943, '44, and '45. Bob Joyce was the ace in those three years, winning 20, 21, and 31 games. Lefthander Tom Seats won 25 in 1944. Henry Steinbacher (2-105-.318) led the offense in '43 and Bill Enos (.346) was the big hitter in '45.

And that brings us up to 1946, where this book really begins.

◆ CHAPTER 2 ◆

1946:
The Best Ever?

First place: W 115 L 68 .628 4 games ahead
Governor's Cup
First round: San Francisco over Hollywood, 4 games to 0
Second round: San Francisco over Oakland, 4 games to 2

Even though the Seals had won the previous three Governor's Cups, the team had not actually finished in first place in league play since 1935. Some purists even said their last *real* league title came in 1926 because the '35, '31, and '28 titles came when the league played split season schedules.

In the preseason, the 1946 team was considered to be strong, but was only considered to be one of perhaps four that could contend for the pennant. The war was over and returning players strengthened teams at all levels of baseball. The Seals benefited in this manner, but another new face to the team also played a major role.

Paul I. Fagan, a millionaire whose fortune was derived from banking, shipping, and Hawaiian pineapple, bought a partial interest in the team from Charlie Graham. Initially it was believed that Fagan would be a silent partner and Graham would continue to run the team, but that was far from the case.

Fagan's goal was the major leagues, not just for the Seals but for the rest of the PCL as well. He began this quest by upgrading Seals Stadium to major league levels.

He had the previously unpainted ballpark painted forest green. The ads on the outfield fences were removed and the fences, too, were painted solid green. The right field fence was shortened from 385 feet to 350 feet and bleachers were added in right field, increasing seating capacity by 2,000.

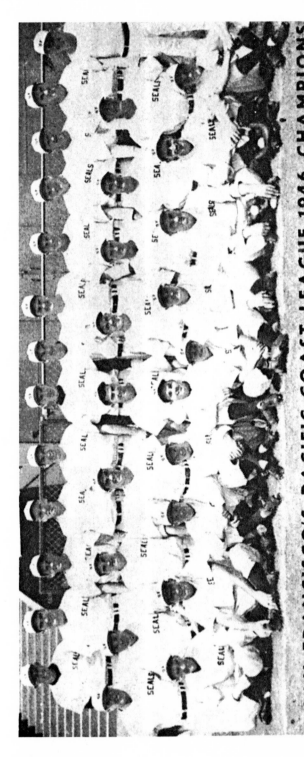

SAN FRANCISCO'S PACIFIC COAST LEAGUE 1946 CHAMPIONS

Back Row, left to right: Cliff Melton, Rino Restelli, Joe Sprinz, Al Lien, Bill Werle, Bones Sanders, Larry Jansen, Frank Seward, Ray Harrell, Doug Loane, Jim Tobin, Emmett O'Neil, Trainer Leo Hughes.

Second Row: Manager Frank "Lefty" O'Doul, Bernie Uhalt, Don White, Sal Taormina, Ted Jennings, Roy Nicely, Joe Hoover, Mel Ivy, Del Young.

Front Row: Ed Stutz, Neill Sheridan, Bruce Ogrodowski, Don Trower, Ferris Fain, Mascot "Winky" Morris, Hugh Luby, Frank Rosso, Vince DiMaggio, "Chuck" Mazzen, Ball Boy.

1946 PCL champion Seals (courtesy Richard T. Dobbins collection).

The clubhouses were upgraded. Shoeshine stands and a barbershop were added. Flower boxes were placed in the office windows. Uniformed female ushers were hired to show the fans to their seats. The wire backstop was replaced by Plexiglas (which, for several reasons, proved to be a bust).

And to make the operation major league in all respects, he raised the team's minimum salary to $5,000, the same as that in the major leagues.

Fagan's efforts and the Seals' excellent play paid off handsomely. The team set an all-time minor league attendance record with 670,568 fans paying to see the games. This record stood for nearly four decades. It was a great year for attendance in the Bay Area as the Seals and Oaks combined for more than 1.3 million in paid attendance.

Fagan flew the team to Maui for 1946 spring training. There were those who warned that rain and lack of competition would prevent the team from being properly prepared, but the weather was beautiful and a

Seals Stadium with part of the record-setting minor league attendance in 1946 (author's collection).

team of local all-stars was formed to give the Seals the competition they needed. And at the end of spring training, the Philadelphia Athletics flew to Honolulu to play a four-game exhibition series with the Seals. The Coast League team defeated the major league team in all four games.

When the '46 season got underway, the Seals had Cliff Melton, Ray Harrell, Frank Rosso, and Hugh Luby from the New York Giants. These were in payment for Bob Joyce, the 31-game winner of 1945. Back from the military were Bill Werle, Al Lien, Don Trower, and Ferris Fain — and Larry Jansen, who had been frozen on the farm rather than drafted into the service, was also back.

Fain at first base was the offensive leader, backed solidly by Luby, Don White, Neill Sheridan, Ted Jennings, and Sal Taormina. Luby at second base and Roy Nicely at shortstop were a solid double play combination. Fain had been a Seal before the war, from 1939 through 1942, and he had been a .240 hitter. In '46, however, he showed the form that would eventually make him a two-time American League batting champion. He batted .301 with a league-leading 112 RBIs.

Jansen won 30 regular season games, the last PCL hurler to do so, and added two more in the playoffs. Melton won 17, Frank Seward 15, and a total of six pitchers won in double figures.

Jansen had been a useful pitcher for the Seals before the war, winning 16 games in 1941 and 11 in '42, but he showed nothing that would hint at the pitcher he was in '46. He was allowed to work his farm instead of being drafted, and in late 1945 he was told he could return to the Seals.

While on the farm in Oregon he played for a local semi-pro team. Jansen explains his emergence as a great pitcher: "A couple of things happened to

Manager Lefty O'Doul (courtesy of Don Trower).

me. In 1942, the last year I had played, Larry Woodall, who was a coach, taught me how to throw a slider. I was having a lot of trouble. I wasn't fast. I had a curveball and a changeup, but he said I was gonna need another pitch if I was gonna keep pitching 'cause the hitters were all sitting back waiting for me. I was just starting to master the slider when the season was over. During the summers up here, I played ball twice a week and was working on the slider all the time and by the time I got back in '46 I had it mastered to a tee. I had great control of it."

In addition to his league-leading 30 wins, he led in ERA (1.57, the second lowest in PCL history) and winning percentage (.833).

As the season entered the home stretch, it was the Seals and the cross-bay Oakland Oaks fighting it out for the

Top: Pitcher Cliff Melton in spring training in Hawaii, 1946 (courtesy Richard T. Dobbins collection). *Left:* Joe Sprinz, longtime Seals catcher and coach (author's collection).

top spot. The Oaks took a percentage points lead in late August, but it lasted only 24 hours. In the end, the Seals prevailed by four games. Their 115 wins were the most by a Seals team since 1928.

In the playoffs, the Seals swept the third place Hollywood Stars, four games to none. Jansen won game one, 8–0, with help in the form of two RBIs from

Sheridan. Lien won game two, 3–2. Werle won game three, 7–5, in relief. Sheridan had two hits, including a home run, but the winning runs scored on a two-run double by Frenchy Uhalt, who pinch hit for Sheridan in the eighth inning. The sweep was completed when Jansen won game four, 6–5, in relief. He also homered and Taormina drove in two runs.

Sheridan batted .571 in the series, and reserve Trower, platooned with Jennings at third base, batted .667.

The Oaks needed the full seven games to defeat fourth place Los Angeles.

The championship series opened in Oakland and ended six games later in San Francisco with the Seals four games to two winners. Lien won game one, 5–2, with four RBIs from Luby. Oakland came back to win game two, 5–4, despite Uhalt's three hits. Werle lost game three, 5–3, in relief of Jansen. Werle hit a two-run home run, but he gave up two home runs.

Oakland now led the series, 2 games to 1, but Frank Seward won game four for San Francisco, 6–3. Don White had three hits and he and Sheridan each scored twice. Harrell scattered 10 hits to win game five, 4–1, as Nicely drove in two runs with an infield out and a sacrifice fly.

Lien tossed a four-hit shutout to take game six, 4–0, and the series. White homered and drove in two and Nicely had three hits. Lien got the only run he would need in the first inning when Trower led off with a single and went all the way to third on Uhalt's sacrifice, then scored on a wild pitch.

For the series, Sheridan batted .454, White .435, Fain .412, and Luby .409. It was the Seals last Governor's Cup victory.

FERRIS FAIN

Seals 1939–1942, 1946

Ferris Fain left high school two weeks early in 1939 because the Seals needed another first baseman. He was a bit overmatched that year, and the next was not much better, but he found his stroke in 1941, batting .310. His 1942 season was terrible, but the military gave him the next three years to develop and mature, which he did.

Upon his return in 1946 he was a Hitter with a capital H. His 112 RBIs led the PCL and at season's end he was drafted by the Philadelphia Athletics. That began a nine-year major league career during which he led the American League in batting twice, with averages of .344 and .327, and was selected to four All-Star teams.

Ferris Fain (author's collection).

BK: Talk about the 1946 Seals.

FERRIS FAIN: I just think that that was the best ballclub that I've ever played on, including major league. I mean, as a *team*. And I think that it was as good a Triple-A ballclub in my era that I know of. It was the best Triple-A ballclub going.

We played a four-game series in spring training against the Philadelphia Athletics and we beat 'em all four games. Sure, it's spring training and we had our whole nucleus; that doesn't mean that the A's did, *but* we nevertheless beat 'em four ballgames. What I saw of their pitching was basically the same thing that I went back to the next year with 'em and we [Seals] had a hell of a lot better pitching than they did. And overall I just think we had a better ballclub than the Philadelphia Athletics of 1947.

I shouldn't say 1947. This isn't ego talking, but when Joost and I joined the ballclub we improved the ballclub quite a little bit because there were two weak spots in the A's lineup. But even with that, I thought the '46 Seals were a better ballclub than that '47 Philadelphia ballclub.

BK: There is reason to believe that the '46 Seals was the best the franchise ever had.

FF: I believe that. I take it position by position. There really wasn't any weak spots. When you get to the pitching staff, that was our strong point. That was the year that Larry Jansen won 30 ballgames and we had Cliff Melton, we had Bill Werle. We had one hell of a pitching staff. To get those kind of numbers that we had that year you gotta have pitching.

The only thing I can say about Jansen is every time that he walked out there I was tickled to death to see him 'cause it looked we were gonna have a "W" in the column. I didn't realize what a good pitcher he was until I finally got to hit at him in an All-Star game. I could see where he not only got by, he excelled with that good slider that he had.

Of course, when you're out there in the field you're not much concerned about anybody else's position. You've got all you can do to handle your own, so you're not zeroed in on how's this guy doing, how does he look. I'm not the manager; I'm just a player. Like I say, it wasn't until I got to hit at him one time or two in an All-Star game that I realized just what great stuff he did have.

His big asset was his uncanny control. He puts me in mind of the guy I think in today's era is a hell of a pitcher — Maddux. I like those guys who can throw the ball where they want to. Every hitter is gonna have a problem, some place or another he doesn't like that particular pitch and if you're able to pitch to that area as Jansen could and would, he had to be successful. He just was one hell of a good, steady pitcher. You knew you were gonna get a win when he got out there.

BK: Before the war he was a good pitcher, but after the war he was a world-beater.

FF: As you get older you get a little smarter. [Laughs] Larry just was one hell of a pitcher.

BK: Werle came back from the service and won 12 games.

FF: Like I say, my main purpose was going out there every day. That was not only '46, that was '39 and 1955 in my last year of baseball. My big thing was doing *my* job and concentrating my whole thought and effort on that, rather than try what somebody else is doing.

I just know that Bill Werle was on the ballclub. I know that I put 13 months in at Hickham Field during the war and when we got out of the service, by God, we went back there to Honolulu for spring training.

But again, there was a tough son of a buck. He went to the big leagues. Cliff Melton had come down from the big leagues. Big Cliff was tough. They were two tough lefthanders.

Then we had some other guys. We just had one hell of a good pitching staff.

BK: Your double play combination in '46 was Nicely to Luby to Fain. It was probably as good as any in baseball.

FF: Well, I would say it wasn't quite as good as Joost to Suder to Fain. That was a remarkable infield, but if there was a second place I would say that I would give it to Nicely, Luby, and Fain. It was easily the best in the Coast League.

A lot of us put three years in the service. As we said, you get a little smarter as years go on, and another thing, you get a little maturity. Like in my own case, there's some people that mature at 20, 21 years old, others it takes a little longer. Physically and mentally — the whole damn thing. I think the three years that I put in the service, and, of course, I had the good fortune of measuring what the higher leagues would be when I played against so many of those major league ballplayers that were in the service. It was a pretty good ruler to go by. They didn't look like they were God and the experience and the confidence that I gained in those three years was invaluable.

Confidence goes with experience. You learn things and then you can execute. Hell, I'm looking at these guys. That's why I'm saying the '46 ball-club of the Seals was better than the A's of '47, minus Joost and Fain, truly. That isn't any bouquet to either of us, other than the fact that we did help that ballclub in two horribly weak spots.

BK: The older you got, the better you got.

FF: I think in any form of athletics, but particularly in baseball, I've seen these other guys and myself that I think reach a peak of being able to *do* what you've learned when you're in your early 30s. 30, 31, 32, 29 — there's a period of four or five years there that you know what you wanna do and, God willing, you do it. As you get older, then you know what you gotta do, you've really got it mastered, but then the reflexes aren't there. [Laughs] You're just a day late and a nickel short.

BK: Statistically, in your early years with the Seals you appeared to be just another ballplayer.

FF: It was, again, that maturity, the experience that I got playing for three years. Actually and frankly, in 1942, the last year before I went in the service — I went in the service in early '43, March of '43 — I had had such a horrible year in '42 and it persisted. It stayed with me when I went to McClellan Field and we were playing baseball there — basically, that's what they had us there for — and I couldn't get unraveled it didn't seem like.

My father had gone from being a jockey and had outgrown the

saddle — he got too big to ride — and he went into boxing. He passed on some of that knowledge to my brother, who was a year younger, and I thought, "I can't seem to get untracked." Had I not been shipped out — they decided after we were there 13 months at McClellan Field, they gave us a 10-day or a two-week furlough and in that period of time I was to have my first amateur fight. I'd gone into the gym and said, "To hell with this. I'm gonna see how this other endeavor works out." I was gonna give that pugilistic career a shot.

But as it turned out, and very likely for the best, I never got to get in the squared ring. I'd had no official fight, but more than just one bout with the gloves on.

It's a funny thing. There was a one-eyed guy that was a janitor at McClellan Field and we were in the gym. He used to clean up the gym when I was in there farting around, thinking I was gonna be the next Sugar Ray Robinson. A big heavyweight came in and wanted to spar, so I was the guy he selected. I'm 162, 163 pounds, so we got on the mat and went to it. As I recall he was a piece of cake.

After the thing was all over, this one-eyed guy, who later turned out as I remember went by the name of Young Joe Gans, so he was an ex-pugilist — he came over and said, "Young man, who are you? Have you got anybody handling you?" I didn't know what he was talking about. I said, "No, I'm here all by myself." He said, "I'll tell you what. I'd love to handle you. You're the best-looking white boy I've seen in a long, long while." So apparently I must've had some ability.

As it turns out, I'm glad that I didn't have to find out just how much. I knew I could punch, but you also have to take one, too, so I don't know what my pugilistic career would've been, but I'm just as glad it was bypassed.

BK: We talked about the double play combination, but the 1946 Seals were solid defensively everywhere. Frenchy Uhalt was in center field.

FF: Great. Great. Frenchy was a *great* outfielder. Didn't have the greatest arm going and I think that's probably one of the things that kept him out of the major leagues for any time. See, in those days, you didn't go to the major leagues and be an on-the-job learner. You either had it then or you didn't. There was only eight teams in each league so if there were some things you could not do, hey, they'd find somebody that *could* do all of 'em. Frenchy, I think, his arm kept him out of the major leagues, but, thank goodness for that 'cause he was our center fielder and one hell of a center fielder. His arm wasn't *that* horrible or he wouldn't have been playing center field as well as he did.

We had Neill Sheridan there that year. There was an arm in right field.

That guy could throw and run and he used that triple-threat USF ability to no end. I can remember hearing that guy coming; he'd be hitting behind me and I'd be rumbling around third, trying to get in to score, and he'd be right on my tail and it sounded like a herd out of the Kentucky Derby coming. He ran hard and loud and fast. And he had good power.

In left field we had Don White and he did an excellent job for us. Defensively, he was a hell of a good outfielder.

Even [third baseman] Ted Jennings, who was not reputed to be the greatest fielder going, he did a respectable job. He was more than adequate.

Now you're going to Nicely, who was one *hell* of a shortstop. It's a shame the guy couldn't hit a little bit more than he did. He was a tremendous defensive player, *great* arm.

Luby with his experience reminded me an awful lot of who I saw in the big leagues, Lou Boudreau. Lou wasn't the fastest, didn't cover much ground, but when you hit a ball he seemed to be standing right in front of it, wherever it was. That was just purely experience. Well, this is Luby.

Then, of course, I had my good moments at first base. I can remember, too, old Sam Gibson was with us before '46, when I first came up. I left school in 1939, a couple weeks before graduation, to join the Seals. When I finally did get in the lineup, which wasn't until the last three weeks of the season to beat that draft situation. Had I played in June and sparingly, that would have counted as a whole year against the draft that was prevalent in those days.

Old Sam, if he had 20 runs, would say, "Goddamn it, get me more runs!" I don't know if we were ahead or behind or what, but I screwed up at first base, did something wrong, and here's Sam, "Get that goddamn kid outta here!" He talked *real* high and he'd eat a whole box of those cube sugars every time he pitched. He crammed those sugar cubes in and in between sucking on one of those cubes, he'd yell, "Get that goddamn kid outta here!" [Laughs] I couldn't've been the greatest ball of fire in my earlier years with the Seals and I wasn't and I know that.

Again, a few years under your belt remedies a lot of that.

BK: You were a good fielder. Would you have been a Gold Glove winner in Philadelphia if that award had been given then?

FF: No, I don't think so because if I didn't lead the league I was close to it in errors.

I had great range. I had a great arm. I could throw like a son of a bitch, and accurate. My defensive ability — I'm not gonna compare myself to anybody, that's not my style — if there's any comparison's to make let the viewers do it.

I've yet to see the guy that could throw as well as I could, as strongly, as accurately, had the range. I won't be adverse to giving myself a little bouquet with having a little bit of more than average baseball intelligence. So, putting 'em all together, I think I did a pretty good job, except that it just wasn't in my realm of things to say that.

If there's a chance of knocking that lead runner off, that was my whole ambition when I was playing. That was my whole thought. I knew that you had to start at home plate and you had to go from first to second to third, back to home. The closer you got to home, the easier it was to score, so anytime I got a chance to keep that guy at first base instead of giving him the easy play to second, just take the nice easy throw — anybody could do that. And they do. And they did.

Rather than take a shot at second base and knock that lead runner off, oh, no, we're gonna let the guy go over there, I don't wanna dare make a misplay here. I don't wanna ruin my dandy little record. My whole thought was that lead runner; if there was any chance at all, I'm gonna get that guy, whether it's going to third or second, home, I don't care. We're gonna try to keep 'em from getting close to home plate.

BK: Let's go back to 1946 again. Bruce Ogrodowski.

FF: Bruce? Well, there it was again — the old veteran. Bruce handled those pitchers just great. Again, I'm viewing this from first base where I'm not paying a hell of a lot of attention to what the other folks are doing, other than if they drop a pop fly they should've had. I can remember that.

We had Ogrodowski and we had Joe Sprinz and we had Mel Ivy. I haven't thought of that name in 50 years. Mel Ivy was also on the ballclub; didn't play a lot because you had Ogrodowski and Sprinz. The history of catchers, their main objective was to be sure to handle the pitchers and if you could hit a little more than average that was even better. But the basic thing was get those guys back there that aren't gonna screw up behind the plate. They're the ones who get every pitch.

What I recall of Oggie is the same as Joe Sprinz. When they got back of the plate, they weren't gonna hit any .350, that's for sure, but they were gonna give you more than a competent job behind the plate. That's what they were there for.

An experienced catcher is so important. You can see it in today's game; like this black guy that's catching — Charles Johnson. Got $10 million and his claim to fame is he handles pitchers well. $10 million!

BK: What would you make today, a two-time batting champion?

FF: I don't know, but I'll take it. [Laughs] I know one thing, it would beat my tops of $45,000.

When I went to the major leagues in '47, the minimum salary was 5500. Now it's over 200,000! And then I see a .214 hitter gets a three million dollar raise. Johnny Pesky took a 25 percent cut after he hit .335.

It reminds me of a story about Joe Orengo, used to be an old Cardinal and was the PR guy with the San Francisco Seals. He used to love to tell this story at these hot stove league sessions. When Branch Rickey sent him out his contract he looked at it, put it back in the mail with a note saying, "I make more money out here in my native California picking oranges than what you offered me here to play next year." And he said, "I got the shortest telegram ever was back from Rickey: 'Pick 'em.'"

And that's where they had you. I know no matter what they paid it beat driving trucks, but it was nothing compared to what this is. Now you don't even have to drive that limousine. You have somebody else do it. [Laughs]

BK: When you were drafted, the A's didn't want to pay you as much as you made with the Seals.

FF: Totally, I made $6500 with the Seals. I made $5500 base salary — five and a half months. I can remember when I came out of the service and my first day at home. It was probably mid February and Charlie Graham called me and said, "Ferris, how would you like to be the first Seal to sign this year? Come on over and we'll get it done."

So I went over to the office and we went through the inevitable nothing talk and then, finally, "Well, what do you think you oughtta have to play this year?"

I debated it pretty seriously for quite a while and I said, "I just got to have $700 a month. That's all there is to it."

He said, "Okay. I'll be right back." He came back and laid the contract down and said, "There you are. Sign it."

I looked at it and I looked at him. It was a $1,000. He had got some play money from Mr. Fagan that helped to get me that extra 300, but he didn't have to do that.

Then we played five and a half months and that's where my 5500 came in. At the end of the season, I had Lefty O'Doul call me down. He said, "I want you to stop by the bar. I got something for you."

So I go down there and he gives me a brand new 16 gauge Ithaca shotgun. I have always liked to hunt. "This is for doing a hell of a job for me."

Now just before Christmas, here comes a $1,000 in the mail from Charlie Graham, a bonus of $1,000. I think I'd already been drafted by Philadelphia and I guess I got ten percent of the draft price at that time. So, totaling it all together, I'm 6500.

The first contract I get from Connie [Mack] is 6,000 bucks. I finally battled him and we argued and I said, "I gotta take a cut to go to the major leagues? Stick it in your ear." I ended up getting a big fat $500 raise over the 6500.

I'm dickering with the ballclub in one of those years. I'm holding out. So Earle Mack says, "Okay. We'll give you that, but please don't tell Mr. Mack." [Laughs] That was the organization of the amazing A's in that era. I think that was one of the reasons I got traded after the 1952 season. They anticipated — and they were right — we were gonna get some money.

Even so, I go over to the White Sox and another one of my mistakes occurred. Frank Lane [White Sox general manager] calls me. "How would you like to sign?" "I'm ready." And he says, "Well, what do you want? What can we give you that'll make you happy?"

I said, "I want $45,000." I knew the minute he said, "By God, I'll have a contract in the mail for you tomorrow," that I'd blown it. [Laughs] I should've said, "What's your offer?"

The odd part of that is it wasn't 20 minutes after I agreed to 45 grand with Frank Lane, I get a call from this guy and he said, "Hello, Ferris?" And I said, "Yeah." He said, "This is Ty." I said, "Ty who?" He said, "This is Ty Cobb. I just wanted to call you and help you out a little bit. Have you signed your contract yet?" "I just agreed 15 minutes ago, Ty."

I don't know yet what his bit of wisdom was gonna be, but I know one thing: it was gonna be better than that 45. [Laughs] And had I let Lane make the offer, it would've been more'n 45, I'm sure.

I just managed to become a pretty good hitter. Mainly, I got up on the bat about three inches or more and that made all the difference in the world.

BK: Lefty O'Doul was your manager with the Seals.

FF: The greatest manager, the greatest guy, my idol was Lefty O'Doul. You couldn't help but love him because he wasn't the aloof Paul Richards type, the guess-what's-coming-you've-got-two-strikes-on-you-here's-the-take-sign Connie Mack, Jimmy Dykes strictly by the book, you could dictate every move that man made, that we're gonna bunt at the end of the fourth inning. My guy in the big leagues that I thought was a good manager — I liked his style — was Billy Martin. I didn't like the guy personally, but he was one hell of a manager. He played a you-try-to-figure-out-what-I'm-doing game. I liked that. That was Lefty O'Doul. Billy learned that from O'Doul.

I had the good fortune of joining the Seals as a kid right out of high school two weeks before graduation — no father — and I'd say that he might have been somewhat of a father image. He saw something in me that I hoped I would be and he just worked his ass off helping me become a good ballplayer.

BK: Some say he was the best batting coach who ever lived.

FF: Of course, they were independently owned and they made their money basically by selling ballplayers to keep their head above water. O'Doul had a theory that the scouts loved to see pull hitters and he just worked on me all the time. "Whip that ball to right field! They love to see that." And that just was not my type of hitting.

The year [1941] that I hit .310 or so was the year Lefty had got hit in the eye in the bar and was out a lot of the season. Well, then Tony Lazzeri and Larry Woodall took over. I can remember it like it was yesterday; we're on a train going up to our two week sojourn in Portland and Seattle and they said, "Forget this pull-pull-pull-pull. Hit the ball wherever you can hit it! We don't want you to just keep pulling-pulling-pulling." Well, I had a good year. Lefty came back at the end of the season, the very end.

Now the next year we're back to the pull-pull-pull and when I went in the service I'm still trying to pull the ball and that's when I pulled myself into the gym. But finally I got unraveled to where I started hitting the ball to the opposite field, to center field, move the ball around. It was just not my style. I wasn't one of those guys that had those good wrists, who could roll those wrists. I was more of a forearm and shoulder hitter. When I was in the service I was on my own and that's where I hit. I had great success.

When we come back to spring training in '46, O'Doul sees what I'm doing and I'm having tremendous success. The word had gotten out that, "Hey, this guy is looking pretty good in the service," and there was never one word about let's be a pull hitter.

But his basic knowledge of the game — you don't lunge, how do you keep from lunging. It's one thing to say you don't wanna do this, but there aren't many people that have the remedy. How do you keep from lunging?

Here's how he did it. I can remember him standing back of the batting cage with a rope tied to my belt and when I started to go forward with my body I ended up in the back of that batting cage. [Laughs] He yanked on that rope and there I'd go.

He also had the idea of how you keep from lunging. O'Doul's theory — and it was the greatest that I've ever heard — there aren't too many people know that 'cause there's not too many people wanna listen — is that it's a physical impossibility to take your body forward and keep your head back six, seven inches. And it is impossible to do just the opposite. You can't stick your head out there seven inches and keep your body back. So the two combined — your shoulder and your head — if you don't let them go forward, your front foot you just pick up and put back down. That's more or less a rudder that takes you in and out in the direction of where the pitch is. If the pitcher pitches outside, naturally you're gonna go out across the plate a little bit, or toward the plate, to get the ball, to get a whack at it. Inside, you're gonna step a little bit away.

We'd have a few milkshake drinkers on every ballclub I played, but there were more guys that'd have a snort every once in a while than the milkshakers. His thing was, "If I ever walk in a bar and you guys are all in there, don't you get up and run. Sit right down here and we'll both have a couple of drinks together." He was a human being and he treated you like a human being, where these other superior bastards just made my ass ache.

I can remember Paul Richards. I'm supposed to be one hell of a fielder. He might have been one hell of a catcher, but when he's telling me how to play first base we've gotta talk about that. When we got through with the conversation, he went along with my idea.

BK: One more Seal. Sal Taormina.

FF: Sal was a good hitter, but again I can't relate why guys that show this ability don't eventually go to the top. I think the thing is I can't look in their head. I'm not implying that Sal Taormina was a dumb guy, but I don't see why he didn't go further with the ability that he looked like he should've had. He was strong and he could run pretty good. Those are the main things that I recall, but I think that Sal should've gone further than he did. What the reason, I don't know. But he helped our ballclub, but I thought that he probably could've been a better ballplayer.

BK: How were you originally signed?

FF: We had one hell of a high school ballclub. Out of the guys in my senior year at Roosevelt High School, seven of those guys went into professional baseball. Two of us went to the major leagues: Ed McGah, who is the basic owner of the Oakland Raiders, and me. I remember when we used to go steal peaches together at the cannery. Now he's got jillions and jillions and more jillions. He went to the Red Sox for a couple of years and I was with the A's.

With this ballclub that we had, in those days every ballgame we played there was scouts from the various major league ballclubs. We were the draw. You got to know that guy's with Cincinnati, that's St. Louis Cardinals, that's Joe Devine with the Yankees. They were always out at our ballgames.

There was a local that was scouting for San Francisco, Doc Silvey. Doc had endeared himself to me. I liked Doc; he wasn't pushy like some of the others that I'd seen. Doc had made arrangements for me to go over and work out with the San Francisco ballclub.

My senior year in school, my mother was the only support of the family. I had a drunken father that was absolutely no good. My brother and I were on a 50 cents a week allowance and we didn't always get that.

I go over and work out with the Seals. Starting the year — my senior year — they made a deal to have me come over and work out with them when they were in San Francisco and then when they came to Oakland — and I'm an Oakland kid — I'd come over and work out with the ballclub there. It was worth $200 a month to me. I went from 50 cents a week allowance to $200 a month. The football coach couldn't understand why I couldn't play football for him that year and I couldn't tell. They're giving me $200 a month not to. [Laughs]

So come June, the first baseman — I think it was Harley Boss — got hurt and so they came and they got ahold of my mother to see if they could get me signed. She had to sign for me. And then they went to the school, got that okayed. I was student body president and they talked them into letting me out two weeks before to join the ballclub, to take the place of Harley Boss. That's how I ended up with the Seals.

The Yankees wanted to send me to any college in the United States I wanted to go to, as long as it had a good baseball coach. They would've taken care of everything. The guy that I would've had to compete against if I *ever* had any idea of going to the major leagues was a kid by the name of Lou Gehrig.

The Seals had impressed in me that "We're an independent ballclub. You can go to *any* major league ballclub from our team, whereas if you sign with Cincinnati or the Cardinals or the Yankees or whatever, you belong to that ballclub." And in those days they could shove you back and forth from the International League to the Coast League. They could bury you in the minor leagues.

My main thing was I'm not gonna sign and fight against a guy by the name of Lou Gehrig. But who was to know that a year later he was gonna die?

I was lucky to get drafted by the A's. I gotta be happy with what happened. I got no complaints, other than I think I could've made a little more money someplace other than the A's. [Laughs]

I was an aggressive ballplayer. Not dirty or nasty; I played hard and there were a lot of people that didn't like that. I would argue with the umpires; now I'm a hothead and everything else. That wasn't it. I had one hell of a good eye and the longer I played the more I proved it. I didn't get all those base on balls because I was lucky. I could see where that pitch was and if it's not on the plate I'm not gonna choose a bad pitch like they do now, under the plate. I kinda like that idea of hitting that 2-and-0 and

3-and-1 pitch because then you could take a look and say, "I think I'm gonna look for that fastball."

Or, like a ballgame I beat poor little Bobby Shantz — one of my good buddies — when I went over to the White Sox. After watching Bob and Joe Astroth work for several years, I noticed they loved to pull the string on the 2-and-0 pitch. They liked to throw up that dead mackerel. So I retained that when I went to the White Sox.

We were in a ballgame and they've got us beat, 1-to-nothing, and I'm 2-and-0 with a man on and I said, "Well, I think I'll just look for that dead fish." And sure enough, and now the score's 2-to-1. [Laughs] And that's the way it ended up. I beat poor old Bobby only because I could look for a pitch.

This was the type hitting that I did. It's like reading somebody's mail. If you *know* you get 2-and-0 and you say, "I'm gonna look for the change of pace," or "I'm gonna look for the curveball," or "I'm gonna look for the fastball" and you get the pitch, it's up to you to do what you can with it. If you guess wrong, it's 2-and-1. So what? You can still do the same thing. Particularly a singles hitter. They're not gonna walk you. They're gonna make you hit the ball, so you look for a pitch again. If you miss again, which is unlikely — you're not gonna miss it twice in a row — you're 2-and-2 and it's like you started off when you walked up to the plate. This was my theory of hitting and I maintained it as long as I played.

My first year with Connie Mack, he must've had an idea when I joined the ballclub in '47, to score a run we're gonna get four base on balls. That's the way he managed. I'm not kidding. When you'd look down there — and why you'd look anyplace with two strikes is ridiculous because there's only one thing you can do is hit the ball — but I happened to look down to third base and I've got two strikes and Al Simmons is the third base coach and he gives me the take sign. It came from the bench.

I'm 2-and-0 and 3-and-1 two different times at the plate in Yankee Stadium and here comes the take sign. In both instances I didn't do anything. I hit a 14-hopper to the second baseman, struck out the next time on a 3-and-2 pitch. I am incensed. I got in the dugout and I pranced back and forth and finally stopped in front of Connie Mack and I said, "Why don't you take that take sign of yours and stick it in your ass!" I'm just a rookie — a 26-year-old rookie — coming up from minor leagues, but he was killing me.

At the end of the game here come the coaches. "You oughtta go talk to the old man." I was ready to go back to San Francisco. At the end of the day, though, I got to thinking over that second beer, "This is a pretty good place to be playing. The major league is all right." I figured, "Well, I'll talk to the old man next time I get a chance."

He *never* got to the ballpark before five minutes before game time. The lineup was always made by Simmons, Brucker, and those guys; he didn't do it. So I'm gonna go down and get my bat and go and get some batting practice for 50 or 60 minutes before game time. And who's sitting down right at the bat rack? Connie Mack. Now I lose my guts. He'll never know who I am; I'll just turn my back to him and get a bat and get up to the cage. Well, I got ahold of a bat and he said, "Oh, boy, boy, boy! Come here."

So then I start, "Oh, Mr. Mack. About yesterday…" and I'm whining like a son of a bitch. He says, "I know. I heard everything. Now I wanna tell you something." I figured, "Well, here's the good news. I'm outta here." And he says, "I have noticed that you play a mighty fine game of baseball, so from here on you don't have to look for any signs." [Laughs] So help me goodness. For the rest of the six years that I was with the A's I was on my own.

I think that was one of the things that did *not* endear me when Jimmy Dykes took over. "No, I don't have to. Mr. Mack said I could do this." [Laughs]

FERRIS ROY "BURRHEAD" FAIN
Born May 29, 1921, San Antonio, TX
Died October 18, 2001, Georgetown, CA
Ht. 5'11" Wt. 180 Batted and Threw Left
First baseman

Year	Team, Lg	G	AB	R	H	2B	3B	HR	RBI	BA
1939	SF, PCL	12	33	4	7	2	0	1	8	.212
1940		146	446	64	106	21	7	7	50	.238
1941		174	649	122	201	27	8	5	66	.310
1942		162	519	57	112	17	4	4	53	.216
1943–1945				military service						
1946	SF, PCL	180	615	117	185	35	6	11	112	.301
1947	Phi., AL	136	461	70	134	28	6	7	71	.291
1948		145	520	81	146	27	6	7	88	.281
1949		150	525	81	139	21	5	3	78	.263
1950		151	522	83	147	25	4	10	83	.282
1951		117	425	63	146	30	3	6	57	*.344
1952		145	538	82	176	43	3	2	59	*.327
1953	Chi., AL	128	446	73	114	18	2	6	52	.256
1954		65	235	30	71	10	1	5	51	.302
1955	Det/Cle, AL	114	258	32	67	11	0	2	31	.260
1956	Sac., PCL	70	147	18	37	6	0	0	16	.252

*Led league

FRANK SEWARD

Seals 1945–1947

Frank Seward joined the Seals in 1945, sent there by the New York Giants. He entered the starting rotation and had the second best record (18–13, after losing his first five starts) on the team, behind Bob Joyce's 31–11. Then, in the Governor's Cup playoffs, he won two more games, giving him 20 for the year. In four games in the playoffs, his ERA was 1.07.

In '46, he pitched well again, winning 15 and losing 13 with a 3.12 ERA. His biggest game of the season came in the second round of the Governor's Cup. Oakland had won two of the first three games and another victory for the Oaks would have made a San Francisco championship very difficult. Seward started game four and had a no-hitter through six innings before allowing a run in the seventh. Dale Mathewson relieved him with one out in the ninth and got Billy Raimondi to hit into a double play and the Seals won, 6–3. It was the turning point of the series; San Francisco won the next two to earn their fourth straight Governor's Cup title. In addition to his pitching in game four, Seward got a base hit and scored a run.

Frank Seward with the Seals in 1946 (courtesy of Frank Seward).

FRANK SEWARD: We had a pretty good league when I was out

there. We went first class with San Francisco. We were the first in the PCL to fly.

Lefty O'Doul was a great manager. He was the type of manager that if the guy's going good, he doesn't suck up to them; he just leaves them alone, they're already on cloud nine while the guy who was struggling, he would trip over them, or pat 'em on the back or the rear end. He used the reverse psychology since most of the managers, for example, Alex Rodriguez, they give him anything he wants. He's not going to improve by getting all these perks and he's got the talent to produce with or without those extras, but to bring out the hidden talent of other ballplayers who may not have that same degree of talent, and some managers overlook them and they never develop. But O'Doul got more out of his players collectively than any manager I ever played for. He joked around a lot.

BK: I've been told by several people that he was truly a players' manager.

FS: Yeah, and you know Mel Ott was just the opposite; Mel Ott was a great ballplayer, but he thought that everybody else should be as talented as he. He didn't have to think about anything; he would just come up there and hit the ball out of the park.

I was with him when he was managing — I was just a kid then — and I'd have a rough inning and he'd come out, he'd just grab a ball right out of my hand. "You're through," he would say.

BK: That's kind of hard on the self-respect and the ego and everything.

FS: And yet, he was a great hitter. And a good outfielder; he just couldn't handle people.

BK: That's a talent. And I don't think that's a talent that can be learned; I think that's a talent that you have to be born with.

FS: Right.

BK: Ok, start with your early career. Who signed you?

FS: Well, actually, I was signed by Connie Mack of the Philadelphia A's in 1938. Atlantic White Flash, a petroleum company, held a tryout about ten miles away, conducted by Ira Thomas, who was a scout for the A's, and Jack Coombs, who was a famous no-hitter pitcher and the coach of the Duke baseball team. I was a junior in high school and my older brother took me to the tryout. The morning session had kids running and other kids throwing. I was with the pitchers. Out of the group, there must have been about 50 kids there and they chose 18 kids and that afternoon had an intersquad game. I was one of the pitchers that was pitching for one team. I had played semipro ball before then; we used to play against the Cuban All-Stars and the Bacharach Giants and the House of David.

They used to tour back in those days and I played for the Pennsauken Indians. I used to pitch for them and during the game they'd pass the hat in the crowd. I'd count up my quarters and get about a dollar fifty. I thought that was great.

Anyway, getting back to the tryout, each pitcher pitched three innings. I pitched my three innings and I struck out eight of the nine guys. Well, they were swinging at anything, trying to make an impression. [Laughs] As I was walking off the field Jack Coombs, up in a lifeguard stand with a big megaphone, said, "This young man is attending Duke University next year." And this struck me like a bolt; I'd never talked to Jack Coombs, I never saw him before. So after it was all over, he said, "I want you to come to Duke on a scholarship." And I told him that I was only in my junior year. He said, "Well, finish your senior year and come on down. We have a great team: Crash Davis, and Ace Parker, and Eric Tipton." Hank Wagner, Bill McCann, Billy Werber all played at Duke. I told him that I had a scholarship to Western Maryland." He said, "Come to Duke and you'll never regret it."

I went home and I had to go my senior year and all during that year I didn't know whether to go to Western Maryland or Duke. It just happened Duke was in the Rose Bowl that January, I guess New Year's Day of my senior year, and they lost, three to nothing, on a last-minute field goal. My brother and I listened to the game and afterwards he said, "It's better off being a small fish in a big pond than a big fish in small pond; I think you should go to Duke."

So, I went to Duke and my freshman year I worked in the Union; you had to work to get your meals and I worked at the Union, which is like a cafeteria. One night it was pouring rain and you weren't supposed to walk on the grass—they had hedge all around the grass—so I jumped over the hedge, running across the field to my dorm and I had crepe soles on, and I slipped while jumping, catching my foot on a hidden wire concealed by the hedge. I landed on my right arm, fracturing my forearm. Consequently, I didn't play my freshman year.

In my sophomore year I made the varsity, getting my letter. I won two or three games. Then in my junior year I got appendicitis in the fall and I wasn't interested in more schooling and I really wasn't getting anywhere. My desire was to play baseball. So I quit school and took a bus to Florida. I was a walk-on at the Baltimore Orioles, which were in spring training there in Hollywood, Florida. They were in the International League — Double A — at that time. They let me work out with them and at the end of the stint down in Florida, Tommy Thompson, the manager, came over to me and he said, "We can't take you on the way north, but if you're still interested in playing ball I'll give you a letter for you to take to Connie Mack." And I said, "Fine", because I lived in Pennsauken, New Jersey, which is only about 4 or 5 miles from Philadelphia, across the river, to Shibe Park. I'd been there many a-time watching Jimmy Foxx and Al Simmons and guys like that, so I took this letter and went over to Shibe Park and gave it to the business manager and he told me I could pitch batting practice and they'd give me 50 dollars a week." I thought, "Boy, that's great." That lasted for two weeks.

The A's were going out to California and they said again that I wasn't ready to be part of the squad. At that time they had Jimmy Dykes and I don't know if Jimmy Foxx was there, but they had Mickey Cochrane, and Lefty Grove, Earnshaw, etc. They had a good ballclub. The business manager told me that Mr. Mack wanted to talk with me. His office was up in the Ivory Tower they call it, it's up on the third tier of Shibe Park. I walked in there shaking. He had pictures all over, and trophies, and a little settee, a small couch, made of baseball bats, for the back and the seat and the arms were all bats. He told me to sit down. Everybody called him Mr. Mack. And all the players that he talked to, he called Mister.

He said, "Well, Mr. Seward, I don't think that you can make it as a pro ballplayer." And I said, "All I want is a chance." He said, "Well, if you're that eager, you take this letter and you talk to"—I forget the business manager's name—"and he has railroad tickets for you and I want you to report to Newport News." And I said, "I'll be there." That evening I went home and told my pop and he took the letter and he got a kettle, a teakettle, and steamed open the letter. The letter in essence said that I had talent and to pay this boy a hundred dollars a month.

So we sealed up the letter again and I had to leave there ready to travel that night. I was on the Pullman bound to the end of Delaware, had to take a boat over to Newport News. So I got to Newport News and the general manager met me there and took me into a motel room and gave me a contract—and it's the first time I ever saw a contract—but I did see a hundred dollars a month. I said, "I'm not gonna play for $100 a month." And he said, "What are you going to do?" I said, "I'm going to go home." "Well, how much do you want?" I said, "A hundred twenty-five." He said okay. So it was $125. And I played for Newport News that year and won 10 and lost 13. We were in last place; we didn't have that great a ball club.

BK: So, you were what, 20 years old at this point?

FS: Yeah, I would say around 20. When I was at Duke, Bill McCann and Eddie Shokes were on our team. And Bill McCann was the guy that pitched a no-hitter for the Philadelphia A's and Eddie Shokes went up to

Cincinnati. We had a pretty good ballclub at Duke. But getting back to my story, that league folded, the Virginia League; that was a Class D league. So I came back and I hooked on with the Phillies and they took me to spring training and again I wasn't ready so they sent me up to Springfield, which was Class A. That was Springfield, Mass. Spencer Abbott was the manager. Bucky Harris was the manager for the Philadelphia Phillies at that time and he had a connection with the Washington Senators and Spencer Abbott was also connected with the Senators. I pitched for Springfield and won about 13 games and I lost 19. And again we finished in last place, but we had a fairly good club. My roommate at that time was Whitey Lockman who went on to the New York Giants. He was on base when Bobby Thomson hit that famous home run off of Brooklyn's Ralph Branca.

BK: Whitey was just a baby then.

FS: Yeah, well, Whitey was 16 years old when he joined Springfield; that was his first ball club.

Anyway, getting back, toward the tail end of the year, there was a scout from the New York Giants, Hank DeBerry, and he scouted me. I didn't know there was a scout in the stands, but I was walking into the lobby — we were on the road, we were in Binghamton — and Spencer Abbott was up. We had a night ball game and we went out and got something to eat, came back to the hotel, and he called me over, and he said, "You're leaving tonight for New York. The New York Giants bought you." Boy, that was something. So, again I had to get on a train down to Jersey City, taking the ferry over to New York. I think that the Giants had a downtown office, around 53rd or 54th Street, so I walked from the dock up to 54th Street and I met John Swartz. Horace Stoneham was the owner of the club and we signed a contract and I signed for 500 bucks a month, which is a little better than $2500 a year. That was the minimum salary at that time. I never had ridden on the subway, and, really, had only been in New York a couple of times as a kid, so he told me to take the subway and go up to 145th Street to the Polo Grounds. So somehow I managed to get there and I rapped on the clubhouse door, the trainer came out and asked, "What do you want?" I said, "I'm Frank Seward and I was just bought by the ball club." And they didn't believe me. [Laughs] He wouldn't let me in. And so finally they contacted somebody and I got in. I was just in awe there. There was Ernie Lombardi, Joe Medwick, Babe Dahlgren, Carl Hubbell, Hal Schumacher, Dick Bartell, Mel Ott, and I sheepishly walked in. They gave me a locker, so I got a uniform. Dick Bartell and Billy Jurges and Gus Mancuso, they really befriended me and came over and were talking to me. I pitched some batting practice.

And we were about ready to go on a western swing to Chicago, St. Louis, and Cincinnati. Ott said, "I'll start you in Chicago. I don't wanna start you at home; it's too much pressure." So I started in Chicago against Paul Derringer at Wrigley Field. And he had won 199 games and I was trying to win my first. And I got beat in 10 innings—I pitched the whole 10 innings—and I got beat, 3-to-2. It was customary to go the distance back in those days. I don't know what they do today, but the day after you pitched, usually the next night or day you would pitch batting practice to loosen up. And that was the last game in Chicago that I pitched. We took the train to St. Louis. And I was pitching batting practice in St. Louis. They'd always set a net in front of you and I didn't want a net 'cause that disturbed me, so I had them take the net away and I was pitching to Joe Medwick. And, you know, you just throw 'em right down the middle about three-quarters speed so they get their timing. And he hit a shot back at me, right through the mound. I couldn't react; I threw up my arms to protect my face and the darn ball hit me on the forearm and fractured my forearm so I was through for the rest of the season. The next year I came up and I made the team and when we came north I did mostly relief. I won three and I think I lost two ballgames and then they sent me to Jersey City and I won a couple of games over there and then they brought me back in the fall. Then I didn't pitch anymore. I think I pitched about 25 games that year.

The next year—1945—they optioned me out to San Francisco and I played for the Seals. And out there my first five home games I lost and I wound up the year with I think it was something like I won thirteen or fifteen games and lost twelve or thirteen.

BK: I have you as eighteen and thirteen.

FS: Well, that was my second year.

BK: No, second year you were fifteen and thirteen, according to what I have anyhow.

FS: Oh, I think it was just the reverse. The second year we won the pennant and we won the playoffs. And we got a nice ring out of it, a nice diamond ring.

BK: You won the playoffs both years you were there and you pitched very well in the playoffs both years.

FS: Yeah. The second year my record during the year was 18 and 13 and then I won two in the playoffs. So it was considered in those days the playoffs was part of your record, which would make it 20 and 13. That's the year that Larry Jansen, he won 30. I guess Cliff Melton, he probably had 15 or 16 ballgames

BK: You had Melton, Harrell, and Bill Werle.

FS: Yeah. We had a good ball club. We outdrew Washington that year; we drew something like 700,000.

BK: The Seals set a record for minor league baseball that wasn't broken until the 1980s.

FS: Yeah, I remember Seal Stadium. That Rainier Brewery, right along beside it.

BK: How was Seal Stadium to pitch in? It was a cavern as far as the hitters went.

FS: See, I was big, I weighed about 210, 215, about 6–3, and I didn't mind the cold weather. When I went to Sacramento and L. A. I'd lose ten or fifteen pounds in dehydration, it was so hot. But I liked the Seals Stadium because I was strong, I felt strong because it was always cool. The fog would roll in about 6:30 and it was hard to see, then about seven, 7:30 it would clear off. It was cold; we used to have electric jackets that we'd plug in just keep warm and we used to drink clam broth.

BK: I remember going to night games there as a kid in July and August and having to wear a coat.

FS: Oh, yeah. The second year with the Seals we trained in Hawaii and we flew to the islands.

BK: I guess the Seals were the first team to go to flight all the time. Is that right?

FS: Yeah.

BK: Everybody who played for them seems to think they were treated very well and paid very well. Were you?

FS: Yeah, yeah. Charlie Graham, he was the owner. And there was a guy who was part owner, a guy named Paul Fagan and he was a relative to the Dole family — pineapples — and that's why we went to Maui. We trained in Maui. That was through his connections. But, no, I considered Frisco better than the majors.

BK: A lot of fellows did.

FS: It was, you know, pleasant. In the big leagues, it was cutthroat. Nobody would help you out; I mean, nobody ever told me what to do. They'd just give me the ball and say, "Throw it. Get 'em out." But we didn't have any kind of exercise machines, whirlpools, etc.

BK: Talk about some of your teammates there in San Francisco.

FS: Well, you know, Ferris Fain, Hugh Luby, Roy Nicely, Neill Sheridan, Dino Restelli.

BK: Was Roy Nicely as great a shortstop as many claim?

A: Well, he was very good. He couldn't hit, but he was good. He was like Bruce Ogrodowski. I used to like him as my catcher. He used to catch Dizzy Dean; I mean he was a good catcher, but a lousy hitter.

BK: That glove can save as many runs as a good hitter can bat in.

FS: Yeah. Nicely was a good shortstop. Hugh Luby was a good second baseman and Fain was great at first. We had a good ballclub.

BK: Frenchy Uhalt was in center field.

FS: I don't know if he's still living or not.

BK: I understand that he is. He's 90 something, I've been told. Someplace around Oakland, I think.

FS: Well, you know, Casey Stengel used to be managing Oakland. Jimmy Dykes used to manage in Hollywood. Marv Owen in Portland, Pepper Martin in Sacramento.

BK: In the '46 Governor's Cup, the second round, the Oaks were ahead, 2 games to 1. You pitched that fourth game and won it. Do you remember that game?

FS: It was a daytime game, I think it was on a Saturday or Sunday. I had a good fastball that day.

BK: You had a no-hitter through six. You pitched eight and a third innings.

FS: I had good stuff that day. But you know, it's funny when you're a pitcher, when you're warming up, you think, boy, the ball is popping; you're feeling great and then you go out there and you get hammered. And then other days, when you don't feel too well, you go out and pitch a great ball game, and I think a lot of it is your mental attitude.

You think, "Boy I'm strong; I'll throw that ball right past 'em." But you can't do that. And it's good to have hindsight. The thing that I objected to back in those days, maybe not, the way the game was played, but nobody ever told you that you had to concentrate, and you know, that's the whole thing in playing ball today. I mean it's just like Roger Clemens. He doesn't know where he is half the time; he's so wrapped up in the game.

And you know, nobody ever approached me and said, "Well, why don't you shorten your stride," or "lengthen your stride," or try this or try that. You know, I was thinking, but I would just throw the ball. I wasn't really a pitcher; I was a thrower.

BK: Well, the coaching, from your day 'til today is, was so different. When we played I was a pitcher and they gave me the ball and said, "Pitch" and that was the extent of the coaching. Now they show them, they correct their mechanics. Nobody ever taught me; I'd hear of pitches and I'd go out and try and throw it the way that they say it's thrown, but nobody ever taught anybody anything. And I understand what you're saying.

FS: Yeah, now it's a business. And they know their weaknesses, and you know they used to tell us to have a meeting before every game with the Giants, and essentially what they would say was pitch 'em high and tight and low and away. [Laughs] Everybody does that, or they try to do it. No, I have no regrets.

BK: As well as you pitched in San Francisco, why did you not get another shot in the major leagues?

BK: I don't know. I was up there twice. And in my third year with San Francisco in the spring I got bursitis. And I had trouble. That was, I guess, 1947. I was in the bullpen, oh, I would say for about half of the year. And then they released me and I went with Hollywood.

BK: You were only with Hollywood for a very short period of time there at the end of the season.

FS: Yeah. I was there for only about a month or a month and a half. And then they released me. Then I went with Syracuse in the International League. And I'd lost my fastball and I'd lost practically my curve. It was a slider; I don't know what happened. I was just having trouble with my arm. Then I guess I must have thrown too much with my arm and my back started bothering me and I was having trouble with my vertebra, and I had to get that worked on and finally I just quit. I retired.

BK: And you were, what, 28?

FS: Yeah. I guess so.

BK: What did you do when you left baseball?

FS: Oh, you know, I couldn't get a job. I didn't have any experience. I never worked. I'd go and they would say, "Well, what kind of experience do you have?" So I finally went with Sun Oil Company and I worked at the gas station, the company station, then I worked my way up and became manager and then I became salesman and I guess I stayed with them three years. Then I had an opportunity to go with National Homes; they were a fabricator and I stayed with them for something like 14 years. And I worked my way up to vice president and manager of one of their big plants. And finally, it's like being a coach or a manager, if you don't produce they can you. And we weren't selling too many houses. And the mortgage money was tight, so I got fired from that. And then another fellow and I, we started our own business using government money to rehab low income families' homes. We did that for 10 years. It was a non-profit organization. We did that for 10 years and then I retired.

BK: When did you retire?

FS: '86.

BK: You've enjoyed it ever since then?

FS: Oh, yeah. It's the best job I ever had.

BK: Okay, go back to baseball. Who was the best player you saw? You saw some awfully good ones in New York.

FS: I would have to say that the best player I pitched against was Stan

Musial. I guess the best player, well, two I would say, Carl Hubbell, of course he was on our team, I used to watch him pitch, and then Ted Williams with Boston. We'd play exhibition games; I think they trained in Sarasota, Florida, and we were training at that time down in Miami in the Orange Bowl. I would say that Hubbell and Musial and Williams. I never played with Willie Mays; he came after me.

I mean there were a lot of good ballplayers: Phil Cavaretta and Lou Novikoff. When he played for the Cubs he used to wear me out; and when he went to the Pacific Coast League — the L. A. Angels — I'd pitch against him and he was a big out then. It was just funny.

BK: How did you avoid World War Two?

FS: I had a perforated eardrum.

Frank Seward with the Seals in 1946 (courtesy of Frank Seward).

BK: That's too bad, but I guess I'd rather have a perforated eardrum than go over there and shoot at people.

FS: Yeah. All of my three brothers were drafted and I was the youngest and they left me alone.

BK: Would you be a ballplayer again if you could go back?

FS: Oh, yeah. You know, in my mind I'd be a smarter ballplayer. [Laughs]

BK: Well, yeah, we learn as time passes.

FS: Learn too late.

FRANK MARTIN SEWARD
Born April 7, 1921, Pennsauken, NJ
Ht. 6'3" Wt. 210 Batted and Threw Right

Year	Team, Lg	G	IP	W	L	Pct	SO	BB	H	ERA
1942	NwptNws, Va			10	13	.435				
1943	Spgfld, EL	35	234	10	19	.345	68	73	267	3.46
	NY, NL	1	9	0	1	.000	2	5	12	3.00
1944	JC, IL	11	71	4	6	.400	17	24	83	3.17
	NY, NL	25	78	3	2	.600	16	32	98	5.42
1945	SF, PCL	37	257	18	13	.581	113	106	284	3.85
1946		36	219	15	13	.536	72	79	214	3.12
1947	SF/Hwd, PCL	28	63	3	3	.500	28	29	89	5.29
1948	Syr, IL	30	70	6	2	.750	19	28	62	4.37
1949		10	15	0	1	.000	0	5	23	8.40

DON "JEEP" TROWER

Seals 1940–1943, 1946–1948

Don "Jeep" Trower could have made it to the top, but it was not to be. The Boston Red Sox had an interest in him in 1943, but Uncle Sam stepped in and while Trower was in the service he suffered a knee injury that limited his previous excellent range at shortstop. He recovered sufficiently to be a valuable backup for the 1946 championship Seals, but he was not the same as he was before.

In '46, most of his playing time came at third base, where he'd take over at times for the erratic-fielding Ted Jennings. He also filled in occasionally for Roy Nicely at his natural position of shortstop. Trower's greatest value that season came in the Governor's Cup. In the first round against Hollywood, he played third base in games 1 and 3, went 2-for-3 in each game (including a double), scored twice, and played errorless ball in the field.

In the championship series versus the archrival Oakland Oaks, he started games 1 and 6 and came in in the late innings defensively for Jennings or Nicely in the other four games. In the decisive game 6, he led off the contest with a single, advanced all the way to third on a sacrifice bunt by Frenchy Uhalt, and then scored on a wild pitch by Oakland starter Gene Bearden. It was the only run that Seals pitcher Al Lien needed as he shut out the Oaks, 6–0, to give San Francisco its fourth straight Governors' Cup championship. In the playoffs, Trower batted .545 (6-for-11) with four runs scored.

There were other highlights in his career, but when asked his greatest thrills he named only team accomplishments.

BK: How were you originally signed?

DON TROWER: I was working for PG&E after I graduated from high school because they had given me a job to play baseball for 'em. That was in 1938. We finished the job up in February of 1939. I had signed with the Oaks in 1937, but I had an interview with the owner and

Don "Jeep" Trower (courtesy Don Trower).

he told me that I should finish high school and then come back and sign with 'em. So I said okay and so I came back and finished high school and then I went to work for PG&E and played ball for 'em in the Twilight League. Then when they fired a hundred of us, then I signed with San Francisco.

I went to Salt Lake City as a second baseman, but I played shortstop in high school. About a month into the season they shifted me to short because they were having problems there. The fellow couldn't catch the ground ball. I played all that year at Salt Lake City. I was 19. I had a good year. Eddie Mulligan was our manager.

When I went to spring training in 1940 with San Francisco, he thought that I would be the shortstop because I had a good spring training, too. I hit .333 and the speed was good. I stuck around there for about two or three months and Harvey Storey, who had had surgery and was the short-stop prior to my signing with the Seals, came back. He was a power hit-ter, but not too much on the range in the field or a good glove man, but he had power at the bat, so he started the season at shortstop. Finally they optioned me out to Tacoma, Washington, which was Class B. I played up there for a while and then I was recalled and spent the rest of the year with San Francisco.

In '41 I played second base and Nanny Fernandez was the shortstop. We were a bunch of young fellows playing and there was a few older fellows, like Sam Gibson. Sam had been there for years. And Brooks Holder was there.

They had bought Tony Lazzeri to play second base in 1941 and he didn't work out. His legs were bad, so he played about a month or so. He was working with me at second base and showing me how to make that double play so I took over at second base and played the rest of the year at second base for 'em.

And then they bought Bill Lillard in 1942 and Bill had the same problem as Storey. He couldn't catch a ground ball. I'd been playing second base and then I was moved over to shortstop. That was the year that Bill Rigney was with Oakland and there was kind of a rivalry between the two of us. I could move and I had a good year at shortstop. I hit .256, I think it was, that year. Bill hit .282 and he was sold to the Giants. But as a young shortstop with San Francisco, I led the league in assists in 1942. I had more assists than any shortstop in the league. I finished second in fielding to Lindsay Brown up in Portland.

Then in '43 I was there and opened up at shortstop and was doing all right. I think Del Young was playing second base at the time and we were leading the league in double plays. Then Uncle Sam took me in June, but the Boston Red Sox, they were wanting to buy my contract from San Francisco, but that didn't develop because Uncle Sam had first choice. Charlie Graham didn't want to sell me at that time because I was just developing. He thought if I could come back and have a good year he'd get more money out of me probably.

When I went into the service I had maybe four or five bases that wanted me to come and play ball for 'em. A lot of the fellows did that; they went in and they got stationed in a place and they played ball for 'em and they got easy jobs. I wanted to fly so I went into cadet training. I ruined my leg, but things happen. Some of those fellows that went in there, they never came back. Or they came back with more severe injuries than what I had. I saw Dr. Hitchcock up there in Oakland and I had him examine my knee and he said, "Well, it's a 50–50 chance. Fifty percent you'll be a stiff-legged man and 50 percent you can use it." But nowadays, with this surgery that they do, it's possible that they could've fixed it.

Like I said, I ruined my knee in the service. I was in pilot training and I was running an obstacle course. I was in good shape at the time because I had played ball. This barrier that I had vaulted over on a western roll, why it was on grass and it was wet early in the morning and my left leg hit the ground and twisted. I slipped and it popped like a double-barreled shotgun going off and I tore everything in my knee.

That ruined my career. I had to wear a brace. I didn't tell San Francisco anything about my knee because I knew I'd be down the river, so I just put that knee brace on in the bathroom or with guys around me in the locker.

I stuck around there for three years: '46, '7, and '8, but I just couldn't make that double play like I used to and I couldn't move like I used to. I was just utility. I could play third, second, or short, and I even played right field.

I roomed with some pretty good characters, like Ferris Fain. Brooks Holder was another good roommate of mine.

Ferris, he was hot-tempered and he wanted to do everything right, you know, and he wanted to win all the time and he wanted to hit every ball for a base hit. And he would fight at the drop of a hat. His dad was a boxer, so he taught him quite a few things. Ferris was a good ballplayer. He was aggressive and like he told me, when he went up he'd look at Connie Mack and he'd tell him to be taking and he'd take and he'd want to be hitting that ball. So finally he wasn't hitting good and he told Connie, he said, "You can take that take and shove it." [Laughs] That's the type of a ballplayer he was. So he started hitting and he led that league.

He wasn't a home run hitter and when you played with Lefty he wanted you to pull everything. That's what Charlie Graham — he was the owner — told me. "Jeep," he said, "punch that ball around. You're not a home run hitter." Then O'Doul said, "Pull, pull, pull!" You were between two people. But, anyway, after I started managing I sprayed that ball and hit to all different fields. I wish I'd've done that when I was playing up there.

BK: You hit really well as a playing manager.

DT: I did a lot better, naturally, in Class C. I learned to wait for the pitches that I wanted.

In 1949 when I went down and managed Phoenix, they had never drawn over 70,000 people and we won the pennant that year and we drew 140-some-thousand people there. I signed and I was like Reggie Jackson when he signed with California down there; you know, he got 50 cents a head extra bonuses. I got a nickel a head extra. [Laughs]

We had a good ballclub and I enjoyed managing, but I didn't like the scouts to come in. They were drinkers, a lot of 'em, and we'd go out after the game and talk about the fellows in the league. I didn't drink; I'd nurse a coke until two in the morning and hear about what all they had done and so forth. Then we'd talk about the ballplayers and they'd be drinking those beers and when we'd go outta there I don't know whether they knew what day it was. I didn't go for that. I'm not a political guy and I called a spade a spade. [Laughs]

Joe Devine, who recommended me for the job, was the head West Coast scout for the Yankees. Joe was behind me and he knew what I could do with the kids. I was managing Twin Falls—he got me that job up there—and he said, "If you do good, you'll go on up."

Well, Joe passed away. Cancer or something. He had said, "As long as Jeep's with the Yankees I'll see that he moves on up." I had had a first place in '49 and 1950 I think we finished third, and then in Twin Falls we finished fourth.

No one on the East Coast knew me because all of mine was on the West Coast with San Francisco, so Weiss, who was the fellow back in New York, he didn't know me and when Joe passed away all the other scouts were pushing their boys. I called him and talked to him and I says, "I think with my record I'm deserving of a Class B situation." He said, "They're all filled right now. We can send you down to Class D in Paducah." I said, "No, thanks," because Chet Murphy, who was the business manager of Phoenix, had kept in contact with me and he says, "We'd like to have you back here in Phoenix." So I went back there in 1952.

And then in '53 I took a job with an automotives company out of Cleveland, Ohio. I interviewed for the job because I was getting kind of fed up with baseball, not being able to go ahead. If you don't have somebody pushing you you're not gonna make it, you might say. So I went to selling and I played ball for Phoenix and sold up until about June of 1954 and that was it.

The area just opened up for me. I was working on straight commission, traveling the whole state, but I'd play ball in Phoenix and then I'd work Tucson and if they'd go into Bisbee-Douglas, I'd work Bisbee-Douglas and so forth. I'd work all the areas around there, calling on all the new car dealers, body shops, the mines, and so forth. Ranchers.

I quit then in June and the area just opened wide open for me. People got to know me and could depend on me calling on 'em. I started in '53 in November, I think it was, and in 1955 they took 12 men out of the sales force and put 'em into management and so I just went on up in management and took an $8,000 a year cut to go into management. I didn't have to get out and beat the bushes every day and call on accounts. I just worked with the salesmen, which was worse than what I was doing. [Laughs] I didn't realize it, being younger and wanting to advance.

I had 11 western states that I supervised — district manager — and called on all of the new car dealers and trained these men on how to sell the product. After six years of that, of being away from the family, I told 'em I'm gonna go back to selling. They couldn't believe it. I said, "I don't want to be away from my home and children anymore. Just give me a territory." "You can have any area in the United States." I said, "I'll take Fresno."

They had a man there, but since I was district manager over this kid and he wanted to go to L. A. in the industrial end of it, I told 'em he wanted to transfer down there. So they transferred him down there and I took over the Fresno area and I sold here for about a year-and-a-half. It was terrible; the area had been abused by salesmen — packing the orders, putting extra ciphers on the hundreds and giving 'em a thousand and so forth — so I just laid groundwork with all these people. Because I had played ball here when I was younger a lot of 'em knew me. I started asking 'em, "Would you buy from me if I had my own business?" "Definitely." So I did that. I had enough money to buy a little merchandise and I started selling to 'em and got more merchandise and kept growing. We had the business for 14 years. Then I sold out and retired. I was 53.

I was born in Colorado, but lived most of my life here in Fresno. I was a year-and-a-half old when I came out here. Dad came out and had 40 acres and I grew up on a ranch. Then he'd sell that and we'd go into town and buy a house and fix it all up and trade that for a ranch. We moved 32 times in my life. [Laughs] Dad was kind of a go-getter. He worked his job during the day and he'd come home and go to work. Us boys, we had to help. We had cows at one time and he'd come by and, "Boys, it's time to get up." Five o'clock in the morning, we'd milk those cows and then we'd have to go to school.

I played all the sports in high school. I was a football player, and basketball and baseball and track. I did 'em all. In 1999, in fact, the high school that I went to inducted me in their athletic hall of fame. That was quite a surprise to me.

BK: The 1946 Seals.

DT: I got back out of the service and went to spring training in Hawaii on the island of Oahu. We played Philadelphia [Athletics] over there. They came over for exhibition games. I was just doing my job, playing and enjoying the ocean and swimming and so forth. We would work out real early and then O'Doul would let you have the rest of the afternoon off.

I didn't play too much in '46. I played a little third base. Luby was at second base and Nicely was the shortstop. Nicely we picked up when I was in the service. I'd relieve him because he was not really a strong kid. He'd get sick and he had trouble with his stomach, I believe, so I'd go in and play short. Then he'd get better and go back in.

We had a good ballclub. We had some good pitching. Larry Jansen was there, and Al Lien and Bill Werle. I saw Bill up in Oakland a while ago. I go up there and visit with a few of the old-timers. Old Bernie Uhalt, I've seen him. He's 90 years old now. Dario Lodigiani. Bill Rigney. When I managed Phoenix the Giants had spring training down there and Bill and Larry Jansen came out to the house and the wife fixed dinner for 'em and we sat here and chitchatted. He's done real well for himself, Bill has.

Jansen was one of those pitchers who could more-or-less thread the needle and he developed this slider that I don't know whether too many guys had seen one at that time. Larry had good control and he threw that fastball and he'd twist his wrist a little bit and that thing'd slide off and hit 'em on the end of the bat. He had a real good year.

And Larry was a good hitter for a pitcher, too. He was like Bob Joyce. Those guys swung the bat because they wanted to win ballgames, not get up there and just swing at the air.

We had a good balanced ballclub, although one or two guys asked me about Ferris. He hit real good one year and the next year he hit about .200-something. Lefty wanted you to pull everything 'cause he could do it.

I guess Lefty had good reason to be loved. He just loved baseball and he knew hitting and developed some very, very good ballplayers, as you know. They went on up. Lefty never put any restrictions on you; you did what you wanted to do. If you wanted to go out and carouse all night, if he found out about it he wouldn't say anything, but if you did that and then you started going downhill on your hitting and fielding, then he'd jerk you out and let somebody else play and then tell you to get your life in gear and do what you're supposed to do. Like I say, he just knew how to work each and every individual.

When I came back out of the service as a pilot, he wanted to sit by me and know about what was happening to the airplane. I remember one night, we were coming back from Hawaii there in '46 and we were on the TEM Mars and that thing lost the autopilot and that thing dropped about 8 or 900 feet. Boy, the first thing I know here's Lefty in my bunk wanting to know what happened. [Laughs] I say, "Lefty, I don't know. It took me some time to find out. Later on, when they got things under control I talked to the boys up front and they told me they lost the autopilot. I told Lefty and he was satisfied then.

My son flies with Alaskan Airlines now and I've been in those simulators and, I'll tell you, everything is so different from what it was then. I've flown that simulator — that's the MD80 — and that's just like flying an airplane. They train you right there in that thing and not have to spend all of that money for gasoline.

Getting back to ol' Lefty, he was well liked by everybody in the movie industry. He worked down there and when we'd go to Hollywood all of the fellows would come to the ballgames. George Raft would come into the clubhouse, and Eugene Paulette, and tell their stories to us and travel on the trains from Hollywood or L. A. to San Diego and go down with us. We enjoyed talking to those guys because they had a lot of tales that they could tell you about the movie industry. They were around all the ballplayers; they knew the Hollywood Stars and they knew the Angels.

BK: In the 1946 playoffs you did particularly well. Were you a good clutch player?

DT: I just played every day to give it everything I had. I loved to play ball and I knew I had good hands and I had good range because I was quick. I just did the best I could and that was it. Whether I was a clutch player or not, I don't know. You just get up there and do the best you can.

I know one time when I was leading off, Forrest Joe Orrell was pitching for Portland. It was the second game of a double header and I was leading off and he threw at my head and I went down. I didn't think anything about it. Joe was about six-foot-four or so and he looked like a giant out there on that mound when he was throwing at you. But, anyway, I was up there and I was trying to get on base and the next time, down I go again.

Gilly Campbell was catching for Portland. Gilly was the type of a guy who would talk to you all the time; he'd just yack-yack-yack. He'd say, "Jeep, what d'ya want? You want a fastball? I'll call for it. Let me know." And he'd get you thinking and you might be in trouble. [Laughs] I told Gilly, "If that guy throws at me again and knocks me down, I'm going out after him."

Of course, you know that I went down again and, man, there I got hot under the collar. I'm pretty even-tempered, but when I get mad I don't know what's going on. So I'm out on the mound with my bat and I'm menacing ol' Joe and here come both dugouts out and it's kind of a melee out there. There's a picture in the paper the next morning of me looking up at big Joe and it says, "David and Goliath." [Laughs] I'm about 5-8.

But I enjoyed the game for all the 14 years I was in it.

BK: Here's a tough question. Nicely has the reputation of being one of the best fielding shortstops who ever played. You also had the reputation of being an outstanding fielder. Who was better?

DT: [Laughs] That's a hard one to answer. I don't know if Roy ever made the record books for fielding or not, but I know I led in assists and I'm in there.

BK: Nicely made a lot of errors, but he was making errors on balls that other shortstops could not have gotten to.

DT: By leading the league in assists, you have to be moving to cover ground. I've run the hundred in ten flat in high school. I was quick and I could move quick. I had good range. I feel that I saved a lot of base hits by being able to get over there and stop 'em and then getting up and throwing guys out.

When I see some of these plays that are made today — the game has changed so much — I don't see the fellows getting in front of the ball all of the time. They'll run to the side and scoop it up with their left hand and then take another step to throw it and all of that. I guess that's the way they let 'em play nowadays. When I was playing they always told us to always get in front of the ball. You'd go to your right and you'd slide into the ball and come up throwing.

BK: Do you remember much about the tie in 1947?

DT: Not much of anything. We played L. A. and we set there waiting for them to finish up. Jack Brewer started the game for us. I don't even remember if I played in that game or not. It was a heartbreaker. Somebody hit a home run and that broke the game wide open.

BK: What do you remember about Oakland's Nine Old Men in '48?

DT: I see Billy Raimondi all the time. I don't remember much at all. If I was Sam Gibson I could tell the pitch that I made to a guy 20 years ago, and the score and where it was and everything else. I used to sit there in amazement listening to him talk about that. Some guys are like that; they can remember everything that happened to them during their career. But I couldn't tell you what happened in my career. I do remember that incident with ol' Joe Orrell and a few things like that.

And when we were playing Philadelphia in an exhibition game and I was at shortstop and here this pitcher came into second base and he just threw his leg back and shoved his spikes into my leg and cut me all up. I've got a blood vessel that's got a little knot in it to this day. I said to him, "What are you, a busher? You're trying to ruin my career. You could slide into second base without trying to rip my legs all to shreds." I think he thought he was Ty Cobb. Those things you remember.

BK: What was your biggest thrill?

DT: Oh, gosh. Probably was winning the pennant in 1946. And then in '43, when I went in the service, we won the Governor's Cup playoff and I got a ring out of that.

I'm not too much on the individual things. I played with some good ballplayers that went on up and it's always nice to know that you played with some of 'em like that.

BK: Who was the best one?

DT: Oh, I think Larry Jansen and Ferris Fain and Nanny Fernandez. He was good with the bat and he was not really a good fielder, as far as that goes.

I have enjoyed playing with players on the Seals and also the players on the other teams. I have many friends that I keep in contact with. Baseball is a great sport and I hate to see it so commercialized.

DON "JEEP" TROWER
Born December 10, 1919, Hartman, CO
Ht. 5'8" Wt. 150 Batted and Threw Right
Infielder

Year	Team, Lg	G	AB	R	H	2B	3B	HR	RBI	BA
1939	S.L.C., Pio	120	514	108	148	20	11	3	42	.288
1940	Tacoma, WI	101	361	64	95	23	8	7	44	.263
	SF, PCL	19	49	8	8	0	1	0	1	.163
1941	SF, PCL	126	394	56	97	22	4	3	36	.246
1942		165	607	192	153	17	4	1	35	,252
1943		64	263	34	58	9	0	2	18	.221
1944–1945		military service								
1946	SF, PCL	98	193	34	40	4	0	0	11	.207
1947		71	76	21	17	1	0	0	9	.224
1948		53	109	13	20	6	0	0	8	.182
1949	Phoenx, AzTx	146	543	149	172	32	10	5	70	.317
1950		101	391	128	134	33	8	4	59	.343
1951	TwnFls, Pio	135	484	112	132	24	1	11	68	.273
1952	Phoenx, AzTx	131	499	96	132	26	4	5	76	.265
1953		39	161	44	64	14	3	1	33	.398

CHAPTER 3 ◆

◆

1947:
The First Tie

Second place: W 105 L 82 .561 1 GB
Governor's Cup
First round: Oakland over San Francisco, 4 games to 1

As the 1947 season dawned, the Seals team that took the field was very similar to the 1946 champions. But the changes, although few, were major. Gone were 30-game winner Larry Jansen (to the New York Giants) and RBI leader Ferris Fain (to the Philadelphia Athletics).

Both Fain and Jansen initially balked at being promoted to the major leagues. The Giants offered Jansen less than a $1,000 increase over his PCL salary, but the pitcher arranged a conditional contract that would pay him well if he produced well, which he did. Fain's offer from the A's was actually for less than the Seals had paid, but after some discussion the amount was increased and he signed.

Jansen's replacements appeared to be more than sufficient. Bob Joyce, the 31-game winner of 1945, was back, and he was joined by Jack Brewer, who came from the Giants in the Jansen deal, and Bob Chesnes, up from Salt Lake City, who was an excellent hitter as well as a promising pitcher.

The offense missed Fain, though. Joe Brovia was recalled from Salt Lake City and replaced Frenchy Uhalt as an outfield regular, Ray Orteig did a fine job as the new third baseman, and Sheridan stepped up as the offensive leader, but first base was a problem. Chuck Henson, who had led the Pioneer League in batting (.363) at Salt Lake City in 1946, was awarded the job in spring training, but illness ended his season and career after only 12 games. PCL veteran Bill Matheson took over but produced (4-69-.250) only about half of what Fain did in '46.

The first base situation eventually caused the end of the Seals' working agreement with the Giants. New York still owed San Francisco players in exchange for Jansen, who was having a brilliant rookie season in the National League, and O'Doul and Charlie Graham wanted Jack Graham, a slugger who had 34 home runs and 121 RBIs at Jersey City in 1947. Instead, the Giants traded Graham to San Diego, where he hit 48 home runs to lead the league in an injury-shortened 1948 season. Charlie Graham terminated the working agreement after the '47 season.

The 1947 pitching was perhaps better overall that '46's, other than for the loss of Jansen. Chesnes, the top pitcher in the Pioneer League in 1946 at Salt Lake City (18–6, 1.52, a league-record 278 strikeouts), won 22 and lost only 8. Brewer won 16, Melton won 17 for the second straight year, Joyce, who did not succeed with the Giants in 1946, came back to win 15, and Bill Werle won 12 as he did in '46. Once again, the Seals had six pitchers with double figure victories.

1947 San Francisco Seals. *Back row (left to right):* Bill Werle, Roy Nicely, Ted Jennings, Frank Seward, Joe Brovia. *Second row:* "Battle" Sanders, Frenchy Uhalt, Bob Joyce, Dale Westley, Hugh Luby. *Front row:* Don Trower, Dino Restelli, Lefty O'Doul, Jim Gladd, Sal Taormina, Joe Sprinz (author's collection).

Hugh Luby, veteran second baseman (courtesy of Jack Brewer).

The best pitching performance seen by the Seals in 1947 was not by a member of the team. It was by former Detroit Tigers' ace Tommy Bridges, now pitching for Portland. On April 20, Bridges no-hit them, 2–0.

Sheridan's 16 home runs and 95 RBIs topped the team, and Brovia batted .309, Orteig .299 (a poor last weekend of the season cost him a .300 average), Don White .292, and Dino Restelli, also .292. The middle infield combination of Hugh Luby (9-70-.266) and Roy Nicely (8-73-.253) was again among the best in professional baseball.

During the season, the PCL became determined to be a major league in 1948. When the proposition was put to Commissioner A. B. "Happy" Chandler, he at first gave hope, but the major league owners overruled him. Major league status was not to be granted.

There was a league first in 1947, just as there had been in the National League in 1946 and would be in the American League in 1948. Never before had a tie for first place occurred, but when the dust cleared at the end of the season both Los Angeles and San Francisco had identical records of 105–81.

Los Angeles led most of the year, but the Seals caught and passed the Angels in mid September. The Angels overtook them again before the month was out and it was neck-and-neck down the stretch. Either team could have won the pennant outright with a win in its final regular game, but both lost those last games.

The Seals came out on the wrong end of a questionable ninth inning umpiring decision in that final game against the San Diego Padres. Max West's three-run home run in extra innings won it for the Padres and forced the Los Angeles— San Francisco playoff game, which was played in Wrigley Field, so decided by a coin toss.

The Los Angeles Angels won the coin toss and therefore the game was played in Wrigley Field on September 29. The ballpark was filled with 22,006 people, among them the third-place Portland Beavers, who finished the season in Hollywood. If the Angels won this game, they would stay in L. A. to play them; if the Seals won, they would fly to San Francisco.

SF	AB	R	H	RBI	LA	AB	R	H	RBI
White, cf	4	0	0	0	Garriott, cf	2	1	0	0
Luby, 2b	3	0	1	0	Schuster, ss	4	1	1	0
Sheridan, rf	4	0	0	0	Sauer, rf	2	1	0	0
Restelli, lf	4	0	0	0	Maddern, lf	3	1	1	4
Orteig, 3b	4	0	1	0	Ostrowski, 3b	4	0	0	0
Matheson, 1b	4	0	1	0	Barton, 1b	4	1	2	1
Nicely, ss	3	0	1	0	Stringer, 2b	4	0	1	0
Gladd, c	4	0	1	0	Malone, c	3	0	0	0
Brewer, p	2	0	0	0	Chambers, p	3	0	1	0
	31	0	5	0		29	5	6	5

Pitching	IP	H	R	ER	SO	BB
Brewer (L, 16–14)	8	6	5	5	7	3
Chambers (W, 24–9)	9	5	0	0	5	2

SF	000	000	000	0	5	2
LA	000	000	05x	5	6	3

E: Luby, Matheson, Sauer, Ostrowki, Stringer. LOB: SF 6, LA 5. HR: Maddern (15), Barton (18). Double Plays: Stringer to Schuster to Barton, Luby to Matheson, Ostrowski to Stringer to Barton, Schuster to Stringer to Barton. HBP: Sauer by Brewer.

It was an even match-up. In addition to tying in the final standings, the two teams evenly split their season series. Given the pitching assignment for L. A. was southpaw Cliff Chambers, the league's top pitcher that season. Lefty O'Doul gave the ball to righthander Brewer. Both pitchers were working on only one day's rest, but for seven innings neither man seemed to tire.

The only evidence that perhaps Brewer was not at peak form was his control, which was not as sharp as usual. He walked five and hit a batter. Chambers led off the Angels' eighth and was out, then leadoff batter Cecil Garriott walked, Bill Schuster singled, and Brewer hit Eddie Sauer with a pitch to load the bases. Cleanup hitter Clarence Maddern homered to make the score 4–0. Brewer retired John Ostrowski and then Larry Barton homered to end the scoring. Chambers retired the Seals in the ninth and L. A. won, 5–0. It was Chambers' 24th win of the year.

The now second-place Seals had to play fourth-place Oakland in the first round of the playoffs, but this was not the same Seals team that it had been before the tie-breaker with the Angels. Oakland's Will Hafey tossed a two-hitter to shut out San Francisco, 2–0, in game one although Joyce pitched very well in defeat. Then Chesnes was hit hard in game two and the Oaks won, 7–6, despite Matheson's 4-for-4 with 3 RBIs.

The Seals took game three, 4–3, in 11 innings. The winning run was scored by Hugh Luby, who led off the bottom of the 11th with a double and scored on a single by Orteig. Bill Werle pitched the first ten innings, but the win went to Mike Budnick, just down from the Giants, who tossed a perfect eleventh. It was his first appearance for the Seals all season.

Oakland came back to win game four, 8–4, roughing up Melton for six runs in six innings, and Hafey pitched his second shutout of the series in game five, winning 4–0 and holding the Seals to only four hits. For the five games, San Francisco batted only .234, a microscopic .194 in the four losses.

Los Angeles defeated third-place Portland, four games to one, in the first round, and won the championship series against Oakland, also four games to one. It was the only time the Angels won the Governor's Cup.

JACK BREWER

Seals 1947–1949

Jack Brewer joined the Seals in 1947 as part payment for Larry Jansen. Early on it looked as if Brewer would be a washout because his arm turned up sore at the end of spring training. With the help of a trainer, however, it came around and over his first two years with the club he won 31 games and led the team in innings pitched. He was the staff ace for those two years.

He faltered in 1949 and that was his last season with the Seals. He did not play in 1950 and tried a comeback in 1951 in the Western International League, but was unable to perform up to his earlier level, so he retired.

JACK BREWER: I went up to the Giants [in 1940] from USC, where I graduated. I had pitched with the Trojan team for three years; we won two championships. I had a scout following me around my last year. He worked for the Giants; his name was Frank Brazill, an ex-ballplayer. He played in the Coast League and was quite well known. An infielder, I believe.

I signed for what at that time was a pretty generous bonus: $10,000. I went up to New York directly, even though I didn't get a chance to pitch. That was in '41. I was with some Hall of Famers up there, including Mel Ott and Carl Hubbell. That was quite a thrill for me. I was about 22 and had never been out of California.

The Japs had bombed us in 1941 and I joined the Navy in 1942. I knew that I was gong to be called so I joined and got a commission as an ensign in the United States Navy. I spent '42 and '43 in the South Pacific and at the very end of '44 I received an honorable discharge and joined the Giants about August of '44. I hadn't been in training and wasn't really in shape except for pitching a little batting practice.

We went to Philadelphia and Mel Ott, our manager, handed me the ball and said I was the starter that day. I managed to pitch a four-hitter and beat the Phillies, 4-to-1. What a thrill!

I had a pretty good year in '45. I won 8 and lost 6. In '46 I figured that I had earned a starting role at the beginning of the season so I became chagrined when I wasn't being used as a starter and went over Mel Ott's head, which I know now I shouldn't have done, although everything turned out right in my overall life through God's grace.

I went over Mel Ott's head and complained to Horace Stoneham, the owner at that time. He said he had the ability to option me to

Jack Brewer with the New York Giants in 1945 (courtesy of Jack Brewer).

Minneapolis. I went down and I won 14 games. We got in what they called in those days the Shaughnessy playoffs, in which the first and third and second and fourth teams had a playoff series. We ended up losing to Indianapolis.

The Giants recalled me then but I had really pitched hard and long at Minneapolis and the season was still going on in New York but I was tired so I chose not to report. I found myself being traded to, originally, the Hollywood Stars. I went to spring training with them and there was some kind of a mix-up and it was supposed to be the San Francisco Seals, so I reported to the Seals. I was there in '47, '48, and '49. I started the season in '50 and was traded for Joe Grace to Sacramento.

I enjoyed my Seals' experience immensely because the weather conditions are so much nicer along the coast. All the teams were up and down the coast and travel by air allowed us to have Mondays off each week.

I enjoyed particularly playing for Lefty O'Doul. The first year, for example we trained in Maui, Hawaii, in a quaint little town. The little village was owned by the vice-president of the Seals at that time, Paul Fagan, who had bought in to the San Francisco Seals organization. As a kind of promotion deal be brought the Seals over there because he was opening a beautiful hotel-motel. Hana, Maui, was the town.

We trained over there at the little schoolhouse grounds. They had a baseball field there and it was a wonderful experience. The pitchers and catchers went over about a week or two in advance with all the equipment in a DC-7, a non-commercial plane.

I had always had a fear of flying. When I talked to Fagan

Jack Brewer with the Seals in 1947 (courtesy of Jack Brewer).

when I reported to the Seals, he called me up to the office and told me of his elaborate plans. I thought we were going over in a cruise boat and when he said we were gonna fly, I thought flying over that 2,000 miles or whatever it is across the water I wasn't too keen about it. I was a ballplayer, not an aviator. Fagan said, "When it's your time to go you'll go." I said, "That's okay, but I don't want to go when it's the pilots' time."

At any rate, he ended up giving me a sleeping pill, so we left late at night — 10:00 in the evening, dark all the way — and I literally went to sleep and didn't wake up 'til early the next morning. As I looked out the window dawn was just breaking; I noticed one of the propellers was not turning. [Laughs] The co-pilot must have known I was a chicken. He came back and he said, "Don't worry. We can fly this ship if necessary on one propeller." I said, "I sure hope you don't have to do that." [Laughs] They sent a Coast Guard plane out to kind of accompany us in the last few miles. I understand the [San Francisco] *Chronicle* had quite a write-up about the incident. They expected the plane to crash in the Pacific Ocean.

We had to take small planes over to Maui, kind of like a little taxi service. That was a little spooky, too. As the years went on I had to learn to fly because that's the only way we traveled with the Seals, except when we played Oakland and Sacramento. I got over my fear, 'though I was always tense during landing and takeoff.

We had a wonderful time in the islands. The whole team flew over to Honolulu and we were to play the New York Giants. I was going to pitch the opener and I was going to show the Giants organization what they missed by not retaining me — kind of a sour grapes thing — but, lo and behold, I came up with a sore arm. I had the sorest arm I ever had. I guess they thought I was chicken or something, but it really was [sore]. And it's amazing because in that hot weather over there in the islands it was ideal training conditions.

They rushed me downtown to a doctor and he shot my arm with cortisone. I went back to the hotel to have a light lunch before the game and I couldn't lift my arm up to my mouth. I just lost control of my right arm entirely, so that was no remedy and I missed the series. I think it was three ballgames.

Then we came back to San Francisco — Seals Stadium — and we played more games there but all during that I thought, "I guess I'm gonna lose my job" because the reporters were on my case every day. There were 15 or 20 young pitchers that were vying for a job on the team. Sportswriters soured on me because they felt I was jakin', and I had been traded by the Giants for one of the Seals' greatest pitchers, Larry Jansen, who had won

30 games and pitched them into the Pacific Coast League title in 1946. When Lefty O'Doul announced I was gonna pitch the opener it was headlines in the sporting pages: "Brewer's pitching for his job."

The trainer, a fellow named Schaeffer — I think his first name was Mickey — with the Giants liked me very much when I was with the Giants. During the time the Giants were there he called me up at the Fairmont Hotel. He heard that I had a sore arm and he worked on me. Every night I would go up there and he'd lay me out on the bed there with hot towels and [use] manipulation — deep manipulation — with his thumbs and kneading and so forth and he found the sore spot that was bothering me and worked that out. I pitched pain free for 300 innings that year and in that cold and windy San Francisco Bay area. It was a miracle because I never missed a start. At night sometimes it was so cold we had to wear electric jackets to keep warm. Some nights there the fog would roll in and the game might be called because of lack of visibility.

The Lord really blessed me to be able to pitch there three good seasons and I pitched my share of innings each year. We won that opener, 4-to-2, as I recall, but I didn't receive credit. I was relieved in the eighth inning by a pitcher named Ray Harrell. He got credit. He came in with the score tied at 2-all and we won it in the ninth.

The most important thing about that game was while I was warming up in Seals Stadium that day. I had met a girl while I was in the Navy at an Officers Club dance and became very much infatuated and felt that it was probably time for me to start figuring on finding someone for life, but the Navy sent me down to Coronado Isle, San Diego. I opened an amphibious base there and went overseas eventually and lost contact with her. I hadn't seen her for three or four years and thought I never would again.

But during warming up for that opening game in San Francisco her dad, who I had met — a wonderful man and a great baseball fan, never missed a game — came down to the railing and said, "Hi, Jack." I looked up and said, "Hi, Herb." His name was Herbert Manners. He said, "Look up in the stands," and he pointed up and there was Dorothy sitting up there pretty as a picture with a big smile on her face. I waved to her and had to continue warming up, but when I got back to the hotel that night there was a call from her father inviting me to dinner.

Dorothy had married and had a little two year old girl, but she was in the process of a divorce. The man that she married turned out to be very abusive, even to taking a gunshot at her mother. They were near the end of the final decree; he had been jailed and then released with the parole obligation of staying out of the state.

I told Herb that I'd be right out for dinner and that started it all off.

That was '47. In '48 at the end of the season I thought about having a wedding out at the ballpark with the ballplayers with crossed bats, but I noticed the other ballplayers were getting a little envious. Lefty O'Doul put the kibosh on it, so we were later married on November the seventh, 1948, in Riverside at the famous Mission Inn.

I was in the Larry Jansen trade and if I hadn't been traded that wouldn't have happened. The Giants did all right and I did well; I got my million-dollar baby and we have just celebrated our 52nd anniversary. I wouldn't trade her for all the million-dollar salaries of today's ballplayers.

Joe Brovia and I roomed together several times. Joe was a very amiable Italian boy who was born right there near San Francisco. He was a terrific hitter; he just literally attacked the baseball. He was like a *vicious* hitter; he could hit the long ball. His average always bordered on or was over .300. His only problem, he wasn't much of a fielder. He had a chance with Cincinnati but he really didn't get a good break at all.

We also had Dino Restelli, also an outfielder, who had a good year in '48 and was signed by the Pittsburgh Pirates. He went up and they had that great home run hitter, Ralph Kiner, and Dino was competing with him homer for homer there for a while, but I guess, as the old saying goes, they started curving him [laughs] and he tailed off.

The real star in '47 was Gene Woodling, our center fielder. He went to the Yankees. Casey Stengel called him up. He had a sensational year with us. Lefty O'Doul really made a hitter out of him. I remember in spring training he was a punch-and-judy hitter. He faced the pitcher in such a way that he couldn't get much power in his bat. Lefty worked with him; he used to tie a rope around his waist to get him in the proper stance. To keep him from lunging he'd work by the hour with Gene and pulled that rope so he wouldn't lunge out in batting practice. He got his timing right and, boy, he was knocking down the fence during that season. He led the league in every department and had great years with the Yankees, including two World Series against the Brooklyn Dodgers.

Lefty was a marvelous instructor of hitters. Ted Williams—he noted his ability when he joined San Diego. He told Ted, "Don't change a thing. That swing of yours is great." Of course, Lefty is an unacknowledged Hall of Famer. That's one of the crimes of all time. I can't understand how they've avoided getting Lefty in the Hall of Fame because he was a marvelous hitter. He led the National League in hitting twice. He had some great years with the old Phillies. And as an instructor he was, in my opinion, the greatest.

We had Bill Werle, a lefthander. He was a terrific pitcher, a starter and reliever. Werle was a lefthanded sinkerball pitcher. Bob Chesnes, also a pitcher, had a terrific year and went to the Pirates. He had a fastball about as fast as anyone could throw. We didn't have measurements in those days, but I imagine he was in the mid 90s. He had a good curveball and all the physical equipment to be a superstar, but I understand he got a sore arm and eventually gave up baseball.

Roy Nicely, he was the best [shortstop] I ever saw. I remember Lefty was always on him for not being able to hit higher. He was a .240–.250 hitter, which nowadays he'd be making a million dollars with his all-around ability. We were crossing the bridge one time; Lefty and Roy and all of us were going over to Oakland to play that crosstown morning game. Lefty was kidding Roy a little bit about his inability to hit. It was kind of a kidding way, but it was needling. Lefty was saying, "I'd be able to hit .300 in this league if I used a rolled up magazine." [Laughs] "What you oughtta do is jump off this bridge when we're halfway out there. You oughtta be ashamed of yourself." He was always on Roy. But he made up for anything with his glove. And he would somehow or another come up with a clutch hit when we needed it, even with the low batting average. He was a pretty good clutch hitter.

Neill Sheridan had some good years while I was there. Played right field, long ball hitter. Ex–football player, pretty rugged guy, very intense ballplayer.

At second base was the veteran Hugh Luby. I pitched a playoff game in '47 against the Los Angeles Angels. I had a no-hitter for seven innings, but in the eighth inning I walked [Cecil] Garriott, a little lefthanded hitter, and had one out, then [Bill] Schuster hit a ball right to where Luby was playing. I never quite got over it because it would have been a double play ball. Roy had given the signal that he was gonna take the throw at second base in case Garriott stole but it was a hit-and-run and Luby ran over to cover second base and Schuster hit the ball right where he should have been. That started a rally and finally the number four slugger, Clarence Maddern, hit a high slider over the left field wall and it was a four-run inning. Larry Barton hit a solo of me and that was the ballgame. We got shut out by [Cliff] Chambers, their ace pitcher.

We were tied at the end of the regular season. We'd been playing in San Diego. I'd won a ballgame down there and I only had one day rest when I pitched that playoff game. Monday night, I believe it was, the second to last game of the regular season; all we had to do was beat San Diego Sunday because Rex Cecil had beaten the Angels, 1-to-nothing, in their last game of the regular season. Rex Cecil was a boyhood buddy of mine from Long Beach. I was so proud of him when I saw the scoreboard; it gave us the opportunity to sew up the pennant.

We had a chance to win that game in San Diego and Lefty I must say made a real bad move as third base coach. We had the bases loaded, we're trailing by one run in the ninth inning. Roy Nicely was up and Lefty had the runner on third try to steal home on a hit-and-run. On a 3-and-2 pitch and two out and the bases loaded, Roy took the pitch, which he should've — it was way over his head — but the umpire called strike three and the ballgame was over.

The attempted steal was reckless, but would have been successful if the umpire had called ball four, forcing in a run. The catcher never tagged the runner. We had a chance to win the game if we were able to go another inning or more. But that's history and along with my playoff game I have some painful memories.

JOHN HERNDON "JACK" BREWER
Born July 21, 1919, Los Angeles, CA
Ht. 6'2" Wt. 170 Batted and Threw Right

Year	Team, Lg	G	IP	W	L	Pct	SO	BB	H	ERA
1940	Knoxv'lle, SA	20	78	3	0	1.000	30	53	77	4.50
	J.C., IL	4	12	0	1	.000	10	7	17	9.75
1941	Clinton, III	21	143	7	11	.389	109	71	150	4.15
	military service									
1944	NY, NL	14	55	1	4	.200	21	16	66	5.56
1945		28	160	8	6	.571	49	58	162	3.83
1946	NY, NL	1	2	0	0	—	3	2	3	13.50
	Mnpls, AA	27	190	14	9	.609	106	74	185	3.46
1947	SF, PCL	38	287	16	14	.533	122	81	278	2.79
1948		37	242	15	11	.577	96	61	291	4.28
1949		34	139	5	11	.313	63	51	171	5.12
1950	did not play									
1951	Tri-City, WI	23	112	4	13	.235	59	33	158	5.79

ROY NICELY

Seals 1945–1950

Almost everyone who saw him play says Roy Nicely was the greatest fielding shortstop the game has ever seen. This was said by teammates, opponents, scouts, sportswriters, and fans. So many people have said it over the years that it *must* be right. One or two people can be wrong, but dozens and dozens can't.

His bat and the fact that some perceived him to be "delicate" kept him out of the major leagues, but he was a clutch hitter with a little punch who played in 90 to 95 percent of the games in schedules that sometimes were 200 games long. So he stayed with the Seals for six years, during which time the team made it to the Governor's Cup playoffs four times.

Nicely teamed with Hugh Luby to give the Seals a middle infield combination that could compare with any in baseball, at any time.

Roy Nicely (courtesy Doug McWilliams).

BK: You had played professionally for a few years before you joined the Seals. How did they acquire you?

ROY NICELY: I belonged to Jersey City — that was in the International League — in '44. I got out of the service in the middle of that year; I had ulcers so they let me out. And I joined them. Then the next year I wanted to try to play on the [West] Coast somewhere, so Jersey City said they had a player in San Francisco that wanted to come back there and they traded us for each other.

BK: Were you from the coast?

RN: No. I was from Missouri.

BK: Who signed you originally?

RN: Originally, with Knoxville, Tennessee. And then I went from there to their spring training, which was in Valdosta, Georgia. From Valdosta, Georgia, they sent me to Salisbury, North Carolina, and from there the [Jersey City] Giants were down there looking for a pitcher that had pitched a no-hitter and they came down to watch him pitch the next game and it ended up they bought me. Then I belonged to Jersey City.

I was outrighted to San Francisco. I played there six years and then I came back and played a half a year at Oakland to end up my career. That was in '52.

BK: Your manager in San Francisco was Lefty O'Doul.

RN: He was one of the best. He wasn't hard on the players and that made you want to play for him. He wasn't a strict bed-checker and all that, which some guys probably needed. He was the type of guy that might put a pitcher in to pinch hit; he was a hunch player and it worked out. The rumor was he could've gone to the big leagues any time, but that was his hometown and he wanted to stay there.

BK: It was said that he was making more money in San Francisco than he could have made in the majors.

RN: Some of the players didn't wanna go to the big leagues because they got a cut in salary.

BK: Larry Jansen was one of your teammates.

RN: He may be the originator of the slider. I'd never heard of a slider. That was in '46 when we had the good ballclub. You know what the players called it — a piss curve. [Laughs] A curve that didn't break much.

Bob Joyce is the one; I never played behind a guy that was any better. I mean, they were gonna hit through the box. Righthanders and lefthanders. It sounds funny, but a lefthander hitting against a righthander, he more or less hit it on his fists and it would be back through the box. And a righthanded hitter would hit it on the end of the bat. You could play closer to the bag because you knew what he was throwing.

I was looking through my scrapbook today and what I found you can't believe. My wife and I got married in '46 — in January — and we had reservations in Carmel. Gosh, we got lost going down there and ended up getting there about three o'clock in the morning and they'd already rented our room. [Laughs] We were supposed to show up about ten, I think. They give us another room and I was looking at this bill today. It was five days. It was called the Pine Tree Inn and it was the fanciest at that time and our bill for five days was $36.00. [Laughs]

BK: You probably paid that and thought, "Boy, this is expensive!"

RN: Yeah. A dinner was a dollar and a quarter or so. That was board and room; that wasn't just room.

BK: Nobody was getting paid $250 million back then, either.

RN: Isn't that awful? There's no sense to it. He's [Alex Rodriguez] not that good a ballplayer. I've watched him 'cause we get Seattle on our television games and I've watched him and watched him. He's a real good ballplayer, but I've never seen him do much with men on base when they *needed* runs. He'd do a lotta home runs with nobody on or the game was 7-to-3 or something. But get the bases jammed or something and need two or three runs, he didn't get 'em.

BK: If someone wants to pay me that kind of money to do what I do, I'll take it.

RN: Yeah. That's the whole thing. If they're crazy enough to pay you that, I'm crazy enough to take it. [Laughs] If somebody offered you 500 bucks—"Here, take it"—you wouldn't turn it down.

BK: It's the guy who's giving who needs his head examined.

RN: Yeah. Texas, they've got some pretty good salaries. That catcher, [Ivan] Rodriguez. I don't know how they'll make money. I guess they raise the admission tickets.

BK: Were you the greatest fielding shortstop ever?

RN: Don't give me that question. I did what I did and that's all I did. I couldn't tell whether I was the best. Everybody around there thought I was.

You remember they got Joe Hoover in '46? They had just won the World Series—Detroit—and they got him from Detroit. Well, I was expecting to not even be with the club, but he wasn't showing anything. He was all form; he'd catch the ball and he had to come up to a certain place to throw it. Well, by then there was two or three steps being taken when he was doing that. O'Doul let him run his rope out and he put me back in.

BK: O'Doul was on you a lot about your hitting.

RN: Yeah. I don't know. I hit fairly good with men in. One guy went to the trouble with statistics. He put the amount of assists and putouts I had against hitting and all that. He said I would have been hitting almost .400, taking hits away from other players.

BK: There's no difference between driving in 100 runs with your bat and saving 100 runs with your glove.

RN: That's right. I know one thing, all the pitchers liked me. One night, we was leaving San Diego to come home and there wasn't enough room on the plane. That was back when you could only get 27 or something on the plane. Well, we had a fella named Tony Buzolich. Him and I, they put us on the train. We got delayed; we got to the ballpark and the game was about half over at San Francisco. Oh, man, the pitchers were disgusted. We really got our fannies eat out, but it wasn't our fault.

BK: The Seals were in the Governor's Cup your first four years with them and you had a high percentage of the team's RBIs in those games.

RN: I guess I just concentrated more or beared down more when they needed it.

See, I had ulcers and a lot of times I was playing and I didn't even feel like it. Sometimes you get up there and think, "The quicker I can get out of here...." [Laughs] A lot of the scouts told me later, even after I moved up here, that they weren't worried so much about my hitting in the big leagues. It was health, if I could play so many games.

BK: You didn't miss many games.

RN: I know it. That's what I told 'em. We had 169 games or something and I'd be playing in 155 or -60. We had 200 games some years.

BK: You had pretty good punch. How big were you?

RN: 'Bout 155. One year Don White, I believe it was, was the club's leading RBI man. I think it was 87; something like that. I had 72 and I was hitting about .250 and he was hitting about .320 or so.

I remember two or three games. One of 'em was a 16-inning game and everybody, their hearts fell out when O'Doul says, "Get up there and get me a hit." Well, we won that 16-inning game. With the bases loaded I singled, two outs.

Another time there was a game that they thought they should've put a pinch hitter in and I drove in two runs in that game.

When I grew up my brother played ball and I was always around a ballpark with him. We lived about two blocks from a ballpark in Joplin. That was me; I didn't even learn how to swim 'cause I wanted to play ball. [Laughs]

BK: Some say the 1946 Seals were the best team the franchise ever had.

RN: Everybody played together. It wasn't what you'd call any all-stars or anything. We all just played when we had to. I don't know; I'm sure they had some awful good teams before that.

I was just looking in my scrapbook and there was a triple play that we had. They didn't know how far back it had been since they had a triple play. It was '46 or '47, I forget which. The whole thing was I never even touched the ball. That was the amazing thing.

The third baseman says, "Don't give me the credit for the triple play. Give it to Roy," because I told him where to throw, see. It was man on second and first and they hit a ball to him, one hop — Shofner — and he was gonna fire to first for the double play and I kept screaming at him, "Second base! Second base!" 'cause I saw the guy running and he wasn't going very good. He wasn't running hard. So he threw to second and then to first for the triple play.

BK: An around the horn triple play is rare.

RN: Usually it's a line drive and somebody steps on the base. Ol' Shofner, everybody was talking about it and he says, "I don't want the credit. Nicely done the steering of me to throw to second. I'd've never thrown to second 'cause I was just gonna make the throw over for a double play." Normally you would, but when I saw the guy was slow getting out of first base I saw that was the play. I believe it was against Hollywood.

BK: You played with Ferris Fain in 1946.

RN: I couldn't figure it out at first. He used a softball net for first base. They're smaller, big pocket, but he could sure scoop 'em up. He was a good ballplayer, good hitter. Well, he had to be to lead the American League a couple of years.

BK: Nicely to Luby to Fain was a great double play combination.

RN: Luby and I played good together. What Luby liked was I could get the ball to him quick and he didn't have the worry of somebody sliding and knocking him down. He mentioned that about Hoover. He was just getting slaughtered on double plays; he wasn't getting a chance to throw to first 'cause he [Hoover] had to come up and throw overhand. Well, I'd just catch the ball right by my feet and just flip it to him and there it was. He got it probably two steps before he ever got to the bag and he knew what he was gonna do.

That was one of my assets, I guess, being able to throw from anywhere. I could get just as much on the ball throwing it a foot off the ground instead of up shoulder high. My arm was accurate. A lot of guys thought I hadn't even looked at the base and threw 'em out. [Laughs]

BK: In 1947 you were a key figure in the last game of the season with San Diego that caused the tie with Los Angeles.

RN: I was at bat and the count on me was three balls and one strike. Restelli was on third. To this day I don't know if he was sent or just went on his own, but here the ball was over shoulder high and outside. Well, the umpire called it a strike, then he calls him out at home and he slid *way* before he could come down with the ball. It was just a nightmare right there. That would've won the ballgame. I wake up sometimes now and think of that. We could've had two pennants in a row.

O'Doul, he just fell over backwards on the ground, like he passed out. [Laughs] First, he called it a strike on me. That was bad enough, and then called the runner out when there was no chance they could've got him because the ball was way up high and outside. By the time he'd catch it and dropped to the plate, Restelli had already quit sliding.

BK: That seemed to break the team's spirit because you guys didn't play at all well in the tiebreaker or the Governor's Cup.

RN: No, we didn't. It took the steam out of us, even that one-game playoff.

BK: Restelli was a very good natural hitter.

RN: He was kind of a streak hitter. I think good hitters don't go into a slump for five or six days or so. They get their one or two hits. That seems to me to be a steadier ballplayer. You couldn't hardly get him out when he was hot. He went up for a little while.

BK: Who was the best player you saw?

RN: I'll tell you one of the smartest players that I ever played with was Uhalt. Bernie Uhalt. He was the only player that I ever played with that wanted to know what the pitcher was throwing. I'd give him a sign. As soon as I got the sign from the catcher I'd relay it to him. That gave him a couple of steps jump on the balls that's hit to him. The other guys didn't want to do that, never had anybody to ask me.

BK: He'd been around many years when you played with him.

RN: He was about through in '45. He's still alive last I heard; he lives over in Oakland. You know, there's not many of us still around.

BK: Joe Brovia.

RN: Oh, he was a character. I liked ol' Joe. One night we was playing in Seattle and I says, "Joe, let me borrow your bat and I'll hit a home run." [Laughs] And he says, "I'll bet you 20 bucks you don't." I says, "Okay, I'll just call you." The second time up that night I hit one out. [Laughs] They had a garden; a guy had a truck garden out back of left field and people set out there on the bank and watched the game. I hit one up into the crowd out there with his bat.

BK: Did he pay you?

RN: No. [Laughs]

He pulled a good one one night at San Francisco. The winning run for the club was on third and they hit a long, high fly out in left field and it was foul, way foul. He went over and caught it. Well, the guy tagged up and walked home because it was hit that far. We couldn't holler at him to not catch it. If he caught it, it just makes an out and they get the winning run. But he didn't know that. He thought he was making a great play.

You're a veterinarian, right? Are you ever around the Thoroughbred racers?

BK: That's all I work on. Strictly horses.

RN: You know, that was one of my bad habits. I liked to go to the races. I was fairly lucky. I would say over the years I went I'm still ahead of 'em.

BK: How did you get to Oregon?

RN: My wife was born and raised here.

BK: Al Lien.

RN: He was my roommate. He was a good, steady pitcher. A lot of people didn't think he pitched good, but he was a good pitcher. He was there way before I got there.

Did anybody mention Bruce Ogrodowski? He used to catch Dizzy Dean. You know, Dizzy'd change his pitch while he was winding up. He'd decide he wanted to throw something else. This can mess a catcher up and a lot of catchers didn't wanna catch him. Oggie'd catch him because he wanted to play.

I went to Birmingham after the '50 season and I jumped the Kansas City ballclub. I was traded to Kansas City and I found out later the reason Kansas City — that was the Yankees farm team — they wanted me to be close to 'em in case they needed a shortstop real quick, but I never did know anything about that until afterwards.

Anyway, I was in spring training with 'em and they were so cheap. The ballclub, the owners and managers and them, they were eating in the dining room at the hotel. We were stuck off in a little side room and the menu had three items on it, so you had your choice of the three things. That was okay.

Then we started to break away from spring training and we went into a marine camp. Paris Island. They give us a mattress and sheets just like we was going in the service. We had to take 'em into the barracks there and make our own bed and everything. I'd done that because I'd been in the army. That still didn't bother me.

But what bothered me was after one of the games, to dress — there was no hot water. We took a shower in cold water, then we get upstairs and had no towels. I just took the sheet off of the bed and I just happened to say something. I said, "You know, I think I've had enough of this. I think I'll head home." And the guy right there in the bunk by me, he played at Kansas City the year before and he said, "Where do you live, Roy?" I says, "I live in San Francisco." And he says, "I live in L. A. Let's go."

So we went into town and caught a bus to Louisville, I think, and then we got the plane into Kansas City 'cause I had my car in storage there. We drove all the way back to California. He said, "They got so cheap at Kansas City at the end of the season we had to borrow bats from the other team." [Laughs] He said, "I don't blame you for wanting to leave."

At one time they had a barbecue, a big barbecue. We was in Lake Wales, Florida, for training that same year. They had this big barbecue for the team. Well, I couldn't eat that kinda food with my bad stomach so I just went in to the dining room to eat. Then I got billed for it. [Laughs] That kinda teed me, too, you know. They said, "Nobody is supposed to be eating here. They're all supposed to be up at this picnic." "I can't eat that food." "We'll have to bill you." I said, "Go ahead and bill me."

This other area where we're eating in, if you wanted another glass of milk you had to pay for it. I mean, it was just little things that were eating you up. *The Sporting News* after that said it was great to be a Yankee, but not a Yankee farmhand. [Laughs]

BK: You were still a young man when you retired.

RN: Yeah. In those years if you was over 32 or 33 you were through. They didn't want you. But now, heck, they're playing at 40. That money deal is what's ruining the game.

BK: What was your top salary?

RN: 1200 a month.

BK: That was outstanding pay back then.

RN: It sure was. I could even save a little money. Now that's tipping money.

BK: Would you go back and play ball again?

RN: I would. Yes.

ROY MELVIN NICELY
Born February 2, 1918, Joplin, MO
Ht. 6' Wt. 160 Batted and Threw Right
Shortstop

Year	Team, Lg	G	AB	R	H	2B	3B	HR	RBI	BA
1940	Salsby, NCSt	111	464	81	113	22	7	2	62	.244
1941	FtSmith, WA	125	449	60	103	19	8	3	48	.229
1942–43		military service								
1944	JersyCity, IL	43	123	19	21	5	0	0	11	.171
1945	SF, PCL	143	484	51	121	18	2	1	44	.250
1946		133	446	32	98	19	3	1	46	.220
1947		173	637	77	161	29	10	8	73	.253
1948		157	613	61	144	24	3	4	85	.235
1949		156	530	48	103	19	2	0	35	.194
1950		110	283	24	55	9	0	2	20.	194
1951	Birm., SA	69	259	34	62	16	0	0	17	.239
1952	Birm., SA	44	154	10	26	2	1	0	16	.169
	Oak., PCL	42	90	12	19	1	2	0	7	.211

NEILL SHERIDAN

Seals 1944–1947, 1950, 1951, 1953–1954

Seals Stadium was a notoriously difficult park in which to hit home runs. A new live-ball low was reached in 1944, when the entire squad could muster only 14. The team leader that season was a young man from Sacramento who was playing only his first year of professional baseball and he

Neill Sheridan (courtesy of Robert Zwissig).

was there only for half the season. Neill Sheridan hit four before he was sent to Chattanooga in a disciplinary move.

Sheridan was a Seal for all or part of eight seasons of his 11-year professional career, which included a brief stopover with the Boston Red Sox in 1948. A self-described line drive hitter, he nonetheless was annually high among the Seals home run hitters and run producers during his time in San Francisco. Today the PCL fans remember him as a Seal, and, indeed, he thinks of himself as a Seal, but his best season may have been 1948, which he spent with the Seattle Rainiers. Sent there by the Red Sox, he batted .312 with a career and team high 17 home runs

BK: How were you originally signed?

NEILL SHERIDAN: I went to the University of San Francisco. When the war broke out we all went down and joined the Marine Corps or the Navy or something and fortunately I had an asthma attack and, of course, the armed services didn't need me and I went to work at the Richmond Hiring Hall. A fellow there in one of the unions knew Lefty O'Doul and he asked me if I'd maybe like to go over and have a tryout. So I went over to the Seals and had a tryout and they signed me.

BK: You spent part of your first year in Chattanooga.

NS: We were up in Seattle and O'Doul was managing and I was just starting. He asked somebody to pinch-hit and I got pissed off and I left. The next day I was on my way to Chattanooga.

BK: You left periodically but you always seemed to wind up back in San Francisco with the Seals.

NS: It was kind of ironic. When Boston bought me I didn't want to go back there 'cause they didn't want to pay me anything. I made more money in the Coast League than I did in the big leagues. Boston ended up sending me to Seattle and then eventually I went back to San Francisco. I've forgotten how that came about. I guess that was in 1950. Then I ended up in San Diego; they traded me for Buster Adams. In '51, I went to

Minneapolis. When Mays went to the Giants I went to Minneapolis and took his place. [Laughs] I didn't do too badly, either. That was about as close as I got to going back to the big leagues, I guess.

BK: The 1946 team was maybe the best the Seals ever had.

NS: We won the pennant; we won the playoffs. That was the first year with Paul Fagan involved with the Seals. He was married to one of the Big Five people from Hawaii; I don't know if it was a sugar family or whatever.

We went to Hawaii for our spring training. We trained in Honolulu and played the locals there, and then we came back to San Francisco and I think we won 13 or 14 games straight and we pretty much led the Coast League the whole year. A lot of the fellows that had gone into the service had returned and they were pretty much in their prime and we had a pretty darn good team.

Larry Jansen I think won 32 games. Ferris Fain went to Philadelphia. Don White, I think he went to Philadelphia. Bill Werle went to Pittsburgh. Most of the people on that team ended up going to the big leagues and the ones that didn't had all come back from the big leagues.

We played big league teams in spring training and as I remember we were .500 against them.

The quality of baseball today has deteriorated, I think. 'Course, maybe I'm getting too old and don't realize what's going on. The fundamentals of baseball, the people don't hit the cutoff men, they get thrown out. The World Series was a good example of people not knowing the fundamentals, running the bases and so forth. It's kind of exasperating to me.

And another thing is the hustle. When you hit a pop fly between the shortstop and the outfielders, or the second baseman and the outfielders, and you loaf to first base, it's unforgivable. The people that I played for, you'd have your ass on the bench, boy, if you did stuff like that. People are paying good money to watch these guys play and they're supposed to be the best in the business and they should produce that way.

The thing that Paul Fagan tried to do was to establish the Coast League as a big league. If the cities at that time had the population, it would've been a breeze. Los Angeles, Seattle, and San Francisco are probably the only three cities that had the population to satisfy a big league. Of course, now it would be wonderful if they would establish a big league on the Coast instead of traveling all over the country.

We traveled pretty much first class. Of course, it was mostly on a train. We went into a city; for instance, we'd go to Portland. We'd play seven games and have Monday off. That would be the travel day. We'd go to Seattle, play seven games, and have Monday off to come home. We stayed in the good hotels. I've forgotten how much meal money we got, but it seemed like we got about seven or eight dollars a day, but it was adequate.

As far as conditions were, it was wonderful. I don't think you could talk to any big league players who ever went to the Coast League that would say any different.

In the Coast League with the playoffs and all that — that was extra money — I think I made $7500 in 1946. In '47 I got a raise. In '48, when I got a contract from Boston, they wanted to pay me the same as I made in the Coast League and I wrote 'em a letter. Joe Cronin was the general manager, I guess, and I said, "Forget it. I'd just as soon stay in San Francisco. I'm not gonna go back there for the same money I made out here where I can be at home." They did send me, I think, a thousand dollars more, so I conceded in going to the big leagues. [Laughs]

I think in spring training I hit around .300. Of course, the big league team I went to was the wrong one. They had [Stan] Spence, [Sam] Mele, [Wally] Moses, [Dom] DiMaggio, and Ted Williams and I was the sixth outfielder. Well, I had about as much chance of making that ballclub as flying to the moon. So at the end of spring training I came back to Boston and I was there about two weeks, I guess, and I had my wife back, and the two kids and they were babies, and all of a sudden they said, "We're gonna send you to Seattle."

I went to Seattle and I stayed there the rest of the season. I hit .315 or .320. Sammy White was on that ballclub in Seattle. At the end of the season, they had a working agreement to take Sammy White to Boston and that's how I ended up back in the Coast League and that's where I stayed.

They did recall me at the end of '48. Sam Mele broke his leg or arm and I did go back. I went to Yankee Stadium and I got my only pinch hitting assignment and I was called out on strikes. That was the only time I got to bat, but I did have a pinch running role at one time. That was my big league experience.

BK: Wherever you played you were one of the top offensive forces. You were a good run producer.

NS: I usually hit third. I could run and throw and the usual stuff that you're supposed to have when you're the third place hitter.

BK: You were well regarded as an outfielder.

NS: I could run very well and I had a great arm. Evidently some people compared me to Clemente. I saw Clemente and I don't know whether I was *that* good. [Laughs]

John Madden was a kid when I was playing and I was his idol. [Laughs] I got a telephone call here one day from John Madden on the radio and we had quite a talk. He was telling me how great an arm I had. I still have the tape. John was a friend of one of the clubhouse boys—I guess they were neighbors –and he use to bring John to the ballpark every once in a while. I didn't know him at the time.

BK: The Coast League was only a half step away from the majors, one way or the other. Who were the best players you saw?

NS: Max West was with San Diego. Jack Graham and Clarence Maddern. Eddie Sauer. [Cliff] Chambers, the pitcher with Los Angeles.

BK: Chambers was the pitcher who beat the Seals in the 1947 playoff game for first place.

NS: Ordinarily I had real good luck with him. He was a lefthanded pitcher and he threw hard and I could hit a fastball pretty well.

The saddest part about that playoff thing is that we should've won in San Diego the day before that. We got kind of screwed. It was one of those things where it was up to an umpire's decision and that really put the monkey wrench in the machine.

There's such a thing as catcher's interference. I think Dino Restelli was on third and I think he was stealing home. The catcher went out in front of the batter so that the batter didn't have a chance to swing and caused a balk. And this was the controversy.

O'Doul just fell over on his back and fainted. And, of course, all around home plate was dust. That would have been the winning run and the decision was against us and that caused the playoff the next day. I think Chambers beat us. Maddern hit a home run. Jack Brewer was pitching for us. We were very disappointed and didn't do well in the playoffs after that.

BK: Talk about Lefty O'Doul

NS: Lefty was the type of guy that was a players' manager. You've heard that expression before. If you hustled and did your best, there wasn't anybody in the world that was better than Lefty O'Doul. If you didn't do your best, he'd chew your ass out and sit you on the bench. There wasn't too many people that didn't hustle for Lefty. He was really a great guy.

It's hard to explain; when you like somebody or when you play for somebody and you respect them, there's not much more you can say about them than that. There wasn't anything bad to say and that's a real compliment, I think, when you can say something like that about a guy. He was first class. He always wore a suit, drove a nice car. I guess about everybody in San Francisco knew Lefty O'Doul. He talked to everybody. They always had an O'Doul Day for kids. It was just a great experience.

BK: Who was the toughest pitcher on you?

NS: I hit against Lew Burdette one time when he was with the Seals.

I was with Seattle at that time. I only hit against him once. He was really tough on righthanded hitters. He had a kind of a goofy delivery and it was hard to pick the ball up on him. A herky-jerky type guy. I think he was probably as tough as anybody.

But when you're hitting good, you can hit anybody. [Laughs] When you're not, almost anybody can get you out.

BK: In the years you played, what was your biggest thrill?

NS: Oh, boy. I was playing with Sacramento and they had a promotion before a ballgame. They wanted somebody to run against a horse. The kid that was supposed to do it — Lenny Attyd — had a bad leg and couldn't do it, so I said I'd do it.

The fellow that was the starter was Hack Applequist. When I was a kid in Sacramento going to Sacramento High School, Hack Applequist was the track coach at Sacramento Junior College and he used to be the starter in track meets that we had. So I ran against the horse and I beat the horse and I introduced myself to Hack afterwards. He said he remembered me but I don't think he did.

But anyway, that same night I hit two home runs. One over left field that was surveyed, and the reason it was surveyed was because the ball went through the guy's back window of his car. He was sitting out on the porch; he had a home behind the parking lot behind left field in Sacramento. He came back the next day and gave me the ball and he told me about it. I told the owner of the ballclub and they surveyed it and it surveyed at 613 feet or something. [Laughs] On the fly.

The same game I hit a ball over the right–center field fence and it was supposedly the only time that a righthanded hitter had hit a ball over the left field fence and the right field fence. That was probably the most memorable thing that happened to me.

BK: Someone said that when you hit a ball there wasn't a park in the country that would hold it.

NS: I hit more line drives. That same year I think I hit 55 doubles. Most of 'em are hitting against the fence, you know. If I had the uppercut swing like they do this day in age maybe I would've hit a few home runs.

BK: You moved around from team to team quite a lot. How was this on family life?

NS: It was the pits. In 1950 we bought our house here where we are now. We moved in in October and I left in March, I guess, to go to spring training. In '51 I was in San Diego, San Francisco, Minneapolis, and then home. I didn't see my family the whole time.

That's another reason I didn't want to go to Boston 'cause I knew darned good and well what was gonna happen. I did have my family with me in Boston for a while and up in Seattle and San Diego. On the whole, I'd much rather have stayed in San Francisco.

BK: Would you go back and do it again?

NS: You know, I'd have to turn back 60 years. It would be hard to say because I've had such a wonderful life *after* baseball that I really don't know if I would do it again.

Actually, my first love would have been teaching. In 1944 I taught at Lincoln High School and coached the football team there and we won the championship. I was— what?— 21 years old, or 22. It was something where I established my own system and it was a wonderful experience looking back on it. I think if I were doing it again I would probably go into teaching.

BK: What did you do when you left baseball?

NS: I went to work for United Wine Sales, which sold different types of wine. I did that about a year or so. It was just a living; it was nothing that I really enjoyed doing. It was a sales job and in those days you had to establish a product and in order to establish a product you had to give half of it away. It just wasn't my bag. I wasn't that much of a BSer, I guess you could say.

One of my customers had gone to school with my dad and owned a liquor store here in Pleasant Hill and I went to work for him on weekends and he bought another store, so I went to work for him full time. I ended up in the grocery business and I worked there 'til '82 when I retired. I enjoyed that. I loved talking to people and people enjoyed me, I suppose.

We had a lot more fun when I played than these people playing ball today. We used to play cards and there was just more camaraderie than they have now. They complain about playing 162 games plus spring training; we played that many games and more and it was a *game*. Good Lord, it wasn't *work*. [Laughs] I think they make it work.

NEILL RAWLINS "WILD HORSE" SHERIDAN
Born November 20, 1921, Sacramento, CA
Ht. 6'1 ½" Wt. 195 Batted and Threw Right
Outfielder

Year	Team. Lg	G	AB	R	H	2B	3B	HR	RBI	BA
1944	SF, PCL	42	150	30	44	5	2	4	21	.293
	Chatt., SA	70	236	41	77	15	10	4	27	.326
1945	SF, PCL	148	527	78	153	35	7	3	68	.290
1946		116	357	58	96	18	4	5	55	.289

Year	Team. Lg	G	AB	R	H	2B	3B	HR	RBI	BA
1947		153	618	94	177	27	9	16	95	.286
1948	Seattle, PCL	140	532	91	166	25	7	17	82	.312
	Boston, AL	2	1	0	0	0	0	0	0	.000
1949	Seattle, PCL	147	486	81	126	19	3	14	67	.259
1950	SF, PCL	104	319	51	98	18	2	12	54	.288
1951	SF/SD, PCL	56	137	13	28	3	1	3	14	.204
	Mnpls, AA	75	304	48	93	17	0	9	50	.306
1952	Toronto, IL	34	73	10	16	6	1	1	10	.219
	SanAnt'o, Tx	72	249	27	55	7	1	6	25	.221
1953	Oak/SF, PCL	170	591	77	173	43	5	13	83	.293
1954	SF/Sac, PCL	22	59	5	9	2	2	0	3	.153
	Vic/Van, WI	95	367	58	113	32	1	11	76	.308

◆ CHAPTER 4 ◆

1948:
Done In by Nine Old Men

Second place: W 112 L 76 .596 2 GB
Governor's Cup
First round: Seattle over San Francisco, 4 games to 1

The Seals were favored in the pre-season polls, but a broken leg suffered by their new outfielder, Gene Woodling, who was the PCL's leading hitter in 1948, probably made the difference in the end. When the season began the club jumped out to a big lead. By late June they had a seven game lead over Oakland, but by month's end it had been reduced to only one-and-a-half games, as both the Oaks and Los Angeles got hot.

The Seals had another loss in 1948, one that cannot be measured in hits or runs. Charley Graham, the long-time and much-loved majority owner of the team, passed away. Graham had been responsible for the signing of many of the players on the team and, although never extremely wealthy, nonetheless paid his players well and "took care" of them. Operation of the club fell to Paul Fagan, who had purchased a third interest prior to the 1946 season, and Charley Graham, Jr., but neither had the baseball brains that Charley, Sr., had. How much this affected the team and distracted the players is impossible to determine, especially more than 50 years later.

The Seals presented a very different lineup than the 1947 team. Mickey Rocco (27 home runs, 149 RBIs, .300) was obtained from Seattle to play first base, Woodling (22-107-.385) came on option, and Dino Restelli became an everyday player. Gone, however, were Neill Sheridan, dealt to Seattle, and Don White, purchased by the Philadelphia Athletics. Dixie Howell (.292), down from Brooklyn, became the catcher in place of Jim

1948 SEALS

Back row (left to right): Charles H. Graham (owner), Felixz Mackewicz, Con Dempsey, Bill Werle, Dewey Soriano, Jack Brewer, Lefty O'Doul, Cliff Melton, Al Lien, Manny Perez, Bob Joyce, Leo Hughes (trainer). *Second row:* Mickey Rocco, Del Young, Dixie Howell, Bill Leonard, Ken Gables, Dino Restelli, Dick Lajeskie, Ray Orteig, Joe Brovia, Bruce Ogrodowski. *Front row:* Albert Boro (batboy), Frank Shofner, Gene Woodling, Hugh Luby, Dan Luby (batboy), Ben Guintini, Don Trower, Tommy Fine, Jack Tobin, Don Rode (batboy).

Gladd, who moved on to Hollywood, and young Jackie Tobin (.301), up from the Texas League, played nearly every day, but some days it was in the outfield and some days it was at third base.

The pitching staff was basically the same, except for Bob Chesnes, who went up to the Pirates. Joyce, however, became ineffective. In place of them were Con Dempsey, up from Salt Lake City, and veteran Manny Perez, acquired from Indianapolis.

Bill Werle had his best — and last — season as a Seal, going 17–7 and leading the league with a .708 percentage. The next year he would be in Pittsburgh. Dempsey was 16–11 with a 2.10 ERA and 171 strikeouts, both tops in the league. Jack Brewer went 15–11, Cliff Melton 16–10, Al Lien 15–8, and Perez 11–8.

Hugh Luby and Roy Nicely were again the premier middle infield combination in the PCL and drove in 77 and 85 runs, respectively. And due largely to them, the Seals set a new record for double plays with 210, breaking the old mark of 206 just set in 1947 by the Seattle Rainiers. Joe Brovia batted .322. It was a solid team, both offensively and defensively.

But across the bay in Oakland there was a team that perhaps did not match up well with San Francisco on paper, but won more games. Two more, to be exact.

It was Casey Stengel's third and last year as skipper of the Oaks, and he made it a memorable one.

The Oaks' ace in 1947, Gene Bearden, went to Cleveland, where he was a 20-game winner. Will Hafey was also sold to Cleveland, but was optioned back to Oakland for the year. Veterans Bob Klinger (pitcher), George Metkovich (outfielder), and Merrill Combs (shortstop) were either purchased or acquired on option. Lloyd Christopher (outfielder) was acquired in a trade, and Earl Jones (pitcher) was purchased from Toledo. Forty year old future Hall of Famer Ernie Lombardi was signed after being released by Sacramento. Ernie had originally played for the Oaks in the '20s. Jack Salveson (pitcher) was also picked up from the Solons' discard pile.

Other veterans were Nick Etten, former Yankee and American league home run king, the team's RBI leader (155, with 42 home runs), Dario Lodigiani, Brooks Holder, Billy Raimondi, and Cookie Lavagetto, spoiler of Bill Bevens' no-hit bid in the 1947 World Series. This age was tempered somewhat by 20 year old Billy Martin. The next youngest player on the team was Hafey at 25.

The nickname "nine old men" did not refer so much to nine individuals as it did to the nine players manager Casey Stengel put on the field on any given day.

The average age of the Oakland team was 33. The oldest team in the major leagues in 1948 was the National League champion Boston Braves at slightly over 30. Oakland's pitchers averaged 33, ranging from Will Hafey at 25 to Ralph Buxton and Bob Klinger at 37. The catchers averaged 35. The two first basemen were both 34. The rest of the infield averaged 28, but it rose to 30 when 20 year old Billy Martin didn't play. The outfield was a mere 28.

Casey platooned; 11 men had more than 300 plate appearances and a 12th had nearly 300. The nine who played the most and therefore could be called the regulars were: Nick Etten, 1b — 34; Billy Martin, 2b — 20; Dario Lodigiani, 3b — 31; Merrill Combs, ss — 28; George Metkovich, of — 26; Brooks Holder, of — 32; Mel Duezabou, of — 27; Billy Raimondi, c — 34; Starting pitcher (any of 4) — 29; The extremes were Martin, 20, and catcher Ernie Lombardi, 40.

It turned out to be a two-team race as the Angels eventually faded. San Francisco led by 1½ games entering the final month and won 21 of 31 games during that month, but the Oaks won 24 of 30. Although Oakland had no individual leaders in any category, the team had the highest batting average (.285) and scored the most runs (1,022).

The Oaks pitching staff was led by relievers Ralph Buxton (13–3) and Floyd Speer (12–3). The top starter, Charley Gassoway, was 16–8, while Jones was 13–6 and Hafey 13–10.

When play began on the season's final day, Oakland held a two-game lead over San Francisco. Each team had a double header, the Oaks with Sacramento and the Seals with Seattle. Oakland won the first game, thereby clinching the pennant. It was the club's first in 21 years.

The Seals closed with five straight wins, but they had lost the first two games of the seven-game Seattle series and those two losses were Oakland's margin of victory. Seattle finished fourth with a losing record, becoming only the second team ever to enter the Governor's Cup playoffs under .500.

Oakland played third-place Los Angeles in the opening round and won, 4 games to 2, winning four in a row after the Angels took the first two. It was not a pretty series; in the six games, the Oaks scored 66 runs and the Angels 55 and the teams combined for 12 errors.

Meanwhile, San Francisco played the fourth-place Rainiers, the team they had just beaten five times in a row. Both teams entered the series handicapped. Woodling had to return home to Ohio because of his father's death and Brewer contracted pleurisy and was unable to pitch.

Seattle, on the other hand, lost Sheridan, one of their top offensive forces, when he was called up by the Red Sox, and their regular catcher,

Mickey Grasso, who was injured and missed the entire series. The Rainiers asked the Seals if they could use Jack Warner, who had joined the team too late to be included on the playoff roster. San Francisco said no, so Seattle played with only one catcher, 41 year old Rollie Hemsley.

Seattle was ready for the series, while the Seals evidently were not. In the first game, Guy Fletcher tossed a four-hitter and defeated Dempsey, 3–1. In game two, Charley Schanz also hurled a four-hitter and downed Werle, 2–0.

In game three, Lien gave up nine hits in seven innings but edged Seattle, 4–3, with relief help from Dewey Soriano. Veteran Ben Guintini, back with the Seals after a three-year absence, had two hits, a run, and an RBI and Nicely had two RBIs.

Bob Hall, in relief of Fletcher, won game four as the Seals defense fell apart. Nicely and third basemen Frank Shofner each committed two errors. Soriano lost in relief of Melton. Howell homered and Luby doubled twice, but three unearned runs were too much to overcome as Seattle prevailed, 8–4.

Hall relieved again in game five and won again, but it took 11 innings. The Rainiers led, 4–2, entering the bottom of the ninth, but Restelli singled, Ray Orteig, who had three hits, tripled, and Nicely singled to tie the score and chase starter Herb Karpel. Seattle scored three times off Kenny Gables in the top of the eleventh, a rally started by Hall's single.

Seattle won the series, four games to one, as San Francisco could hit only .193. The Rainiers went on to face Oakland for the championship while the Seals went home. The Oaks won the Governor's Cup, four games to one.

JOE BROVIA
Seals 1941–1942, 1946–1948

Joe Brovia was a self-admitted designated hitter in the days before the DH existed.

He had a 15-year career spent mostly in the PCL, but he did spend a few weeks in the major leagues in 1955 with Cincinnati. He was 33 at the time. He had a chance earlier but World War II took him instead of the White Sox.

In his 12 years in the PCL he played with four of the original teams: San Francisco, Portland, Sacramento, and Oakland. Everywhere he went he was a fan favorite. In his years as a Seal, he had not yet become

Joe Brovia (courtesy Robert Zwissig).

the feared batter he would be later, but in 1947 and '48 he batted .309 and .322.

JOE BROVIA: Before we get started, let me say this: Judge Landis would have cremated [Pete] Rose. Today they've got unions, they've got arbitrators, they've got lawyers. In our days we had nothing! You were on your own! I'm bitter about this— what he's done to baseball.

BK: Review your PCL career.

JB: I played for the Seals in '41, '42, and '46, '47, '48. In '48 I was sold to Portland, played there '49 through '52, then I was sold to Sacramento and played there in '53 and '54. Then I went to Oakland in '55 and later that year to Cincinnati as an old man.

I was used as a pinch hitter [in Cincinnati]. Twenty-one games, two hits, four RBIs. I played one game, an exhibition, during the All-Star break. I homered and doubled against Detroit. My roommate, Gus Bell, told me I should be playing.

BK: In the early '50s with Portland you were outstanding. What were some of your numbers?

JB: [I hit] 39 home runs one year, drove in over 130 runs. My Coast League batting average was .305 for my career there.

I broke in in 1939 in the old Arizona-Texas League. Hit .383. Went up to the Western International League, Class A, Tacoma. Hit .322. Went to the Coast League in '41 and '42. I was sold to the Chicago White Sox for '43 in October of '42, but I got drafted into the service in November of '42 and the deal was canceled.

I was in combat in Europe and when I came back I couldn't hit my house so they sent me to Salt Lake City in the Pioneer League. Remember Joe Orengo? He was managing. I went 35 or so times without a hit, then I ended up hitting .339, hit in 39 consecutive games. I missed playing on that '46 Seals team that won the championship. Damned good team.

I went back to the Seals, hit .318 in '47, .322 in '48. We had a great team in '47, too; should have won it. They sold me to Portland and I hit 39 home runs, then 36, 32,and 28, then they sold me to Sacramento.

BK: How many home runs did you hit altogether?

JB: I believe I had 194 in the Coast League. I played winter ball in Mexico, so I must have had 350–400 over the years.

I'd go to Mexico, play 80 games, hit 20–21[home runs]. My last year in baseball, 1957, I led the league in hitting. They carried nine Americans: six major leaguers, three Triple-A ballplayers. I hit against Jim Bunning, Whitey Ford, Al Cicotte, Paul Foytack. They gave the major league players $3,500 a month; the Triple-A players they gave $1,000 a month. And I had to pay my own expenses home.

Remember the lefthanded knuckleball pitcher, pitched with Cleveland, Gene Bearden? He was down there, too.

BK: Do you think you would have had a better shot at the majors if you were playing today?

JB: I'd be a designated hitter. I wasn't the fastest runner, but I could hit. They considered me one of the best fastball hitters in the game.

BK: What was your top salary?

JB: $9,000 with the Reds in 1955.

BK: What was your top minor league salary?

JB: Close to that. Today they get more meal money than that. When I was with the Reds we got seven dollars for a day game, eleven dollars for a night game. I started out at $65 a month salary in 1939.

BK: How were you defensively?

JB: Oh, fair. Remember Jake Powell? He ran into the fence. I was just 18 or so, green; they put me in left field in San Diego. I made four errors that night. The media ripped me apart, but I got better. I had a good arm, played right field later.

BK: A short time after you left Oakland to join the Reds, a story appeared in the *San Francisco Examiner* saying that you left your lucky bat behind. Did you ever get it?

JB: No, I never did. Might have made a difference.

BK: What did you do after you left baseball?

JB: I worked with local teams. I drove a beer truck in this area for 15 years.

What irritates me, I paid the ballplayers' association for 20 years and I can't get help. Remember Chuck Stevens, played for the old St. Louis Browns? Wrote and said, "Sorry, Joe, we can't help you." Jack Sanford got help, Marino Pieretti got help. But I saved my money; they turned me down.

Mr. [Peter] Ueberroth wrote and sent forms to fill out. They're playing those old-timers games, 26 a year at the different parks. Maybe I can get some help there. Lots of forms. I pay my dues to the Baseball Alumni each year. I paid my dues in other ways, too.

They say how they help the old ballplayers. Hell, they help the few who can't cope with society. They don't help those who do cope and have problems. You've got to take care of yourself.

I came up during the Depression days. I didn't have a chance to go to school like these boys today. They get a million dollars to sign. Unbelievable.

That's something else. Today in the big leagues you pitch six innings, then go to middle relief, then short relief.

BK: Who were the best players you played against?

JB: That's a tough one. I played exhibition against Joe DiMaggio and others like that, but I won't consider them because they were in the American League and I was in the National League.

Hank Aaron, great hitter. Musial and Mays were good, of course, but I never saw them look too good. But Hank Aaron was a good hitter. Roy Campanella. Man, he could club that ball!

BK: Who were the best pitchers you faced?

JB: In exhibition games I faced Bob Feller in '48 in Seals Stadium. Feller was pitching for the Cleveland Indians. I hit a line drive, almost took his head off.

Another guy, Sad Sam Jones, pitched for San Diego in the Coast League. Later went to the top. Remember Johnny Klippstein? He could throw a hundred mile per hour fastball. He could throw it!

Roger Craig was just starting. I hit against him. Good pitcher. Ryne Duren. Vic Raschi. I'm going back to the '40s and '50s. Rex Barney, remember him? I faced him with Oakland. Then guys like Bill Wight, good control, came down from the White Sox. Hell of a slider, a lefthander.

Another guy, with Sacramento, he could throw rockets! Max Surkont. Hated colored guys. I felt sorry for them; he knocked them down. Went to the Boston Braves later. He could throw through a brick wall!

Color was a problem. Guys were afraid the colored boys would take their jobs. But that's baseball. Johnny Rucker wanted to get the colored players out, wanted us to sign a petition. I wouldn't sign. That's what it's all about — the best player plays. No one took my job.

BK: Did you save things along the way?

JB: Oh, a lot of stuff. Stuff from Mexico.

I've got a trophy from the Santa Cruz Chamber of Commerce. I was elected to the Italian-American Hall of Fame. I've got drinking glasses from the 1947 Seals. My baseball cards—Mother's Cookies—from the '50s.

BK: What do you think of the changes in baseball over the last 50 or 60 years?

JB: They got rid of the reserve clause. I'm glad for the ballplayers. The year I hit 39 home runs for Portland, the reserve clause was still intact. They gave the Coast League Open classification; it was to become a third

Joe Brovia with the Cincinnati Reds in 1955 (author's collection).

major league. Players coming and going to the majors, good players. I called Mr. Walker, general manager of Portland. I said, "Mr. Walker, I want a hundred [a month] raise." He said, "Aw, Joe, you're not a good outfielder." "I had 17 assists from right field; I've got a good arm." "No. Take $50 and forget about it."

Then Curt Flood challenged the reserve clause. Now you can hit .240–.250, play out your option, go to the highest bidder. I blame the owners, not the ballplayers. But they complain.

The biggest change I've seen is pitching. Long relief, short relief. Bad arms. In my day they went nine innings. Now they pitch eight, have a shutout. Short man comes in, gets a save. Why?

Artificial turf. I wish I was hitting off it.

Guys hit a double, pull up lame. A hamstring pull. In my time, we didn't know what a hamstring pull was.

BK: Do you think there are changes that should be made?

JB: I don't know. You've still got to hit a round ball with a round bat. The pitcher's still 60 feet, six inches away.

One thing that irritates me is these guys charging all this money for autographs. I get 12, 15 letters a month. I send pictures to some people; I buy them myself. I don't charge. I love hearing from the fans. Baseball was my life. I owe baseball a lot. I'm lucky to have played the game.

BK: You didn't get the national recognition you should have because of your hitting ability. Would you do it all again?

JB: I got a lot of recognition out here. Yeah, I'd do it all over again. I loved to get up to the plate and swing that bat.

These last few years I've gotten a lot of recognition. Mr. Haas of the A's, Mr. Lurie of the Giants, Mayor Feinstein of San Francisco, Mayor Wilson of Oakland, they gave me a night at the Hyatt Regency Hotel. Eight hundred fifty people. Lon Simmons, the announcer for the Oakland A's, presented me with a large portrait. A hell of a night. They had Sam Chapman there, Joe DiMaggio there. Mike McCormick, the [former] Giants' pitcher, was there. It was for my contribution to baseball in the Bay Area.

Sports History had a story on my home run in 1947 over Seals Stadium. Five hundred and sixty feet. They put a star up there but when they tore the stadium down they tore the star down, too. Didn't give it to me. But they didn't give anything to Joe DiMaggio; they're sure not going to give anything to Joe Brovia.

But the fans in San Francisco had me up there one night; they made me a star.

The story compared my home run to Mantle's in Griffith Stadium — the two longest. July 8, 1988, *Sports History*. Look it up.

JOSEPH JOHN BROVIA
Born February 18, 1922, Davenport, CA
Died August 15, 1994, Santa Cruz, CA
Ht. 6'3" Wt. 195 Batted Left, Threw Right
Outfielder

Year	Team, Lg	G	AB	R	H	2B	3B	HR	RBI	BA
1940	El Pso, AzTx	104	415	73	159	21	19	3	103	.383
1941	SF, PCL	92	195	20	62	6	3	0	27	.318
1942	Tacoma, WI	78	310	54	90	17	3	6	52	.290
	SF, PCL		35		6			0	4	.167
1943–45			military service							
1946	SF, PCL	9	9		1			0	0	.111
	SLC, Pion.	47	183	30	62	16	5	2	27	.339
1947	SF,PCL	114	359	45	111	29	4	10	63	.309
1948		127	444	53	143	28	4	9	89	.322
1949	Port, PCL	117	364	59	114	21	2	11	31	.313
1950		193	649	88	182	28	0	39	114	.280
1951		161	574	76	174	25	2	32	133	.303
1952		170	551	78	160	25	1	21	85	.290
1953	Sac, PCL	165	525	76	165	36	1	20	97	.314
1954		148	504	58	152	32	0	13	91	.302
1955	Oak, PCL	114	372	59	121	19	4	19	73	.325
	Cin. NL	21	18	0	2	0	0	0	4	.111
1956	Buffalo, IL	46	122	12	28	7	0	6	28	.230
	San J'se, Cal	71	252	67	91	18	0	22	90	.361
1957	Vera Cr'z, Mx	23	80	13	25	6	0	1	16	.313

BILL WERLE
Seals 1943–1944, 1946–1948

Bill Werle joined the Seals in 1943 off the campus of the University of California where he had gone 25–2 for the baseball team and had been studying entomology in the classroom. The bugs' loss was the Seals' gain. He became one of the leaders of the pitching staff through 1948 (with 1945 out for the service), when he was sold to the Pittsburgh Pirates

In 1949 he was the top rookie lefthander (12–13 with a horrible team) in the National League and in 1951 he set a team record for games pitched (59). Minor arm problems plagued him and he returned to the PCL in 1955 and continued to pitch there through 1961, when he turned to managing and then scouting.

Bill Werle (courtesy Robert Zwissig).

Fresh from the military, he turned in a 12–8, 2.26 record for the 1946 champion Seals and won 55 games in his four full seasons with the team, including a 17–7 mark in 1948.

BILL WERLE: You had to serve a lot longer apprenticeship when I played; I pitched five years in Triple-A before I ever got to the big leagues. Of course, the war was involved there. I had a chance from what I was told later on — I didn't know about it at the time — to be sold to Cleveland and when they found out I was going in the service they canceled that. Then I came out and had to start all over. I had three more years of Triple-A.

The Coast League at that time had dreams of being a third major league. We had a very wealthy owner with the San Francisco club named Paul Fagan. He and Charlie Graham were the co-owners of the club and hoped to eventually become a third major league, so there was no movement.

It's not like now where they were farm clubs. We had working agreements but that only entitled the club that had the working agreement to have first call on any player that was going to go to the major leagues. If the club didn't meet their price, they were free to deal that player to anybody they wanted to. It was a lot different. San Francisco, at the time, would only let one player a year go and that would be a player that was drafted. It was hard to have much movement.

They [San Francisco] worked with the Giants for a while, then when we sold Larry Jansen to the Giants [1947] they got in a hassle because there were three players included in the deal. We got two of 'em and our second baseman got hurt and Charlie Graham went back to the All-Star game to try and get another player from senior Stoneham — not the one that came out to the West Coast but the father. Charlie supposedly got infuriated and broke off the working agreement and that's when they started working with Pittsburgh. Bob Chesnes went to Pittsburgh the first year [1948], then I followed the second year.

BK: Is it true that when you were sold to Pittsburgh you were reluctant to go because you'd have to take a pay cut?

BW: That's not exactly true. I wasn't reluctant to go. Roy Hamey was the general manager [at Pittsburgh] at the time.

The Coast League was playing 180-some games in those years and there was a little over six months playing time and you were paid by the month. They paid damned good money out here, compared to what the other leagues were paying and in a lot of instances there were players making more than they could in the big leagues. Guys in the major leagues were only making 4- or 500 a month in those days—4,000 a year.

When Hamey sent me a contract, the contract only called for about $300 more than I was making with the Coast League club. I told him, "I always had the understanding it was kind of an unwritten rule that, if you went to the major leagues, you were gonna get about a 25 percent increase over what you made."

He said, "I don't know where you got that idea." He and I went 'round and 'round, but finally he gave me a decent contract and he said, "I'm paying you more than DiMaggio made his first year!" [Laughs]

But I always got along good with Roy and later on, when I was scouting, covering the Coast League, Roy lived in Tucson and I used to see him in Tucson quite a bit at the Coast League games.

BK: You had an excellent year your last year with the Seals: 17–7, led the league in percentage. And you had a good rookie year with a very poor Pirates team.

BW: I've always said that the toughest thing in the world for a pitcher is to go to a weaker type ballclub because there's not much you can do. You go out there and you pitch your best and you're going to lose a lot of heartbreakers. You feel very disenchanted; you give up two, three runs in the first couple of innings, you almost feel like there's no chance to win this ballgame 'cause you just don't have the capabilities on the ballclub. Whereas, you take a guy, if he's a hell of a good hitter, he can play for a last place club, but that's an individual thing. He can go out there and still hit his .300 regardless of what club he's playing with.

But a pitcher doesn't have that type of an advantage. First of all, you're depending on the club to play behind you defensively well and then, by the same token, you expect them to be able to score you some runs.

I remember one time, there was a period of nine or ten games where I gave up something like 12–13 runs and ended up losing five games and winning two and coming off with a tie the others. It was things like that that really almost broke your spirit.

Then you find out clubs like the Dodgers want to buy you. Of course, in those days it was so much tougher to deal and so many players around, if they don't want to sell you there's not much you can do about it.

I think back and wonder what would've happened if I'd have gone to the Brooklyn Dodgers in 1950 or '51. You watch them play and you see guys like Pee Wee Reese and Jackie Robinson and Gil Hodges. They're taking base hits away from your club. And then you see your own club go out there and stagger around — ground balls going through that should be caught and ground balls going to the outfield and the guys don't even slow up, they're going in for standup doubles. It was really tough.

People that I guess were never pitchers don't understand that aspect. They throw back, "Well, you guys are lucky you only pitch once every four or five days," but the thing is, if you're with a tail-end ballclub, you're gonna lose a lot of tough ballgames and there's a lot of things you have no control over.

BK: You were the top rookie lefthander in the National League in1949, even with the poor supporting cast.

BW: Yeah, that's true. I pitched well. The guys on the other clubs would come up and say, "You're tough to hit off of. It's tough to pick the ball up off you."

You think back now, the way baseball has become so specialized, you see lefthanders come in and face one lefthanded hitter. If he gets 'em out they bring in a righthander. You'd have to go through a ton of statistics to dig it out, but I'd almost bet my bottom dollar that all the lefthanders that ever hit off me wouldn't have had a composite .200.

I know Musial went like 0-for-36 before he got his first base hit [off me], and that was actually a fluke because Wally Westlake and Gus Bell ran together on a fly ball in right center and the ball dropped untouched and he ended up with a triple. That kind of broke the spell; I didn't have that luck over him like I had prior to that.

I think Duke Snider got one hit off me that I can remember. I remember guys like Warren Spahn, who was a great pitcher, was worked where he didn't pitch against the Dodgers because of their loaded righthanded lineup. It was a hell of a good-hitting ballclub righthanded and it was a tough park to pitch in. A lot of clubs had the luxury of four or five good starters and they'd work their pitching alignments around to where the left-handers a lot of times would skip Brooklyn, but we didn't have that luxury at Pittsburgh. You took your turn when it fell.

BK: You had excellent control.

BW: Yeah, I did. I had outstanding control. To me, a lot of that is mechanics, but a lot of it is mental, too. So many times you watch a guy warm up in the bullpen and he's throwing the ball over the plate pretty consistently. He gets in a ballgame, he's all over the place. To me, that's got to be mental, whether there's a lack of confidence in themselves against the hitter or what.

I started doing a thing early in my career. We used to throw batting practice about the second or third day after we pitched. I would always play a game with myself to see how many strikes I could throw in a row to the guy taking batting practice. I'd compete with myself. I'd throw eight or nine strikes in a row and then I'd throw a ball or two, then I'd see if I could do better. I was trying to make a game where I was getting something out of it. And I would mentally tab every time they hit a ball whether I thought it as a basehit. All of a sudden, you're letting a guy know every pitch that you're throwing, whether you're gonna throw a curve or a change-up or a fastball, and you're still getting 'em out a majority of the time.

All of this built in to the idea, mentally, I never worried too much about throwing strikes because I eliminated the mental part, which I think is a problem for a lot of pitchers. I think they become almost like defeatists; every time they throw a ball over the plate it's gonna be hit for a home run or a basehit or something like that. One of the biggest traumas most pitchers have is the fact they fall behind so darned much that now they're at the mercy of the hitters.

Left to right: Al Lien, Bill Werle, Don White, spring training, 1946 (courtesy Richard T. Dobbins Collection.

This is all related back to why I had good control. I had it to begin with but this only enhanced it from a standpoint that I made mental notes while I was throwing batting practice.

On the days that I was pitching, when I was warming up in the bullpen I knew I'd have to keep the ball down; I'd have to throw at the knees. If I had a catcher that was lazy giving me a target and [was] just holding the glove in the center of the plate, I'd just start throwing for the knees on my own. I'd try to hit the left knee of the catcher as much as I could. I'd try to make a little box that I'd throw into—an imaginary box. I'd throw maybe 10–11 pitches in a row and then I'd say, "Well now, I've got two strikes on the hitter. I've gotta go upstairs and drive him back, go high and tight." So I'd throw a couple of pitches up there, then I'd go right back to throwing for the left knee again.

You develop confidence so when you get 3-and-1 on the batter, or two balls and no strikes, you really have confidence in yourself to know you can throw a strike. I think a lot of pitchers have a tendency to start aiming the ball and they start really pressing when they get behind and that's the worst thing they can do.

BK: Where did the nickname "Bugs" come from?

BW: I went to the University of California. My uncle was an agriculture inspector for the county down in Stockton. I had a chance to go to Cal on a scholarship and he asked what I was going to take. I said I didn't know and he suggested I take entomology. He said it was a hell of a field.

So I ended up taking entomology but I didn't realize I was going to be involved so much with science courses. [Laughs] it was a tough course! That's where the name came from: studying bugs in school.

BK: You had a marvelous record at Cal.

BW: I only pitched there one year and had a chance to sign professionally and I went right into the Coast League.

Nowadays, if you see a free agent and say, "This guy's gonna pitch in Triple-A" you don't know what you'll give him. The top pitchers in the country all start no higher than A; once in a great while you'll see somebody [start] in Double-A. Not many start over that.

The year I was there [Cal] I only got beat one or two ballgames and we ended up with a tie with USC at the end of the season. We had a one game playoff and I got beat, 3-to-2, in 12 innings. That was my career in college.

I pinch hit then and I played first base when I wasn't pitching, or the outfield. I didn't know it until I went over to Cal to a reunion, but I still hold the record for the highest hitting average in that school and they've been playing baseball for a long time.

BK: You had arm trouble after your rookie year.

BW: It was nothing ever real serious. I used to get a knot in the back of my shoulder.

One year in spring training, I had some problem with a tendon in my elbow where I couldn't get my arm bent all the way back behind my head. I had to pitch almost like holding a runner on position, where you only bring your arm up to your chest. I had to throw from that angle because I couldn't really bend my arm all the way back. They gave me a shot of cortisone and that was the last I ever had any problems with it.

But I did have this problem behind my shoulder, tightening up on me. I was reading an article one day and they were interviewing Satchel Paige and they asked him about a sore arm and he said he'd never had a sore arm but one time in his life. Some older fellow told him, "What you want to do is every time after you pitch, when you feel yourself finally to the point where you're almost through sweating, get off that sweatshirt before the sweat starts turning cold on you and get into a shower and take a towel and lap it over five or six times and let the hot water hit it for five or ten minutes as hot as you can stand it." And he said, "I never had a problem with my arm after that."

So I started doing that every time after I pitched and I never had any more arm problems and I pitched for 19 years.

I asked the doctor one time about it and he said, "Scientifically, what happens is when you put that hot towel with the hot water running over it, the residue, when you use up the energy in your muscle, is what they call lactic acid and that's what makes all the stiffness in your arm. What you're doing [with the hot towel] is you're causing the blood to keep flowing through that area and it takes away a lot of that lactic acid and you find out you're not nearly as stiff," which is true. I could go out the next day and still go out there and throw and never feel the stiffness I used to have, except naturally I didn't have the strength back yet. There was none of the stiffness I used to have before I started doing that.

But I never really had a sore arm, *per se,* nothing that would cause me to miss a turn — just a couple of aggravating things.

Billy Meyer [Pirates' manager] called me in one day and he says, "I've been talking with the pitching coach, Bill Posedel, and he says you'd make a hell of a relief pitcher for us. I want to leave it up to you. If you want to keep starting, I can use Murry Dickson because he's basically the same type except he's a righthander. But I'd prefer you."

I said, "I want to do whatever you feel is the best thing for the ballclub." So then I started going into relieving. They didn't relieve the way they do now. Now it's more of a scientific thing. They have a guy that's a set-up man, then they have a lefthanded short man and a righthanded short man, if they have that luxury. That's what they all like to have on the ballclub nowadays.

They were just starting to keep track of saves but the way they did it was completely different than what they do now. I think the tying run had to be at the plate or on the bases to count as a save.

BK: In your first year as a reliever, you set a Pirates record for games pitched.

BW: At that time. Then we got Ted Wilks over from St. Louis.

BK: You were in the majors into 1954 with the Red Sox. Where did you go then?

BW: After '54, I went back to the Coast League.

What had happened, I had an outstanding year at Louisville that year. I won six games in the post-season playoffs and only gave up four runs in the six games. I beat Stu Miller three games in the playoffs when he was at Columbus. I shut 'em out the first game, gave up a run in the next game.

We ended up going seven games; in the seventh game we ended up in a tie in about the fifth or sixth inning and Mike Higgins [Louisville manager] had me down in the bullpen and he brought me in to pitch. We went into extra innings and a fellow named Bob Broome hit a home run in the bottom of the twelfth for us at Louisville and we won the ballgame. I shut out Stu Miller another six innings.

Then we played Indianapolis and I beat Sad Sam Jones, I think, 4-to-1. Then we played Syracuse and I won two games including the clincher for the Little World Series. So I won six games in the space of a couple weeks.

I was a few innings short of having the record for the fewest walks. I think I only walked nine men in 130 innings or something like that.

Pinky Higgins was the Red Sox manager after that and he said I didn't fit into their plans. He said he'd see if he couldn't get me the best deal the Red Sox could get and so they sold my contract to Cincinnati because Birdie Tebbetts [Reds' manager] had managed Indianapolis and I'd always pitched well against them.

They were on a youth movement at that time and I was going on about 34 or 35 and so Birdie called me in one days and said, "I'm sorry. You've pitched well but we've got all these young kids and we're not going to go anywhere so we're going to give you a chance to go back to the Coast League." So they sold me to Portland for '55.

I pitched through 1961. From Portland I went to San Diego and from there to Tacoma. The last year I pitched, I pitched for Hawaii. That was their first year in the league after taking Sacramento's place. That was in '61. Then I started managing.

BK: Who was the best pitcher you saw?

BW: Hmmm. I thought the majors in those years had some tremendous pitchers. There again, you're getting into my area. To me, there's pitchers and there's throwers—guys with great stuff that win and there's also guys that go out there and they're great pitchers from the standpoint that they know how to pitch to spots and change speeds.

One of my old [Seals] teammates I thought was one of the better pitchers that I'd seen was Larry Jansen. Larry was a great control pitcher and one of the first real slider pitchers.

As far as stuff, I don't know. Spahn was a young pitcher then, and [Johnny] Sain and you gotta like [Don] Newcombe's arm. To me, there were so many great pitchers in those days. Howie Pollet and Harry Brecheen. You have to stop and kind of think of the guys around on the different clubs. There were some *tremendous* pitchers in those days. You hate to put one ahead of the other. A lot of those guys are in the Hall of Fame, or are gonna be in the Hall of Fame.

BK: You mentioned Murry Dickson earlier. He was a heck of a pitcher.

BW: Murry was a great competitor with great control and he was one of those guys that challenged the hitters and threw strikes.

A lot of us in those days believed in the percentages; if a guy was a .300 hitter, that's only three out of ten. What better advantage do you want? A lot of us operated that way and that's the way Murry was. He was a guy that threw strikes and he had a rubber arm. Murry was one of those guys that could start one day and relieve the next.

He probably got a bad break because he came from the Cardinals over to our club in Pittsburgh [for cash]. Then later, of course, we got Howie Pollet and Ted Wilks [along with Bill Howerton, Joe Garagiola, and Dick Cole]; we got three pretty good pitchers from them [St. Louis]. I think Cliff Chambers and Wally Westlake went to the Cardinals.

BK: You had a good pitching staff at Pittsburgh.

BW: Vern Law had just started coming along, and Bob Friend. The club was *just* starting to rebuild.

We had what they called the "sandblower infield" in those days, with Dick Smith and [Pete] Castiglione and Monty Basgall, but he broke his ankle and [Danny] Murtaugh had to come back and start playing. He was gonna be more or less a fill-in type guy but he ended up having to play regular. And Tony Bartirome. We just didn't have that much of a ballclub.

We had fairly decent pitching but the pitching suffered because of the type of club. [Stan] Rojek was still trying to play short and Stan didn't compare with your great shortstops when you look at your Roy McMillan — he never hit much but he was an *outstanding* fielder — and Buddy Kerr with the Giants and Alvin Dark and Pee Wee Reese. You're talking guys that are *great* shortstops. They're making plays, taking basehits away from your players, and you're seeing those same things go through your infield for basehits.

Another thing, too, the guy's in the Hall of Fame and you hate to knock him, but there was *never* any doubt he wasn't much of a defensive player. Ralph Kiner. It was a joke; a guy'd hit a ground ball between third and short and if there was a man at first he'd never even stop and Ralph would end up trying to throw the man out at third and the guy that hit the ball would end up going to second base. So instead of having men on first and second, or even first and third, you'd have men on second and third. It was just a rough place to pitch for.

The Gardens there in those days didn't help you a lot, either. Routine fly balls going for home runs and they used to call 'em "Kiner's Gardens" and that was a joke because when Ralph hit a ball it was over everything. He didn't need that thing; he probably only benefited three or four home runs a year from the Gardens. Most of his were over the brick wall in the back.

He couldn't run, he couldn't throw, and he was a bad outfielder. He had good hands; what he got to he caught but there was an awful lot of balls he didn't get to. [Laughs]

BK: Who was the best player you saw?

BW: I'm a Ted Williams fan, although Ted wasn't that great on defense. I'll tell you one thing about Ted: he was the type of person, if he made up his mind to do something I'm sure he could have done it. I'm sure, if he wasn't as great a hitter as he was, he maybe would have concentrated a little more on his defense and been a decent outfielder.

[Willie] Mays came up in '51 and he has to be high on the list and you can't discount Musial. He was still playing the outfield and then he moved to first base. Jackie Robinson I thought was a *tremendous* ballplayer and participated under tremendous adverse conditions and still played outstanding.

To me, there were so many great ballplayers in those years. Mays was so outstanding in everything. He could throw, he could run, he was a great outfielder, and he hit with power. He did all the things.

BK: Would you do it all again? Any regrets?

BW: I feel that I'm one of the fortunate ones. I had a dream when I was a kid and I was able to fulfill it. So many people want to be so many things when they're young and they either outgrow it or don't have the capabilities to do whatever they want to go into.

In spite of the fact of the money they're making nowadays, I look back and I think there was a lot more camaraderie and I think the fellows had a lot more fun out of the game.

I go back to one thing I've always said in my mind. Most of the guys of my era were kids that were raised during the Depression. My father was a policeman who made $180 a month and his dream was always for me to play baseball. When I was able to do it, he got my first contract and was showing it to everybody in town.

The thing is, I think the fact that we came through the '30s as kids and saw an opportunity to make something of ourselves through sports, I think we appreciated it more and there was much more tenacity about us.

There were so many clubs then. Clubs like St. Louis [Cardinals] had 15–16 farm clubs and guys would go to spring training with numbers like 400 on their backs. It was really tough. And you'd have maybe one coach and he'd coach third base and usually a pitcher would coach first base. And you'd ask and the pitchers would stay together: "It took me ten years to learn this. Do you think I'm gonna give away all my secrets?"

It was all trial and error; you had to watch and observe. There was very little given to you. It was a tough road to go.

You hate to live in the past, but you think of so many players that played Triple-A back in those days with the Dodgers. I remember when they had three Triple-A farm clubs: Montreal, St. Paul, and Spokane. The competition was tremendous.

One of the things I try to keep sight of when someone complains about this guy or that guy because he made a mistake here or there: "Hey," I say, "this guy's only been playing about two or three years. How long did you play in the minors before you got to the major leagues?"

All of a sudden they're saying five-six-seven years. You served your apprenticeship so when you got to the major leagues you basically knew how to play the game. Maybe you couldn't always *do* what you wanted to do, but at least you knew what you were supposed to do: hit behind the runner, hit and run, or whatever. If you were a pitcher, you knew who the next hitter coming up was so you knew how to pitch the guy you're facing now.

I ask guys like Warren Spahn and [Don] Drysdale and guys like that, "How long did it take you to feel that you were an accomplished pitcher to where every situation that arose in a game you were more or less prepared and knew what you had to do?" They'd think for a little and damned near every one of 'em said six or seven years.

We used to have to take the lineup card in front of the whole team and go over how you were gonna pitch to the hitters and it was up to you to be able to execute. If you're gonna pitch a guy inside and down, you'd better be able to do it because the defense is playing 'em a certain way.

Everything is so force-fed now and so escalated that the guys just don't get a chance to learn as well as they should. You see so many mistakes. I watch pitchers pitch and, of course, that's my forte, and you see guys look one time holding a man on second base. As soon as the guy turns his head to go to home, the guy takes off. And they wonder why they're stealing their jock off.

It takes a presence of mind to be able to think, "There's a bunt situation. The man on first base is a guy that can fly. I don't even think about going to second base; I want to go to first, at least have one out, then I operate with first base open and do what I want to do with the hitter coming up." Or, "The guy on first base is a slow-footed catcher. If the ball is bunted pretty hard and I get to the ball right away, I'm going to second base with it unless the catcher for some reason waves me off." But to be able to pre-think and premeditate all that stuff is important.

It's like a guy said one time, "It's like playing pool. Until you've had every shot on the table presented to you so you know how to execute it, it takes playing a thousand games." Same way in baseball. I don't care what endeavor you're in. You can have all the chalk talks in the world on how to do this and how to do that, but until you get in the field of competition in the excitement of the game you just don't know. If you make a mistake and forget to cover first base on a ball hit to your left and the first baseman is left there holding the ball because nobody covered first base and you lose a ballgame one time doing that and it's registered. You say that's never gonna happen again.

You've got to go through all those periods of trials and tribulations. The first couple of years you're learning just to throw the ball over the plate, maybe developing another pitch, then you start going into deeper phases of baseball: game situations, what the guy's gonna be trying to do and you're going to try to counteract it. Man leads off with a double and you've got a righthanded hitter, you say you've got to try to make this guy pull the ball on the ground. So you pitch him inside and if he hits the ball between third and short there's nothing you can do about it, but at least you're playing the percentage. If he hits a ground ball to third or short, the runner on second can't advance. But you talk to guys now, they don't even know what you're talking about half the time.

WILLIAM GEORGE "BUGS" WERLE
Born December 21, 1920, Oakland, CA
Ht. 6'2½" Wt. 182 Batted and Threw Left

Year	Team, Lg	G	IP	W	L	Pct	SO	BB	H	ERA
1943	SF, PCL	9	26	1	2	.333				
1944		36	289	14	19	.424	129	84	331	4.05
1945		military service								
1946		33	175	12	8	.600	72	59	173	2.26
1947		36	205	12	12	.500	80	42	231	3.29
1948		34	250	17	7	.708	136	61	256	2.74
1949	Pitts., NL	35	221	12	13	.480	106	51	243	4.24
1950		48	215	8	16	.333	78	65	249	4.60
1951		59	150	8	6	.571	57	51	181	5.64
1952	Pt/StL, NL	24	43	1	2	.333	24	16	49	5.23
1953	Bos., AL	5	12	0	1	.000	4	1	7	1.51
	Lvl., AA	31	128	13	8	.619	58	25	97	2.60
1954	Bos., AL	14	25	0	1	.000	14	10	41	4.32
	Lvl., AA	14	97	7	4	.636	58	8	103	3.99
1955	Port., PCL	33	221	17	8	.680	76	30	248	3.54
1956		35	247	16	15	.516	82	40	330	4.41

Year	Team, Lg	G	IP	W	L	Pct	SO	BB	H	ERA
1957	Port/SD, PCL	26	174	9	8	.529	58	17	219	3.88
1958	SD, PCL	28	171	10	8	.556	65	34	191	3.11
1959		32	128	5	8	.385	47	29	153	4.36
1960	SD/Tac, PCL	26	134	7	8	.467	66	19	149	4.10
1961	Tac/HI, PCL	23	143	7	8	.467	66	27	159	3.52
1962	did not pitch									
1963	Fresno, Cal	1	.1	0	0	—	0	0	0	0.00

♦ CHAPTER 5 ♦

1949:
A New Regime

7th place: W 84 L 103 .449 25 GB

For the first time since 1942 the Seals failed to finish in the first division and, therefore, did not compete in the Governor's Cup playoffs.

This was the first season in which Paul Fagan was in charge of the total operation. Fagan was a businessman, not a baseball man. He knew he needed help, so he made Lefty O'Doul a vice president late in 1948 as well as the manager.

Fagan continued to campaign for major league status for the PCL, but the other owners, although in favor of it, could not afford to remain apart from the major leagues. They just did not have Fagan's wealth; baseball was the way they earned their money, whereas with Fagan it was only a sideline.

Independently owned minor league teams were losing the battle to the wealthier major league teams and their farm systems. Talent was harder to come by and veterans were expensive, so Fagan directed O'Doul to search out and sign young players. He did. He signed nearly a dozen of northern California's top high school prospects and gave them all roster spots.

Many of these youngsters would eventually contribute to the Seals, but the only one who helped in '49 was Reno Cheso, who played outfield rather than his natural infield and batted .248. The others were sent to a lower classification so they could develop. Those who came back in later years to be important members of the Seals' lineups were Nini Tornay, Mike Baxes, Will Tiesiera, Jim Westlake, and Lloyd Dickey.

The youth-laden Seals started poorly and soon veterans were back in

99

1949 San Francisco Seals (courtesy Richard T. Dobbins collection).

Left to right: PCL President Clarence Rowland, New York Yankees owner Del Webb, Baseball Commissioner A.B. "Happy" Chandler at a meeting concerning possible elevation of the PCL to major league status (author's collection).

the lineup. It did little good; the club finished in seventh place with its worst record since 1933, 25 games behind league champion Hollywood.

Gone were Hugh Luby, to New Orleans of the Southern Association; Gene Woodling, to the Yankees; Dixie Howell, back to the major leagues with Cincinnati; Ben Guintini, to Dallas of the Texas League; Will Leonard, to San Antonio of the Texas League; and Bill Werle, to Pittsburgh.

And gone, too, was Joe Brovia, who batted .322 with 89 RBIs in 1948. He was sold to Portland because, according to Fagan, he "looked sloppy." The style of the day was to wear the uniform pants just below the knees, but Brovia, in a glimpse of things to come, always wore his down to his ankles. This was disliked in many quarters, especially by Fagan, who sent the popular Joe up the coast so he wouldn't have to have him on his team.

Replacing Luby at second base was the veteran Dario Lodigiani, one of Oakland's "Nine Old Men" of the previous year. Replacing Brovia was

Walt Judnich, a major league veteran. Roy Jarvis and Roy Partee replaced Howell and Leonard behind the plate. Jackie Tobin became an everyday outfielder, but was unable to produce anything like Woodling's numbers.

For Partee, a major league veteran, it was his second tour of duty with San Francisco. He first appeared with the team in 1941, when he was only 22 years old. Charlie Graham saw the youthful Partee playing for Salt Lake City in 1940 and liked him so well he bought his contract from owner Eddie Mulligan. The next year he was with the Seals, where he was the third catcher.

"I jumped from a Class C league up into Triple A the next year and I sat the bench

Catcher Roy Partee (courtesy Robert Zwissig).

under O'Doul," Partee recalled 50 years later. "I think I got into maybe 30 ballgames. I only caught the guys that threw too hard and Ogrodowski and Sprinz didn't wanna catch 'em. I had to do the dirty work and ended up with swollen hands and bumps all over me because these were old-time catchers and, 'course, I wanted to play and I got beat up a little bit catchin', but I thought I did pretty good." In 1949 the catching duties were split a little more fairly.

Dino Restelli began the season in Pittsburgh, where he matched home run king Ralph Kiner homer for homer in the early going, but the pitching caught up with him and by mid-season he was a Seal again. Coast League pitching never caught up with him, though; in 268 at bats he hit 10 home runs, drove in 65 runs, and batted .352.

Mickey Rocco was back at first base and although he tailed off somewhat, he again produced well (25-114-.275) and third baseman Frank Shofner went from 2-41-.264 to 15-89-.271, arguably the best season of his career. Roy Nicely, however, batted only .194 and Lodigiani, a consistent .300 hitter as a Coast Leaguer, had his worst season at .269.

The pitching staff, except for the loss of Werle to the majors, was very much the same as it was in 1948, but, although the names were the same, the numbers were not in several cases.

Con Dempsey went 17–14 and again led the PCL in strikeouts (164), but his ERA doubled to 4.23. Al Lien was 17–18, but his ERA, too, jumped, from 3.38 to 4.26. Manny Perez went from 11–8, 3.47 to 9–8, 4.84. Cliff Melton dropped from 16–10 to 5–6.

Jack Brewer apparently did not come back from his bout with pleurisy; he went from 15–11 to 5–11. Newcomers Steve Nagy (15–14, 2.65), from Sacramento, and Elmer Singleton (8–14, 4.02), from Pittsburgh as partial payment for Werle and Restelli, did well.

All in all, however, it was O'Doul's worst and most frustrating season yet as Seals manager.

At the end of the regular season Hollywood was on top, followed by Oakland and Sacramento in second and third. San Diego and Seattle tied for fourth, necessitating a one-game playoff to see which team would play for the Governor's Cup. San Diego won the game, 9–6, with a 5-run ninth and three unearned runs, thanks to Seattle's four errors. Future major league star Minnie Minoso had four hits, including a home run, and four RBIs, in the game for San Diego.

In the Governor's Cup, pennant winner Hollywood defeated surprising third place finisher Sacramento, 4 games to 2, in the first round, and fourth place San Diego downed second place Oakland, 4 games to 3. In game seven, won by San Diego by a 28–2 score, Minoso went 5-for-5, scored six runs, and drove in three.

In the championship round, the Stars beat the Padres, 4 games to 2, to begin a several-year period of success for Hollywood.

CON DEMPSEY

Seals 1948–1951

Confidence in oneself is of the utmost importance in every endeavor. Con Dempsey loved baseball but because he was slow to mature he was unsure of his abilities, so unsure, in fact, that he didn't even recognize that he could throw a ball far better than most boys his age. He was cut from his high school baseball team because he tried out as an outfielder and only made the team when his softball coach recommended him to the baseball coach as a possible batting practice pitcher.

It was still several years — after college and military service — before

Con Dempsey (courtesy Con Dempsey).

he thought well enough of his potential to attend a tryout camp. Finally, in 1947, he attended a Seals camp and overwhelmed the batters he was asked to face. He was signed and sent to Salt Lake City in the Pioneer League that season where he became an all-star, then was an integral member of the Seals' pitching staff the next three years. The Pittsburgh Pirates purchased him conditionally, but Branch Rickey, who probably did as much damage as good in his baseball career, tried to change his delivery. Arm problems resulted and Dempsey's major league career was short and forgettable, but he got there, which is more than most can say.

In his first two seasons as a Seal, he went 16–11 and 17–14 and led the PCL in ERA the first year and strikeouts both years, ranking him among the PCL's best hurlers for that period.

CON DEMPSEY: I grew up here in Redwood City and enjoyed baseball. I had my own team, a neighborhood-type thing. I escaped the needs that other people had in social life that I couldn't quite accomplish and I loved it. I went out for the high school team here at Sequoia — Redwood City — as a junior or senior but never showed a lot of ability. I went out for the outfield but I couldn't hit a person if they ran by me. It was a short-term experience and until the end of my senior year I was playing for a softball team for the school. It was not a fully organized team; it was just a get-together to keep a few people busy, like myself, that didn't think they had the ability — or *didn't* have the ability — to play on the hardball team.

The baseball coach was Al Terremere. He'd been there for years; good man, little bit of a redneck from what I'd heard, but a good coach. He expected something of you and he'd give you as much as you gave back to him.

At the end of my senior year they were still doing well, getting into the championship and the finals as they had done in the years previously. I was envious of those that were on the team and having a uniform would have been the ultimate. Just being a member of the team would have been important to me; I didn't have to be one of the stars.

In this particular case, they were going into the playoffs and they needed someone to pitch batting practice. He asked the softball coach if he had anyone who could possibly throw batting practice and he said, "Well, Dempsey is not bad at it. I've seen him throw some."

So I went and joined with the varsity baseball practice and threw some. At the time my inhibitions had dropped down completely because I had nothing to lose, just go out and pitch batting practice. I threw to the first three or four batters who were *good* batters. The coach was standing on the side and he raised his hand and stopped the practice. He came out and as he was prone to do he was scratching his buttocks and looking at the sky, not at me, and looking around for a minute. Finally his eyes dropped down to my level and he said, "Where in the hell have you been?" He said, "I'd like you to get your butt over there and sit down. When practice is over I want to talk to you."

So he talked to me in his office, asked if I would like to join the team going into the playoffs. He asked if my grades were all right, which they were. I think I pitched in two or three playoff games, in relief, primarily. I don't really remember how well I did. I think we won; we were playing San Jose. I had a half uniform because he had given all the uniforms out and he said, "I'll take one of the other guys' uppers and you do your job for me."

Apparently I did pretty well. I was scared and felt I was dreaming. I think if somebody asked my name I'd have to pick up my wallet to make sure I was giving the right answer. But that was my start.

I think one of the highlights in my life at that time was, if you pitched in the playoffs it either doubled or tripled the number of innings credited toward a block letter. A block letter was quite important to myself. And others. And I attained that goal of a block letter in my four or five or six days with the varsity because I pitched enough innings to triple up and be eligible.

That sort of was the start of organized baseball. Before that it was all sandlot — your team, my team, we'd get together on Saturdays.

I went on to the University of San Francisco. My mother was a great advocate of education. My father was, also, as an Irish immigrant, but he was a man of tools of the trade as an expert carpenter. He came over and worked his butt off to overcome the fact that he was Irish Catholic and got jobs here, there, and everywhere. He never complained. He was the greatest man I ever knew.

We moved to San Francisco. I had a brother who was three years younger than I was who had aspirations for baseball but he couldn't catch cold if he was stark naked in a blizzard. He was academic and social rather than athletic. Eventually became a Jesuit priest. He passed away in1985 here in the Bay Area.

Anyway, I went to USF. They had a baseball team but it was a catch-me-if-you-can type thing. You got a towel to shower with and you dressed and undressed in a barracks they had there. There was no baseball there at all, for that matter.

We had Justin Fitzgerald, who was quite an athlete in the olden days with the Brooklyn Dodgers. He'd coach for maybe four or five weeks and then we'd have somebody else. We were never subsidized by the athletic department.

I was playing semipro baseball in San Francisco with teams that were representing companies. I was enjoying myself because I was playing organized baseball and doing better than I thought I would. I did this for a number of years until I came into the service, as well as playing for USF, which never did get into the realm of true athletic teams. We competed with San Jose State, San Francisco State. We never took road trips. In fact, a road trip was to San Jose. I enjoyed it because it was baseball.

In 1943, I joined the Naval reserve in order to stay in school so I could hopefully graduate, but I was called before I went to UCLA. I went to officers' school and I didn't particularly have any aspirations to be an officer so I didn't goof off but I tried to do something that would avail me after the war, like teaching or coaching, so I took education courses as an incentive program. I was sent to midshipman's school, along with others, to Columbia University in New York City in early '44.

I didn't do very well because I had no true naval preparation, so they decided to send me to what they called a quartermasters' school, which was a navigational and signalman school. That was very easy for me to just breeze through. I was eventually sent to amphibious school, which trained you for landing craft. Then I went over to the Mediterranean and trained there for six months.

In the meantime, there was a team at Bainbridge, Maryland — a Navy team — and I said what the hell so I went out for the team. I was the only non-pro on the team of about 20 players. My biggest game was against a school called Franklin College back there and we won. I felt top-of-the-heap because in looking around I was playing with these guys who were Double-A, Triple-A, and several of them majors and I'm not that far removed. That gave me a bit of confidence that I'd never had before.

Then they shipped me out along with others. Those who were really good athletes stayed and performed for the people at home, and went from base to base, but I didn't have any pro experience and that didn't look good on the dossier or on the program so therefore I was bye-bye baby. I kept in touch with some of 'em: Elbie Fletcher of the Pirates and Buddy Blattner and a few others.

I went to the Mediterranean and trained with the landing craft, which was an LCT at 35 by 100-and-some-odd, just a small flat-bottomed landing ship that carried two tanks and some troops to land on the beaches. In August of '44, we made a landing in southern France in St. Raphael to offset what was going on up in Normandy to draw the Germans out.

Then when the invasion was over and everything was secure, we stayed there for quite some time. We'd been to North Africa and other places and then we did play a little baseball, but it was very limited. There weren't enough people that had the ability in our particular group of 2- or 300 people.

Then we shipped to Okinawa by way of the Panama Canal and we took part in the invasion there. They had one or two teams there that were a little bit more advanced. Then we went to Korea and there was no baseball there. We were there maybe four or five months and then in March of '46 I was shipped home and discharged.

I continued to play semipro baseball in the San Francisco area. At the same time I was developing physically. I was a stringbean before I started, but the development was in my confidence more than anything.

My father, as I said, was an Irish immigrant, and thought that, since my brother was going into the seminary it would be good if I would pick up the tools of the trade, which was carpentry. I tried it to please him. This was right after the service. It wasn't my bag. I was backnailing on the roof of a three-story building with an expert carpenter and he fell down two floors and almost killed himself. He knew what he was doing and I said, "This isn't what I want."

I did want to play baseball, but I didn't think I was good enough. I had aspirations of getting $5- or 10,000 as a signing bonus. I went to a Seals tryout. My mother kind of pushed me out, surprisingly enough. My dad said do what you want if it makes you happy, if it makes your mother happy. So I signed with the Seals 'cause I was very impressive at the tryout camp. They were from everywhere with not too much ability and I had no problem whatsoever in quelling their bats.

I went to spring training in Santa Rosa, California, and I was so elated and so confused I thought I was another person standing beside myself. Me, having the opportunity to play professional baseball?

So up to Salt Lake City I went. I led the league in strikeouts, I was on the all-star team. Everything came all of a sudden. Doors were opened and I was called up to San Francisco after the '47 season. I had a 16–13 record with Salt Lake City.

I started in relief with O'Doul. He said he was happy with me. He said, "You listen and you understand." He says, "I've had people come along from colleges who've had all the answers. They're projecting way beyond their means and needs and ability," but he said, "You seem to have a pretty level head about things."

I had a good two or three years, then Pittsburgh, Cleveland, and a couple of others were interested. The Seals had a working agreement with the Pittsburgh Pirates at the time. I wasn't told about a lot of this stuff 'til the end. One of the biggest sorrows I have is that the Red Sox — my wife is from the Boston area — and the Red Sox were a good Irish Catholic team and a team that had a *wonderful* reputation, but for some reason or another they didn't pick me up. They thought I had a bad back.

Sounds silly, but I carried rosary beads in my back pocket that my brother, the priest, had made out of olive pits. I carried them in my back pocket; I felt it was somewhat of a skyhook with all this achievement that's come all of a sudden. In the old days, the pitchers left our gloves on the sidelines behind the coaching box and then you picked it up as you went out to the mound. And in doing so, rather than have the umpires question why I was going to my back pocket for my skyhook I would genuflect sort of to pick up the glove, one hand going for the glove, one going for the beads to say, "Give me help, Lord. I might need it this inning." I became accustomed to that. And the Red Sox got the impression I had the bad back and couldn't bend over.

O'Doul told me this some time later, said, "I don't think it had a big effect, but you should know it now just in case it comes up later." O'Doul was not a *great* religious man, but he was a wonderful man. I said, "Perhaps other people had the same impression. Perhaps I should stop doing what I'm doing, the genuflection every inning and picking up the glove and hitting on the beads."

In fact, the ballplayers used to hide them on me every once in a while. They knew what they meant to me. It was kind of a joke to them. When I told O'Doul I'd better knock it off, he said, "You're doing well. You're a good kid. That's your thing. I think it's great you have a thing like that. If you stop, who knows? It might change your luck. If it does change your luck, I'll give you a good kick in the ass. You do what you think is right and leave the others to think what they wanna think."

Then I kinda leveled off. It happens to the best of us. My arm was fine, but I went to a 9-and-9. We didn't have that good of a ballclub but, anyway, in '51 I went on a conditional basis: $75,000 and two ballplayers were in exchange for myself. I went up on an option for a 30 day look.

Also, unfortunately, Branch Rickey took over the Pirates in the interim. Talking to Rickey was like talking to a priest in a confessional, which was not my bag. We had spring training in San Bernardino in 1951 and he got me aside and spent a little bit of time with me. I thought maybe he had good intentions, he knows more than I do. I rebuffed some of the suggestions that he made once or twice and he told me he was a man of knowledge of baseball and that he had forgotten more than I knew about baseball and if I wanted to stay I would listen to him.

He said, "I'm going to room you with Vernon Law," who was a very fine gentleman, a Mormon. He said, "He came up with the same stature but with a little better attitude than you." He said, "An overhand pitcher being as tall as you are would be devastating." They didn't have guns in those days; my speed at the time was probably 91 or 92, maybe more.

I said, "I've had success." He said, "There you go. You're telling me something that I've made a study of. I was told by the newspapermen, you being a college graduate, you have your ideas." So he said, "We'll make you an overhand pitcher." I was a sidearm, three-quarters, all my life. So he had me work with [pitching coach] Bill Posedel. Bill knew pretty well that this was not a good idea but Bill was a coach and he couldn't do much else.

So I tried and I was thinking about something I was doing naturally all my life. I wasn't too successful at first in spring training. We got to Montgomery, Alabama, near the end of spring training. Everybody was worried about who would make the team. We had so many pitchers and I was very anxious and excited. And nervous.

We were gonna play the Whiz Kids—Philadelphia. That was one of the last games on the road and they were gonna use their regular team 'cause they were going into the regular season. Bill Nicholson, Eddie Waitkus, Richie Ashburn, Granny Hamner.

Bill Posedel was the coach, manager, bottle washer that night because most of the coaches, including Billy Meyer, the manager, were on their way to see friends and relatives. They were southern boys and this was in the South.

Bill came over to me and said, "The ball's in your glove. Go get 'em." I said, "Bill, can I talk to you for a minute? Can I pitch my own ballgame?

I am so tired of this changing around. My arm doesn't feel that good. I'd like to at least give it a shot."

He said, "I didn't hear what you said, but here's the ball. You do what you think is right." And we beat the Whiz Kids, 7-to-2. I figured I made the team; I got my block letter for this year, anyway. We went into Pittsburgh and I opened my mailbox at the hotel and Rickey wanted to see me. He called me upstairs and I thought he was gonna say, "Rah! Rah! Sis-boom-bah!" Well, he ate my rear out from here to Sunday.

He said, "You got away with it. Nobody was there to supervise." He said, "What did Bill tell you?" I said, "Bill didn't tell me anything except I was the pitcher." He said, "We have films and I've seen them. You weren't throwing the way we were going over. We're gonna make that change for you and make you a much better pitcher." And I said, "I wasn't improving. You know that as well as I do." He said, "Oh, it takes time." I said, "I'm out of the service. I'm not a kid anymore." He says, "There you go again. You've analyzed it; you've got the answers before I ask the questions."

As you can gather, we didn't get along as well as we might have. I was just one of the peas in the pod as far as Branch Rickey was concerned. He says, "We'll see what will happen." After 30 days, they said, "Bye, bye, baby." I pitched in three or four games.

A newspaperman brought me to the airport in Pittsburgh to fly back to San Francisco. I was very dejected, didn't sleep a day or two before. I was impressed with this newspaperman. He was a fellow that never spoke to me before, other than to say, "Hi. Welcome to Pittsburgh." He drove me to the airport and put me on the plane. It was raining; the game was rained out and he didn't have anything else to do, I presume.

I remember him telling me as I left on the plane, he said, "You know, you've got great potential. I think I know what went on behind the doors. You were asked to change." He said, "Get back home and get back in shape. You did a hell of a job against the Phillies and that's made a great impression on some people's minds. I hope to see you back next year."

I was still dejected. I got to the top of the runway and he called to me as I started to go inside the plane. He said, "Con, there's one thing I think you should keep in mind. I'm not a biblical man, but this is an expression I use on occasion. Many are called, few are chosen. You were one of the chosen ones who were chosen to come up and give it a shot. One thing to keep in mind. Even though you don't come back — I think you will — you can tell your grandchildren you pitched in the majors."

It was a cup of coffee and a bubble gum card I got. It's a little bit of an achievement there and I have to look at it objectively.

The Phillies drafted me immediately the next year, but my arm was gone. I contracted bursitis. Denny Carroll was a great trainer for the Detroit Tigers years ago and was in retirement in Sonoma and I learned about it and went up to see him. He examined me and had me do certain exercises for a couple of weeks and come back. I had my dad accompany me. "It was all gonna be worthwhile, Pop," I said.

We went up there and spent the day and he said, "You've got bursitis. How long do you think you've had this?" I said, "Probably only about a year or so." He said, "I don't have an X-ray machine. I'm not hopeful but you never can tell. Do the best you can with the tools you have and utilize every opportunity to improve that arm condition. Usually it takes two to three times the time to come back as it did to get injured and you're not a youngster anymore."

Then from the Phillies I got my free agency. In 1953 I had an opportunity to play with the Oakland Oaks. They had a rather poor ballclub — a last place ballclub — and I went 4-and-10. The pride was gone and I was getting shots twice a week, which I didn't tell anybody about. Nobody knew how to take care of an arm out here at the time anymore than I did, so I was getting cortisone, novocaine. I looked in a mirror one day after almost a year and I said, "Here I am. I can't tell 'em I'm having shots." I could, but they wouldn't touch me. They'd know I wouldn't last.

My brother and my family encouraged me to go back to the University of San Francisco and get a teaching credential, which I had to prepare myself for at the very beginning of my Naval career which cost me from being an officer. At the same time, had I been an officer I would have been in the service an extra four years and as far as baseball goes four years is a long time. So all-in-all it worked out well. Not *very* well, but well.

People tell me, "That's too bad," but I had more than I ever thought I would. I had a cup of coffee in the majors, no cream and sugar. And a bubble gum card. That's more than a hell of a lot of other people had. I'm very grateful for that. I would like for things to have worked out better. Unfortunately, Rickey did not make the deal for me and he wanted his own men in there.

After I hurt my arm it ceased to be fun. My pride was gone, I wasn't able to do what I'd done before. I had a college education so for 34 years I coached and taught in San Francisco.

I consider myself very fortunate. We had a family of six children. We lost one — a young lady — at 22 to Hodgkin's.

Going back, I was on a roll at Salt Lake City in 1947. I was doing something I never thought I would accomplish, such as leading the league in things and doing well. When I came to the Seals, being a hometown boy, I felt that I had to do a good job not only for myself but for the people that believed in me. They called me "Confident Con" but it was not all that inside. I had Irish pride. I almost had to do well and yet enjoyed every minute of it. I had good support.

I had a *wonderful* catcher — Dixie Howell — who helped me immeasurably. He was with the Brooklyn Dodgers a couple of years and he was on his way down. And Roy Partee, who was a catcher with the Red Sox at one time. These two were very influential.

O'Doul was a big help to me. A young man named Harry Eastwood, who no one would probably remember — I see him occasionally at reunions — was a catcher. He was a better golfer than a catcher. At one time during the early part of spring training with the Seals when I was working out hoping to make the team, I didn't do well. In batting practice that's the way they'd rate the new pitchers. It was up in Boyes Springs in Sonoma County in 1948. I was a control pitcher and I was a little bit upset with myself not getting any over and I did want to make the team. They took me out rather disgustedly because I couldn't get the ball over, and I went to the sidelines. In the meanwhile, Charlie Graham, who was the president of the Seals, O'Doul, and a couple of scouts and a couple of other baseball people were there. I was disappointed in myself and not making much of an impression.

I went over to the sidelines with Harry Eastwood and Harry said, "How 'bout you and I playing catch? There's something wrong with my mechanics and I'm not gonna get much help as a rookie." So I said okay and I lazily went out on the sidelines and we played catch easily and he was just kinda lobbing the ball. All of a sudden he got a piece of paper for a plate and put it down with a rock on it. He was squatting and chattering a bit. I didn't know what had gotten into him; it wasn't like him at all.

I kept on throwing and he was throwing back to me and he was encouraging me. We did this for 15 minutes and finally the ball dropped behind me for some reason — a bad throw or something — and I turned around and here are all these people — O'Doul, the scouts, and everybody else — standing in a semicircle watching me. O'Doul said, "*That's* what I was looking for."

It was just a small incident and yet so very important. *Very* important. I still see Harry and we both remember it and kinda laugh about it and reminisce 'cause I could just as well have been out to Timbuktu or wherever.

Then I had the desire *and* pressure of being a hometowner and coming out of the blue. It pleased me and pleased my family and all of a sudden I was somebody that I didn't think I was gonna be athletically, even though I had participated all my life. Somehow or another, with the sidearm and three-quarter and being rangy and fairly fast — velocity of pitch — it got me through. I led the league in strikeouts and ERA and was an all-star. I pinched myself to see if it was a dream.

Then I guess it leveled off a little. I was kinda disappointed about they were gonna buy me — Red Sox and Cleveland — for two years. Then Paul Fagan, who knew nothing about baseball except what it did for him — it made his ego bloat but a nice man — he wanted to maintain the local boys. They always had a drawing power — three or four of us. I thought I was held back a little bit 'cause I think O'Doul was anxious for me to go on to bigger and better things. So in staying, I guess I leveled off. I can't explain that; that happens to a lot of ballplayers. Maybe I got lazy. I don't think I did, though.

When I went to Pittsburgh at the recommendation of some older scouts, who were not necessarily Pittsburgh scouts, whom I knew and met along the way. They were very encouraging and gave me some advice. I remember my high school coach; I went back to see him after my first one or two years with the Seals. He said, "I appreciate you coming to see me, but I didn't do anything with you. I passed you up; I didn't put you on the team. I feel like a jerk. How I missed; I felt I had some talent judgment. I didn't give you the best shot."

I said, "When I was with you that week or two weeks you told me that you saw ability you hadn't seen before and being tall and rangy that I had not developed in the forearm and I said, 'What did you mean by that?' You said, 'Your wrist had not come into play with the rest of your body and when the wrist developed the velocity is going to improve maybe 50 percent and you're going to come with possibly a much better curveball.'"

He said, "I said that?" I said, "Yes, you did. I remembered that because I needed those little perks."

My religion had a lot to do with it, too. I wasn't a born-again Christian, but I knew I had a little help from upstairs with the skyhook and the rosary beads in the back pocket. It didn't cost anybody anything but it was there to help.

Phillies was an experience. I told 'em when I got there, "My arm's not right." They had a guy named Eddie Sawyer, the manager; he wasn't very helpful. He wasn't a personable man and he had a set club with Richie Ashburn, Granny Hamner, Eddie Waitkus, Bill Nicholson, Jim Konstanty. Being a rookie I don't think I got much help and then when I said I couldn't throw but every two or three days 'til my arm got better. Once I threw, the following day I couldn't come back.

I was sold to Baltimore [International League]; I said, "I'm not gonna go to Baltimore with a bad arm." Then I was sold to Seattle and I went up to see Bill Sweeney, who was the manager there. I knew him from the Coast

League. He said to go home and sit it out, so I went home from Seattle down here and sat it out and worked out a little bit. Then I went up to see Denny Carroll and it just didn't work out. I pitched batting practice for the Seals. I could throw for ten or 15 minutes and then I'd be nothing for two or three days because of the bursitis in the shoulder from changing my style.

And I worked out with the Giants. There were no offers made — and I didn't expect any — but I was in the clubhouse with the jocks. I was a little part of the act again and I enjoyed having had the experience I did and enjoyed sort of reliving it again.

The Seals made an important goodwill trip to Japan in October 1949. General Douglas MacArthur contacted Lefty O'Doul and the Seals administrators— Paul Fagan, the owner, and Charles Graham, Jr., the president regarding such a visit. There was some natural unrest in the occupation by U. S. forces. O'Doul was very popular in Japan; he had made several trips earlier and many felt he was the "father of baseball" there. The Japanese *loved* baseball. They would play games on rooftops during lunch times! MacArthur felt our visit would settle some of the unrest.

Twenty players, an American umpire, plus Seal officials enplaned for the month-long visit. We were treated royally; it was outstanding! We were the first American team to visit after World War II. A hundred thousand people waving American flags lined the streets of Tokyo when we arrived.

We were feted with parades and banquets at Tokyo, Kyoto, Osaka, Nagoya, Kobe, etc. Crowds of 80,000 attended several of our games against the Japanese all-stars. We played 13 games; we were 9–0 versus Japanese teams and 3–1 against American service teams. We held clinics at schools, both public and parochial. There were several schools conducted by Jesuit missionaries. We did much sightseeing, were presented with many nice gifts and five picture-filled albums. It was an experience we all treasured.

A highlight was luncheon with MacArthur soon after we arrived. He spent two, three minutes with each of us. What an experience! His final statement at the luncheon was, "Gentlemen, there's no substitute for victory. You are here representing America!" He later publicly stated our visit was one of the greatest public relations events of his time.

We were continually photographed. I was forewarned by American officials to be cautious in interviews as I was the only one who had seen service against the Japanese forces. There was little problem.

The month-long trip was a lifetime highlight!

I still get one or two, sometimes even three, requests in the mail for autographs each week. I run into people that remember and it opens a few doors and it's opened a few doors for my sons and my daughters, so I'm grateful for what's happened.

CORNELIUS FRANCIS "CON" DEMPSEY
Born September 16, 1923, San Francisco, CA
Ht. 6'4" Wt. 190 Batted and Threw Right

Year	Team, Lg	G	IP	W	L	Pct	SO	BB	H	ERA
1947	SLC, P'n'r	39	241	16	13	.552	173	76	235	2.95
1948	SF, PCL	37	219	16	11	.593	171	61	189	2.10
1949		36	262	17	14	.548	164	113	269	4.23
1950		55	194	9	9	.500	100	78	200	4.36
1951		32	92	7	7	.500	51	53	84	3.91
	Pitts., NL	3	7	0	2	.000	3	4	11	9.00
1952	Out of baseball									
1953	Oak., PCL	40	106	4	10	.286	62	61	117	5.18

CHAPTER 6

1950:
.500 the Hard Way

5th place: W 100 L 100 .500 18 GB

Before the season began, Fagan, still frustrated over baseball's refusal to grant major league status to the PCL, threatened to advise the league owners to pull out of Organized Baseball. Commissioner A. B. "Happy" Chandler assured Fagan that the situation would be addressed at season's end and suggested that a new 4A classification may be given the league.

The team improved over the terrible 1949 finish. The .500 finish was an improvement of 9½ games over previous year, although it was still a second-division club, 18 games behind the pennant-winning Oaks, but only one game behind the fourth-place Portland Beavers. For the first time since 1935, there were no Governor's Cup playoffs. When the regular season ended, it was all over.

After several years of declining attendance, the league chose to lengthen the schedule to 200 games, the first time since 1930 that that many games were played. This allowed a record of perhaps dubious distinction to be set by the 1950 Seals. It was the first time in baseball's modern era that a team both won and lost 100 games and it also was the last time — and is likely to remain so — that a team did that. This record should be safe; obviously, a schedule will have to have at least 200 games for it to occur again.

Fagan and O'Doul decided it was necessary to spend some money to acquire quality players. They brought in Joe Grace from Sacramento, giving Jack Brewer to the Solons in return. Don White, a stellar performer in earlier years, was reacquired from the Philadelphia Athletics. Both Les Fleming and Chet Johnson came from Indianapolis. Ray Orteig was brought back from Yakima. Ralph Buxton came across the bay after nine years with the Oaks.

It was a team that was vastly different from the 1949 disappointment. The only regular position player from the previous year to hold a full-time job was Dario Lodigiani, but he was now the third baseman rather than the second baseman. His bat returned to its old form; he hit an even .300 for the year.

Fleming was the new first baseman, in place of Mickey Rocco, who went to Portland. As Rocco had done, Fleming provided the main offensive clout, with 25 home runs, 138 RBIs, and a .292 batting average. Young Jim Moran became the second baseman, a position he would hold off and on until 1956.

Roy Nicely at shortstop had his second straight .194 season and split the job with Jack Conway, another acquisition from Indianapolis. But here was a problem; Conway batted .238, 44 points higher than Nicely, but the defense suffered when Nicely was on the bench.

Orteig, too, was not a defensive whiz, but he batted .300. He had always hit well and in 1947 and '48 he had played third base for San Francisco, but he spent '49 in Yakima to improve his catching skills. He did, but he was only adequate.

The outfield consisted of Grace (13-91-.335), White (.300), and Brooks Holder (11-77-.295), another of Oakland's old stalwarts. Also, old favorites Neill Sheridan (12-54-.288) and Dino Restelli (17-62-.341) were back. Restelli began the season in Indianapolis, where he floundered, but came to life when he once again faced PCL pitching.

The Seals pitching was led by the veterans Johnson (22-13, 3.51) and Al Lien (20-13, 4.11), who had his best season. Cliff Melton

Outfielder–first baseman Joe Grace (author's collection).

1950 SAN FRANCISCO "Seals"

LEFT TO RIGHT, TOP ROW:

Bob Rode, Don Lang, Del Young, Harry Feldman, Earle Toolson, Joe Sprinz, Lefty O'Doul, Con Dempsey, Al Lien, Neill Sheridan, Jackie Tobin, Leo Hughes.

MIDDLE ROW:

Steve Nagy, Brooks Holder, Les Fleming, Manny Perez, Joe Grace, Cliff Melton, Don White, Ralph Buxton, Chet Johnson, Jack Conway.

BOTTOM ROW:

Harry Eastwood (bat boy), Ray Orteig, Dario Lodigiani, Roy Nicely, Jim Moran, Roy Partee, Dino Restelli (bat boy).

bounced back somewhat to finish 11–18, but his 5.10 ERA showed the end was near. Harry Feldman, who a few years earlier had been a member of the New York Giants' rotation, had come out of retirement in 1949 to pitch in relief for the Seals, but in '50 became a starter again, going 11–16, 4.38 in his final professional season.

Steve Nagy, however, had been purchased by the Washington Senators, where he was ineffective, and upon his return to San Francisco in mid-season was doubly ineffective (3–4, 6.19). Con Dempsey fell to 9–9, but, even so, Pittsburgh bought him at the season's end. Elmer Singleton, who had pitched well in '49 and would again in the future, could manage only a 5–10, 4.24 record. And the aging Buxton showed his age, going 6–3, 5.03.

Among the highlights of the season for the Seals was probably a catch that wasn't made by Holder in the 17th inning of a late-season home game with the Hollywood Stars. With no score, the Stars had loaded the bases with one out and a long fly was hit toward Holder in left field. It went into foul territory and Holder could have caught it, but he realized that a run would score if he did so he let it drop. Lien, who pitched the whole game, then retired the next two batters. Going into the bottom of the 17th, the score was still 0–0.

Jackie Tobin doubled to lead off the Seals' half of the inning. It was the team's first hit since the ninth inning. Tobin went to third on a ground out and then reserve and seldom-used catcher Harry Eastwood popped a short sacrifice fly to right field and Tobin, the fastest man on the team, was able to score the game's only run.

Another highlight occurred in late June. Dave Melton, a 21-year-old shortstop out of Stanford University, had just been signed and reported to the Seals in Hollywood. He arrived at the ballpark too late for batting practice and watched as the Stars beat up on his new team, building an 8–4 lead after eight innings. In the ninth inning the Seals had a man on base and O'Doul called for his new player to pinch hit. Melton went up to the plate against Jack Salveson, the eventual 1950 ERA leader, and belted the first pitch he saw as a professional over the left (opposite) field fence for a home run to make the final score 8–6. It was Melton's only home run and only two RBIs for the Seals that year; he was soon on his way to Yakima.

Oakland, under Charley Dressen, edged San Diego by two games for the pennant. Hollywood finished third, 14 games out, and surprising Portland, led by ex–Seals Rocco (26-108-.258) and Joe Brovia (39-114-.280), finished fourth, 17 games behind Oakland but one game ahead of San Francisco.

DARIO LODIGIANI
Seals 1949–1951

Dario Lodigiani was a homegrown San Franciscan but he did not join the Seals until he was 33 years old. By that time, he was a veteran of six years in the major leagues, five-and-a-half years with the cross-bay rival Oakland Oaks, and three years in the military in World War II. In fact, in 1948 he had been a key member of Oakland's "nine old men" that won the PCL championship at the Seals' expense.

Along the way he had shown he was a valuable infielder who carried a useful bat. His career Coast League batting average was .305 when he joined San Francisco and in his nearly three seasons with the Seals he batted .295.

BK: How did you get into professional baseball?

DARIO LODIGIANI: I played in the Golden Gate Valley League. It was the number one semipro league in San Francisco. In 1935, I was signed by the Oakland ballclub in the Pacific Coast League. I played there in '35,

Dario Lodigiani with the Chicago White Sox in the mid 1940s (author's collection).

'36, and '37 and then I was sold to the Philadelphia Athletics. I played there in '38, '39, and part of '40.

Part of '40 I was in Toronto in the International League. Then I came back to Philadelphia. And in '41 I was traded to the White Sox and I played there in '41, '42, then '43, '44, and '45 I was in the service, came back and played with the Sox in '46 and part of '47. Then I came back out to Oakland and played with Casey Stengel there in the latter part of '47, all of '48, when we won the pennant. Then in the middle of the '49 season, over a contract technicality, I was picked up by the San Francisco Seals and I played with the Seals all of '49, '50, '51, and part of '52.

Then I was a manager in the Northwest League and in part of '53 and '54 I was the manager of Ventura and Santa Barbara in the California League. In '55, '56, '57, '58, I was a scout with the Chicago White Sox. In '59 and '60 I was a coach and scout for the Cleveland Indians. In '61 and '62 I was a coach at Kansas City with Joe Gordon and Hank Bauer as managers and in 1963 I came back with the White Sox as a scout. This is my 68th year in professional baseball and I'm still active. I'm still scouting.

Of course, I signed a lot of ballplayers. My first ballplayer that I signed that became a major leaguer was Stan Johnson out of the University of San Francisco. I recommended and signed Jack McDowell out of Stanford. He was a Cy Young Award winner.

And I got a good one now. I signed Kenny Williams out of Prospect High School in San Jose, then he went to Stanford in the off-season. He played with the White Sox, he played with Detroit, and he was an executive in the White Sox organization and he's now the general manager. He was one of my signees. He was a good athlete and a good ballplayer. My God, I thought he did a good job when he was playing. I don't know whether he got injured or what. He ran the rookie club down in Florida for a few years for the Sox and then they brought him back up to the big club and now he's general manager. He's an intelligent son of a gun.

The Sox have got the nucleus of a good ballclub. They've got a lot of youth on the club, they've got enough experience to balance all that, they've got good young pitchers on the club, and I think the experience they went through this year — God Almighty, they won a lot of ballgames during the past season and I think the experience they had in the playoffs is gonna make them a much better ballclub. Jerry Manuel — he's out of Rancho Cordova High School just out of Sacramento — and he's done a great job as a manager.

BK: How did you come to join the Seals?

DL: See, I left the Sox. They gave me my free agency. I had my elbow operated on and Ted Lyons had just taken over as manager and he told me that, instead of waiting for me to go through rehabilitation, they gave me my free agency. So I came home and started working out with Oakland and I signed with Oakland.

And then I was there with Casey Stengel and then Charlie Dressen was manager when Casey went to the Yankees. I was signed by the Oakland club with a bonus and there was a rule then that you couldn't put a bonus player on waivers. Charlie evidently didn't know that and nobody said anything to him, so he put most of the players on waivers to see who would be claimed. My name was one of the names on the list and, sure enough, they found out about it and the San Francisco Seals claimed me.

That's how I got to go over with the Seals. I spent most of the '49 season with Lefty O'Doul. Playing for Lefty was like playing for your brother. He was a good manager and he was lot of fun. We had a couple of pretty good ballclubs the time I was there. I had a couple of good seasons for 'em.

We had Mickey Rocco as first base and the next year we had Les Fleming. I played second base and third base; I switched back and forth. We had a fella named Frank Shofner playing third base and he was a lefthanded hitter and when a lefthanded pitcher pitched against us, then I would play third base and Jim Moran would play second. When a righthander pitched against us, then Shofner would play third and I would play second.

Then the following year we had Eddie Lake. He played second base quite a bit and I played third base most of the time.

I played eight years in the Coast League and two of the years I didn't hit .300. I hit .280-something with Oakland one year and then the year I joined the Seals I think I wound up hitting .270-something. All the other years I hit over .300.

I still say that second base is one of the toughest positions to play. You gotta make the pivot play and you gotta make plays to your right and then go in the hole. I think third base you gotta be a little brave; when they smoke 'em down to you, you knock the ball down, pick 'em up, and throw 'em out. I liked third base; it was easy to play and there wasn't a lot of ground you had to cover. Just guard that line and you're doing a good job. I could throw the ball with anybody.

BK: What are your memories of the last-place 1951 Seals? That was Lefty's last year there.

DL: It was one of those deals where nobody seemed to really do a big job. It was like something was always missing. We'd lose a lot of ballgames by one run or we weren't in the ballgame after the fourth or fifth inning. It was tough; it was the first time I was ever on a real losing ballclub. It's hard to say what really was wrong, you know.

It's a funny thing. I never thought much about that year. It seemed like nothing went right.

Tommy Heath came to the club the next year as manager and I went up to Yakima as player/manager in the Northwest League. I didn't play for Heath.

BK: Talk about some of your Seals teammates.

DL: When I first joined 'em we had Don White — played left field — and Dino Restelli played right field. We had Jackie Tobin in center field. And Neill Sheridan played right field. That was a good outfield, good speed, good power. Jackie kind of sprayed the ball around, but White and Sheridan had good power.

I played third base and Roy Nicely was the shortstop. Second base was Jimmy Moran and at first base we had Mickey Rocco and then we had Les Fleming. Les Fleming hit well for us that year. Catching we had two big righthanded hitters, one from Washington — Ray Orteig. Good hitter, had good power. Then we had Roy Partee part of one year.

We had pretty good pitching. Good night, we had Con Dempsey when he was having a good season, we had Al Lien who won 20 games for us that year, we had Manny Perez. It was a good ballclub.

BK: Some say Nicely was the best shortstop ever.

DL: Roy was a good shortstop. He got a good jump on the ball; he had *very* quick hands. I remember the first time I played second base alongside of him on the double play. I went over to the bag and I was waiting for him to throw it to me after he picked it up and the first thing you know it looked like the ball didn't hit his glove and he threw it and it hit me in the chest. [Laughs] From then on, I went in with my hands up all the time. He had *real* quick hands and he had an accurate arm. He kinda threw sidearm a little bit, but he threw hard and he was accurate.

I thought that Nicely was a pretty good hitter. They said he couldn't hit, but he got ahold of a ball every so often and really drove it. I think that if they didn't make a big issue about his hitting he would've been a good .250, .260 hitter. He was a good clutch hitter.

Surprisingly, when he hit the ball good he had pretty good power. I saw him hit that leftfield wall in Seals Stadium a number of times. Hit the ball outta the ballpark. Everybody was telling him what to do with the bat and I used to tell everybody, "Leave him alone!" Finally, I told Roy, "Don't listen to anybody. Just go up there and just do your own." He was a good defensive ballplayer; it was a pleasure playing alongside of him.

BK: Jim Moran.

DL: Moran was a good ballplayer. He could play second base as good as anybody. Moran was a quiet, kind of an easy-going type guy and he was steady. You put him out there and you never paid any attention to who was playing second base because if he was playing he was always doing a good job. He was a good ballplayer and he wasn't a bad hitter. He would get his basehits every now and then. He was all right.

BK: Jack Graham was there for part of '51. He hit a lot of home runs.

DL: Not very many at Seals Stadium. In the years that I played at Seals Stadium and played with the Seals, I would say that there wasn't 10 balls hit over that right field wall — 350-something feet and there was a wind and a big high fence. Jack Graham *did* hit one over. There's only been one ballplayer in the history of Seals Stadium that hit more than one home run over that right field fence and that was Dolf Camilli. There might've been 10 or 15 other home runs, but they were hit by 10 or 15 different ballplayers. Ted Williams hit one, I know, Max West hit one, big Luke Easter hit one, but nobody hit two. It was a cannon shot over that fence.

BK: Eddie Lake.

DL: Eddie Lake had good power. He could pull anybody. You pitch in on him and, boy, he had the short stroke. For a little guy, he could hit a ball a long way. He hit 27 home runs that year for us. He played second base and he did pretty well at second base. Eddie had been around quite a while; he'd been up to the big leagues and back and then back up again during the war years. He did real well. That year that he played with us at Seals Stadium when he hit the 27 home runs, he did a good job. He was a good journeyman player.

BK: Bill McCawley.

DL: McCawley was a good center fielder. He played real well. He played out there with Jackie Tobin and when they had a lefthanded pitcher pitching, then Lefty would play McCawley. McCawley could pull that ball as a righthanded hitter. He could run; he was a good outfielder. He did very well for us.

BK: Con Dempsey.

DL: Con was a good pitcher. The year that he was with us when I joined the club was just before he was sold to Pittsburgh. I remember when we used to play the morning game in Seals Stadium and then the afternoon game in Oakland. He pitched the morning game against us and he beat us. I remember Joe E. Brown, the comedian; he came up to me and he asked me what I thought of Con Dempsey as a pitcher. I said, "Boy, I'll say one thing. For what he did out there, that kid's got a chance to be a good pitcher. He's got a good fastball and a good sidearm sinker and his breaking stuff was good. He's got a chance." And he was sold a year or so later to the Pittsburgh club. Then when he came back I played with him my last couple of years. He did a good job for us.

BK: Al Lien.

DL: Al Lien was a good pitcher. In '49 he won 20 games. He was always the type of a pitcher that would win 12 to 14 games a year and in '49 he won 20. He did a hell of a job for us. We was always in the ballgame.

I was fortunate enough in '49 to be invited to go to Japan with the Seals. I remember when we got to Japan we had a workout and the next day we had lunch with General McArthur and he made it a point to know something about all of us as we were introduced to him. I remember when he came to Al Lien he said, "Al Lien, my God, I see where you finally won 20 games." I said, "Good night, here's a general taking care of the whole Pacific and he made it a point to know that Al Lien won 20 games."

He was a good pitcher in Triple-A ball, especially in the Coast League. Every year he'd be maybe 15-and-10 or he'd be 12-and-11 or something like that, but this one year he put it all together and won over 20. He was a good solid pitcher.

BK: Is there a game that stands out?

DL: There were so many games. I never stood out like DiMaggio or anybody like that. I think the most important game that always stood out in my mind was in 1938 when we opened the season in Washington and President Roosevelt was there to throw out the first ball, with Vice-President Garner. I was right on top of 'em, wanting to get a good look at the president. I could even hear 'em talking, wishing Mr. Mack and Bucky Harris good luck. He threw the first ball and he threw it over my head. In that ballgame against Wesley Ferrell I hit a double and two singles in five times at bat. That was the first big league game I ever saw and I played in it. It was a game that I'll always remember.

BK: Is there a game with the Seals?

DL: There was a few games where I got a basehit in the latter part of the game, in the ninth inning, to win the game. I remember one day against Seattle when Rogers Hornsby was managing Seattle. We were behind by one run and it was the ninth and with a man on I came up and hit a home run and won the ballgame. We beat 'em by a run. I remember Rogers Hornsby saying, "Jesus Christ, you're lettin' that little shit beat you." [Laughs]

He was something. He had a boy that was playing ball and I asked him one time how his son was doing. All he said was, "He took after his mother." [Laughs] He wasn't the easiest guy in the world to get along with.

He was like Ty Cobb. He was a tough son of a gun. I really got to know him [Cobb] when I was with the Sox. I went to spring training down in Arizona and Muddy Ruel, who was one of the coaches with the White Sox for many years, he lived own there in Atherton [California] and he was close friends with Ty Cobb and he and Ty Cobb came down to Arizona a number of times. Through Muddy I got to meet Ty Cobb. He used to call me "Load-a-jenny," instead of saying Lodigiani. He was great that way, but on the field and in his personal life he was a pretty rough guy.

BK: Who was the best ballplayer you saw?

DL: In the late '30s there was so many great players. They only had 16 ballclubs in the major leagues— eight in the American League and eight in the National League. I played against Lou Gehrig a couple of years, and Charlie Gehringer and Hank Greenberg and all, but overall I would say the best all-around ballplayer was Joe DiMaggio. The best *hitter* I ever played against was Ted Williams. In 1941 I played against both of 'em and one of 'em hit in 56 games and the other guy hit four-hundred-and-six. [Laughs]

Williams wasn't a bad outfielder, you know. He could play that left field in Boston as good as anybody — that big high wall. And then on the road, he played straightaway left field but you had Dominic DiMaggio out there helping him. Anything on his left side or in the hole, Dominic was always there. Ted was a good ballplayer; he had a fairly good arm. But he was hitting .360, .370 all the time 'til he got down to the latter part of the season [in 1941] and he'd start climbing and he'd get up to .380, .390, and then .400. Joe Cronin was gonna take him out and not let him play the doubleheader so he would hit .400. He said, "No, I'm gonna play the rest of the games." He played the doubleheader and he got 6-for-8. [Laughs]

I played in a game when he first came up there and he started hitting that ball the way he did. Mr. Mack walked him with the bases loaded. [Laughs] You figured maybe the old man is losing his marbles, but he said, "I'd rather give 'em one run than give 'em four."

But there were so many great ballplayers in those days. Around the infield there was Charlie Gehringer and Joe Cronin and Luke Appling. Lou Gehrig was great. Jimmie Foxx. Boston had a good ballclub, Cleveland had a good ballclub. And then there were so many great pitchers, guys like Lefty Grove and Bob Feller.

I kinda picked an all-star team from the American League that I played in. I put as the two lefthanders Lefty Gomez and Lefty Grove. The two righthanders were Bob Feller and Ted Lyons. The catchers were Bill Dickey and Mickey Cochrane. First base should be Lou Gehrig, second base was Charlie Gehringer, shortstop was Luke Appling and Joe Cronin, and at third base put Jimmie Foxx. He did play third base quite a few games.

Left field would be Ted Williams. Joe DiMaggio and Hank Greenberg in center and right field. Then there was fill-ins like Earl Averill and Tommy Henrich.

BK: In the Coast League, the players were just a short step away from the major leagues.

DL: The reason for that was ballplayers that couldn't stay in the big leagues they all wanted to play in the Coast League because you got a week in each town, every Monday was off, and the weather was always good. You'd run into some rain early in the year and late in the year in the Northwest, but most of the time the weather was great. You didn't run into that real hot weather and the cold weather like you did in the major leagues on the East Coast. I know a lot of ballplayers, when they left the major leagues all wanted to come out to the Coast League to play.

There were some ballclubs in the Coast League that if they were playing today they would do real well in the big leagues if they had big league pitching. The difference between some of the ballclubs in the Coast League at that time and the ballclubs in the big leagues was the pitching. In the Coast League you faced one and maybe two good pitchers a week, whereas in the big leagues you faced one every day. That was the big difference. Defensively and offensively in the Coast League there wasn't much difference from the big leagues.

BK: Who was the toughest pitcher on you?

DL: There was a lot of tough pitchers. Lefty Grove was a tough pitcher. Bob Feller was a good pitcher. He had an outstanding fastball and a *good* curveball. Then there was Early Wynn. He was a good pitcher. There were so *many* good pitchers, Gomez and Ruffing and those kinda guys. Then there were the borderline pitchers—the middle type pitchers—that were outstanding.

Bob Feller, he was a great pitcher. Opening Day in 1941 I hit a double and a single off of him in three times at bat. Whenever I faced him I never tried to take a big swing; I just tried to meet the ball and I had pretty good luck with him. 'Course, one year he pitched against us, he opened the season in Chicago and we all started with the batting average of .000. When the game was over, we all still had .000. [Laughs] He pitched a no-hitter against us. He had everything going; he had the great pitches, he was just erratic enough to keep you loose, and he had good breaking stuff. Good night, he had a curveball that looked like it hit a rock and took a bad hop.

BK: Would you consider yourself an Athletic or a White Sox?

DL: I would say a White Sox because I played more with the White Sox than I did with the A's. The years that I was with Philadelphia we had a second division ballclub, but we had a *good* ballclub on the field. We didn't have very good pitching. But with the White Sox, we had a good ballclub on the field and *outstanding* pitching. Heck, in '41 I thought we was gonna win the pennant. Geez, we had guys like Ted Lyons and Thornton Lee and Johnny Rigney and Bill Dietrich, Joe Haynes and Orval Grove, to name a few. Edgar Smith. They were just great and it was a pleasure playing behind 'em.

DARIO ANTONIO LODIGIANI
Born July 16, 1916, San Francisco, CA
Ht. 5'8" Wt. 150 Batted and Threw Right
Infielder

Year	Team, Lg	G	AB	R	H	2B	3B	HR	RBI	BA
1935	Oak., PCL	10	38	8	15			1	8	.395
1936		163	554	71	155	32	9	4	60	.280

Year	Team, Lg	G	AB	R	H	2B	3B	HR	RBI	BA
1937		162	538	83	176	35	14	18	84	.327
1938	Wmspt, EL	42	145	25	44	12	4	2	21	.303
	Phi., AL	93	325	36	91	15	1	6	44	.280
1939	Phi., AL	121	393	46	102	22	4	6	44	.260
1940	Phi., AL	1	1	0	0	0	0	0	0	.000
	Toronto, IL	143	494	47	139	23	4	7	78	.281
1941	Chicago, AL	87	322	39	77	19	2	4	40	.239
1942		59	168	9	47	7	0	0	15	.280
1943–45					military service					
1946	Chicago, AL	44	155	12	38	8	0	0	13	.245
1947	Oak., PCL	141	498	83	155	26	2	11	92	.311
1948		162	581	77	176	29	2	7	72	.303
1949	Oak/SF, PCL	181	662	92	178	30	0	10	65	.269
1950	SF, PCL	150	536	88	161	25	2	6	68	.300
1951		120	387	36	117	19	0	5	45	.302
1952	Yakima, WI	123	396	54	126	13	2	3	66	.318
1953	Yakima, WI	38	129	14	37	5	1	1	14	.287
	Ventura, Cal	53	164	21	48	8	3	0	22	.293
1954	ChnlCits, Cal							0	0	.333

CHAPTER 7

1951:
Good-Bye, Lefty

8th place: W 74 L 93 .443 25 GB

As in 1949 the Seals finished 25 games out of first place, but this 1951 team was a *much* worse 25 games out. Twenty-five games out this year meant the cellar. Last place. For the first time since 1926 and only the second time in history the Seals held up the rest of the league.

The PCL left the ranks of Triple-A classification as the season progressed. The push for major league status, spurred by Paul Fagan, resulted in "Open" classification, a half-step above the International League and American Association, still classified as Triple-A, and a half-step — a *big* half-step — below the major leagues.

With Open classification came many changes. The major league draft rules no longer applied and new ones specific to the PCL had to be formulated. Players could still be received on option from the major leagues, but the rules here too were changed. And the salary minimum was raised to accommodate the higher classification.

There were rules put on the ballparks and cities. Presumably, the classification was a step toward major league status (it wasn't) and all PCL parks were now required to have seating capacities raised to at least 25,000. And the total population of the cities in the league had to be 10,000,000.

Fagan increased Seals Stadium's seating by shortening the left field fence to 347 feet (from 365) and lowering it to 10 feet (from 20). In the area thus made available, bleachers were erected. This was called "Paul's Porch" and in addition to increased seating capacity, home run production was increased. The team belted 126 for the year, an all-time club record, but the increase was strictly righthanded.

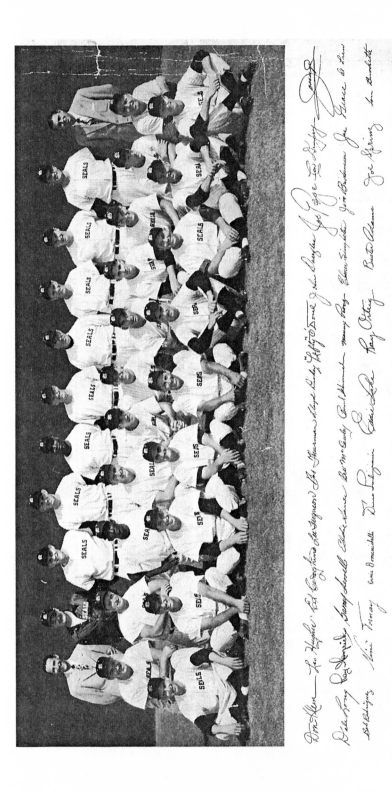

1951 San Francisco Seals. *Back row (left to right)*: Don Klein (radio announcer), Leo Hughes (trainer), Ed Cereghino, Lee Ferguson, Bob Thurman, Lloyd Dickey, Lefty O'Doul, John Douglas, Joe Page, Con Dempsey. *Second row*: Dale Long, Ray Hamrick, Barney Serrell, Ed Sauer, Bill McCawley, Paul Himmichia, Manny Perez, Elmer Singleton, Jim Brideweser, Joe Grace, Al Lien. *Front row*: Bob Rodriguez, Nini Tornay, Ernie Dominichelli, Dario Lodigiani, Eddie Lake, Ray Orteig, Buster Adams, Joe Sprinz, Lou Burdette. (author's collcetion).

Outfielder Bob Thurman (courtesy Robert Zwissig).

Little Eddie Lake, an 11-year major leaguer in his only year with the Seals, was the chief beneficiary of the shorter distance. He bopped 27; he had never before hit more than 19 at any level. Ray Orteig and Bill McCawley each hit 16.

The team's true power, however, was lefthanded and it was still an overnight trip to the right field fences. Bob Thurman hit but 13 and Jack Graham, who could hit a ball out of almost any ballpark, found that Seals Stadium was one of the few in which he couldn't. Graham, acquired from San Diego in the off-season for old favorites Jackie Tobin and Don White, never got untracked for San Francisco and was soon gone, back to San Diego for Eddie Sauer a month-and-a-half into the season.

Transactions such as this one led the '51 Seals to be described as three teams: The one you saw today, the one it replaced, and the one that will arrive tomorrow. This was apparent in the season-opening three-game series in San Diego. (The traditional week-long series were done away with in favor of three- and four-game series.) Lefty O'Doul used 17 different players in that series and by mid-season 13 of them were gone.

The Seals signed a working agreement with the New York Yankees, figuring they would get some high-quality minor league players to fill out the roster. They received much less than they hoped for. The Yankees sent young Jim Brideweser and he proved to be an adequate if not outstanding shortstop. He batted .283 and was steady in the field.

The best Yankee farmhand received by the Seals was pitcher Lou Burdette, whose given name was "Lewis" and for years he was referred to in print as "Lew." However, his favorite player as a boy was Lou Gehrig and "Lou" is what he prefers to be called.

Burdette was the last truly excellent pitcher to play for San Francisco. He won 14 and lost 12 with a 3.21 ERA for the cellar-dwellers, but he wasn't around to see them clinch the basement. On August 29 he was traded, along with $50,000, to the Boston Braves for Johnny Sain and left the Seals before the season ended. He went on to a great 18-year major league career in which he won 203 games.

Burdette might have had one more win but for his love of fishing. He and Lake went on a fishing trip with Seattle's Marv Grissom, Jim Davis, and Hal Brown one night after a night game in Seattle. They drove all night to one of Grissom's favorite fishing spots, caught their limit, and headed back to the ballpark. Sleepless, Burdette and Grissom had to face each other on the mound that night. The 33-year-old Grissom, who tied for the league lead with 20 wins, bested the 24-year-old Burdette, 1–0.

The Yankees sent other pitching, but there was quite a range in age and quality. One was 17-year-old Ed Cereghino from the San Francisco suburb of Daly City. The other was 33-year-old Joe Page, on his way out after a top career in New York. Cereghino, one of the top high school prospects in the country, pitched well for the last-place club and may have done better than 4-6, 5.64 with a better team. Page, however, was ineffective, as were many of the Seals' pitchers.

It was a season of frustration for O'Doul. His club lost its first 13 games, a league record, and settled into last, from which it would escape for only one day all season. That occurred in August, when a seven-game winning streak lifted them to the dizzying heights of sixth place. A loss that day, however, dropped them into the basement again.

From that point until season's end the Seals, Padres, and Solons were in a three-way battle for last. As the closing days neared, San Diego rallied to make a run at fifth place Oakland and entering the last day Sacramento and San Francisco were tied for the bottom spot. Fittingly, these two teams closed the season playing each other in a three game series. San Francisco took the opener, but then lost the last two. Eighth place was theirs.

The Seals' lineup was unimpressive all season. Orteig behind the plate had a good year offensively (16-71-.285), as did Lake at second base (27-58-.261), McCawley in the outfield (16-73-.287), and the veteran Dario Lodigiani at third base (.302), but there wasn't much beyond them.

Thurman (13-63-.274), frustrated by the right field fences, tried, but there was little else. First base was a particular disaster. After Graham's failure and departure, many were tried but none succeeded. Old reliable Joe Grace (2-56-.302) spent some time there as well as in the outfield, but his production was very un–Grace-like. Dale Long (1-23-.266) was sent by the St. Louis Browns to no avail. Actually, the Browns sent the left-handed Long there for O'Doul to convert to a catcher. It was a failed experiment.

The first baseman who had the most playing time at the position was John Douglas, who opened the season with Louisville and then went to Milwaukee. He was acquired to take Graham's place, but the ability he had shown to hit .300 elsewhere was not evident in San Francisco. He batted only .246 with no home runs and only 17 RBIs.

Behind Burdette on the pitching staff were old standby Al Lien (13-10, 3.87), Lloyd Dickey (8-10, 4.90), and Chet Johnson (7-18, 5.67), who found himself in Oakland before the season ended. Con Dempsey (7-7, 3.91) was back, but he was not the pitcher he had been and Manny Perez (5-5, 4.80) was nearing the end; it was his final season as a Seal. The highlight of the year for Perez was the team's first win of the year; he stopped the season-opening 13-game lsiing streak. Elmer Singleton (5-3, 3.04) began the season with Toronto and contributed when he returned to San Francisco. Bob Savage, acquired from San Diego with Graham, was a disappointing 1-5, 5.40. It was a horrible trade.

The franchise that only five years earlier had set the all-time minor league attendance record drew fewer than 200,000 in paid attendance in 1951. Fagan was disillusioned and disenchanted and, indeed, wasn't even present most of the year. He retreated to his ranch on Maui and left the day-to-day operations of the club to general manager Joe Orengo, club secretary Damon Miller, and O'Doul.

Fagan reappeared about two weeks before the season ended and with ten days to go, he told both O'Doul and Orengo that their services would no longer be needed after the season was over. Fagan even threatened to discontinue operation of the team.

The last day of the season was proclaimed "Lefty O'Doul Day," but it was not a happy occasion. Asked what the future held for him, O'Doul replied, "My mother and father were born in San Francisco and lived their lives in San Francisco. Even when I was in the big leagues I couldn't wait for the season to end so I could return to San Francisco. This is my home and I expect to stay here." He didn't.

Lefty O'Doul's record as a Pacific Coast League manager is unsurpassed. His 17 years as Seals' skipper is tied with Walter McCreedie's 17 years at the helm of Portland for the longest with one team. His 2,094 wins are the most and his 1,585 wins with one team are also tops. McCreedie won the most pennants (5), but O'Doul is tied for second with Pop Dixon, Bill Sweeney, and Bill Essick at three. Lefty's 23 total years as a manager in the league is tops.

Lefty O'Doul's record as manager of the Seals: W: 1,585; L: 1,251; Pct.: .559; 2 pennants, 4 Governor's Cup winners.

His record elsewhere in the PCL: W: 509; L: 524; Pct.: .493; 1 pennant (San Diego, 1954).

The Governor's Cup was revived in 1951, but on a reduced scale. The two first round series became the best two-out-of-three and the championship series was three-out-of-five. League champ Seattle downed third-place Los Angeles, 2 games to 1, as Brown won the first game as a starter and the third game in relief. Second-place Hollywood beat fourth-place Portland, the third sub-.500 team to make the playoffs, 2 games to none. George Schmees went 4-for-6 with two doubles, a home run, and three runs batted in and Chuck Stevens went 4-for-7 with two doubles and four runs scored for the Stars.

In the championship round Seattle downed Hollywood, 3 games to 2. Brown won one and pitched 12 shutout innings as a starter and reliever in the series. All together in the playoffs, Brown pitched 22⅔ innings over four games and allowed only 10 hits and no runs. Former Seals' favorite Dino Restelli batted .389 in the Stars' losing effort.

LOU BURDETTE

Seals 1951

Lou Burdette won more than 250 games in a 21-year professional career. Two hundred three of them came in the major leagues, where he was considered one of the top money pitchers of his era. Fourteen more came in 1951, a season he spent with the San Francisco Seals. It was an uncharacteristic Seals team, finishing in last place. Burdette's 14 wins led the team, as did his 3.21 ERA.

He didn't finish the season in San Francisco; at the end of August the Yankees sent him and $50,000 to the Boston Braves for Johnny Sain. It was one of the rare trades where both teams benefited. Sain helped New York to the world championship and a few years later Burdette almost single-handedly pitched the Braves, then in Milwaukee, to the world title over the Yankees.

Burdette was a two-time 20 game winner for Milwaukee and at one time or another led the league in just about everything. His control was his forte; at his peak he averaged only just over one walk per nine innings. Throughout the years, the Seals had several pitchers who went on to major league glory but Burdette was the last to become a true star in the big show.

BK: How did you come to be with the Seals?

LOU BURDETTE: I was with the Yankees organization and they had a working agreement with them and they sent me out there for my third year at Triple-A.

Around Labor Day or a little before I was traded to Boston [Braves], right before we lost our hundredth game. [Laughs] I wasn't there for that. Awful close, though.

BK: After 17 years, that was Lefty O'Doul's last year as Seals manager.

Lou Burdette (author's collection).

LB: I enjoyed playing for Lefty. He was a good guy. He was a real nice man and a good manager and a nice person. I don't know anything bad about him. I don't think anyone said much bad about Lefty. He just went about his business doing the job and he did it pretty well, as well as anybody I've been around.

BK: Why were the Seals so bad that year?

LB: I won — what? — 14 games. We just didn't have a whole lot of power at the plate to score a lot of runs. We had a good ballclub, just no runs.

BK: Your big RBI man was supposed to be Jack Graham, the first baseman.

LB: He didn't have any great year. A lot of the guys had already been up to the big leagues; a lot of Coast League teams were that way at the time. Like Eddie Lake and Joe Grace and a bunch of 'em, they'd already been to the big leagues.

BK: You had two catchers: Ray Orteig and Nini Tornay.

LB: They were pretty good catchers. I enjoyed pitching to both of 'em.

BK: The Seals were very slow to integrate. In 1951 they had Bob Thurman and Bonnie Serrell.

LB: Thurman was a big, strong guy. Good hitter. He was a big swinger, swung hard.

I was a control pitcher and I loved guys who swung hard. I'd love to be pitching today. [Laughs] I think it would be fun. A good control pitcher could foul 'em up something fierce.

They have a big difference in sense of values. I mean, a complete game doesn't mean anything. A nine-inning game doesn't mean anything. They pay the flame-throwers—I call 'em flame-throwers—to come out of the bullpen throwing 95 miles an hour. They pay 'em well to do that. In fact, when I was playing a relief pitcher, that was just something to hang on with, I thought.

BK: What would you have done if you were leading 2-to-nothing after eight innings and the manager wanted to take you out?

LB: I wouldn't have liked that at all. [Laughs] You go that far and evidently you're having success or you wouldn't be leading 2-to-nothing. You're in a groove and you bring a guy in there like nowadays they cock their knee up under their chin. Well, that gives a runner at least two steps and I don't see how in the world a catcher can possibly throw very many runners out.

BK: How much would a man like you with 18 to 20 wins a year be paid today?

LB: Oh, I don't know. Spahn was the highest paid pitcher in baseball and I was second for about six years. Nobody ever regarded me very much. Do you remember when Koufax and Drysdale were gonna hold out for a hundred thousand between 'em? Well, Spahn and I were making more than that then, but nobody knew it evidently. Salaries are not a secret anymore.

BK: You never received quite the credit you should have for the record you had year in and year out.

LB: I'm not in the Hall of Fame, either. I've got a better record than a lot of 'em have. And, you know, almost everything "big" happened to me. The greatest game ever pitched in the history of baseball I won it, but I didn't pitch it. Harvey Haddix did.

I had six one-hitters, I think. I just had a lotta good things happen to me. It just seemed like it didn't mean anything. Like if you beat the Yankees like I did in '57, they forget that real quick. The only thing that means anything is if the Yankees win. If they lose it doesn't mean a thing.

We had one or two writers eligible to vote for the Hall of Fame and if you play in New York or Chicago or Los Angeles there must be 25 or 30 that's eligible in each town. It's not a fair thing. I think it's more of a popularity contest.

Drysdale and guys like that that went into announcing afterwards—
Kiner—they all got in the Hall of Fame because evidently they were up in
the press room with the writers. Buddy-buddy.

BK: If you had pitched in New York or Los Angeles you'd probably
be in today.

LB: Oh, I know I would.

Whitey Ford and I roomed together at Kansas City and I saw Whitey
recently. I was up in Newark at one of the biggest promotion things I've
ever seen. Can you imagine having all the MVPs in the World Series signing pictures of all those guys? I think the only one they said wasn't gonna
show was Koufax. It had to be a big thing. Just the transportation was big.

[At this point, UPS came and I had to leave the phone for a moment.
My dog loves to bark at the UPS man.]

BK: Sorry, Lou. I'm back.

LB: [Laughs] I was laughing at your dog. We've got one here that
barks at every little thing, too. She'll bark and if they're in the house with
her she's sitting in their lap all the time and then she barks 'em back out.
She's a Peekapoo-Maltese. About ten pounds.

We had dogs all the time when the kids were around, then the children got grown and when our last one passed away we didn't have a dog
for maybe ten years.

It happened at a good time, when they had a deal on the cruise ships.
Mary and I did about 70 cruises since about 1985. You give 'em four hours
of your time and you'd get a free cruise. We went all different places. It's
the most reasonable vacation you can take. Nothing else costs you anything. I tell you, it's a great relaxation. We've been on the water 80 weeks.

BK: What have you done since you retired as an active player?

LB: I was pitching coach for Atlanta for two years. I didn't like it, and,
of course, it wasn't paying anything then. I was making 16,500 and I was
the highest paid coach on the team. I took my wife and two daughters—
that's all we had at home then—up to Atlanta and broke even for the season. [Laughs]

Then I went into cable television construction. It's a big business.
They paid me a good salary and an unlimited expense account and a car
to drive. They told me later that if I would've gone piecework that I'd be
a multimillionaire. [Laughs] But I was happy with what I had.

BK: Your infield with the Seals consisted of Jim Brideweser, Dario
Lodigiani, Mike Baxes for a little while, Eddie Lake, and Jim Moran.

LB: We had a good combination at second base compared to a lot of
others. Like I said, I think our biggest problem was the fact that we didn't
score many runs.

BK: Do you remember Al Lien, a lefthanded pitcher?

LB: He stayed there quite a while. He wasn't a bad pitcher. You gotta have runs to win. I don't think you can judge pitching very well when you don't have a team that's gonna get you any runs.

BK: Chet Johnson was there.

LB: Ol' Chet. He was a bird. He was crazy as a loon. He hit Bobby Boyd in the forehead with the ball and he didn't even go down. He just trotted on to first base and Chet threw his glove up in the air and walked right off, right through the dugout and started up to the clubhouse. He was starting up to the clubhouse and Lefty was yelling at him. "Where in the hell do you think you're going?" He said, "Listen, Lefty. If I hit a guy right in the forehead with my best shot and he doesn't even go down and runs down to first base, I don't have it today." [Laughs] He was a nut, anyway.

BK: Did you ever face Boyd?

LB: Oh, yeah. He was a damn good little ballplayer. He could do everything well.

BK: Did you enjoy your year with the Seals?

LB: Oh, yeah. Our oldest child — our son — was born while I was there in '51.

I'll tell you where we lived. You go right straight up Market past the cross on the hill, down on the other side. The sun only shined about six days a year while we were there. [Laughs] We had a *good* home, a nice home. The lady was a widow of a colonel in the service and they also owned a lodge up in the mountains. She gave us a place with very reasonable rent and it was nice, it's just the sun never shined out there. I had to count driveways going home. [Laughs]

BK: How was the San Francisco weather for pitching?

LB: It wasn't too good. It bothered a lot of people. I've pitched games there where it would be 45 degrees. Then you could get in the car and drive a half-hour and it might be 90. The downtown weather there is very weird.

We used to go to the drive-in theaters a lot with the baby in the car and we didn't see many complete shows. Here come the wall of fog. [Laughs] I've seen the ball disappear; leave the bat and go up in the air and it completely disappeared. We had the thermo blankets and jackets that you plugged in in the dugout.

I pitched there when the Giants first came out there again. [Laughs] We played mostly day ball. It's because of the weather.

The Giants never beat me. I went five-and-a-half years once without 'em beating me. I always had good luck with them. Cepeda was the toughest hitter for me. If I kept the guys off base in front of him, well then I never had much trouble.

I found out when Sammy White came over from Boston — a catcher — and Crandall was normally my catcher. We were playing a double header so they put Sammy catching me and Sammy went to Crandall and went over the hitters. He came to me and says, "Crandall says the Baby Bull hits you like he owns you." I said, "Yeah, he does. I just try to keep people off base in front of him." He said, "Could he hit you any better if *he* called the pitches?" I said, "What the hell's the difference in ten rows once it's in the seats?" [Laughs]

Anyway, he came up and Sammy told him that I wanted him to call the pitches and I found out that he did *not* want to know what was coming. He just said, "You can't do that, mon." He wouldn't call 'em and Dusty Boggess, the umpire, told him to get in there. He had me throw three pitches and he's out. So I started calling 'em from the mound, telling him what I was throwing, and never crossed him up and in three-and-a-half years he never hit the ball out of the infield. [Laughs] He did not want to know what was coming.

If he came into the room right now, I'd say, "Hey, Bull. Slider on the outside corner." "No, mon! You can't do that!" [Laughs] He wouldn't give much of an effort to swing at it. The first time I told him three pitches and he popped it up to the mound. I started to catch it behind me and I decided I better not 'cause he didn't even run. He was shook up. I told him every pitch that was coming until I got traded out of the league. I wish I'd have known it earlier. He stood way back and I was a sinker-slider pitcher and he had it all right in front of him. He was a good one.

BK: Did you like Seals Stadium?

LB: It was just in a bad place, as far as the weather was concerned. The field itself, it didn't have any outfield seats. I know they didn't have any seats from foul line to foul line, but then they did after the Giants came out

BK: The owners tried to make it as close to big league as they could.

LB: It was comfortable enough. I never had any complaints about it. It just got cold as hell at times. I'd pitch a ballgame after I got there with the Braves and it'd be in the 40s in the afternoon. We'd go across the Golden Gate Bridge, over by San Quentin, and go up on the mountain to the golf course — Del Rice and I — and it was 85-90 degrees. There'd be 50 degrees difference.

Candlestick wasn't a hell of a lot better. I loved to catch fly balls there because you never knew where they were gonna come down. Spahn and I would have Del Rice hitting balls in the air all the time to us just for the fun of it. I bet Crandall I'd catch as many behind my back as the catchers caught.

One ballgame there, Warren and I went out and caught a few just to see what was going on. In the game the ball went up towards third base, foul territory, and all the infielders went after it. I just trotted over behind first base, over by the Giants' dugout, and just reached out and caught the ball. All the rest of 'em are over by our dugout at third base.

Bill Rigney [Giants manager] ran out and kicked me in the ass. [Laughs] He said, "What the hell are you doing over here? How'd you know where that ball was gonna come down?" I said, "I caught a couple of 'em before the game." The next day he had pitchers out there catching balls " [Laughs]

It was a weird ballpark. When that wind started coming over the mountain you didn't know what's gonna happen. I used to say that's the only ballpark in the world where you can sit on the bench and read the Sunday paper during a double header, with the newspapers coming from the right field fence back around to the left field fence and they'd come right back again in a little bit. [Laughs]

I even hit a couple of home runs there. I hit three game-winning home runs off of Koufax. Not many *hitters* can say that. [Laughs] I beat him five or six times and he never beat me once. And I beat Spahn five times after I left the ballclub. They always pitched us against each other. I was 11-and-0 against the two best lefthanders in the league then.

I loved the Coliseum. I only hit one over that net out there. Where that net came down in left-center field it was just the right distance and that was my general alley to hit the ball in. I hit nine home runs there. I hit two home runs in one game twice. I had some RBI days—five or six — but all I wanted was a win.

SELVA LEWIS BURDETTE
Born November 22, 1926, Nitro, WV
Ht. 6'2" Wt. 180 Batted and Threw Right

Year	Team, Lg	G	IP	W	L	Pct	SO	BB	H	ERA
1947	Amst'd'm, CA	24	150	9	10	.474	79	69	125	2.82
	Norfolk, Pd	6	27	1	1	.500	10	20	23	4.33
1948	Quincy, III	31	214	16	11	.593	185	72	164	2.02
1949	KC, AA	36	118	6	7	.462	51	47	147	5.26
1950	KC, AA	27	139	7	7	.500	77	52	150	4.79
	NY, AL	2	1	0	0	—	0	0	3	9.00

Year	Team, Lg	G	IP	W	L	Pct	SO	BB	H	ERA
1951	SF, PCL	30	210	14	12	.538	118	78	202	3.21
	Boston, NL	3	4	0	0	—	1	5	6	6.75
1952	Boston, NL	45	137	6	11	.353	47	47	138	3.61
1953	Milw., NL	46	175	15	5	.750	58	56	177	3.24
1954		38	238	15	14	.517	79	62	224	2.76
1955		42	230	13	8	.619	70	73	253	4.03
1956		39	256	19	10	.655	110	52	234	2.71
1957		37	257	17	9	.654	78	59	260	3.71
1958		40	275	20	10	.667	113	50	279	2.91
1959		41	290	21	15	.583	105	38	312	4.07
1960		45	276	19	13	.594	83	35	277	3.36
1961		40	272	18	11	.621	92	33	295	4.00
1962		37	144	10	9	.526	59	23	172	4.88
1963	Mil/StL, NL	36	183	9	13	.409	73	40	177	3.69
1964	StL/Chi, NL	36	141	10	9	.526	43	22	162	4.66
1965	Chi/Phi, NL	26	91	3	5	.375	28	21	121	5.44
1966	Cal, AL	54	80	7	2	.778	27	12	80	3.38
1967	Cal, AL	19	18	1	0	1.000	8	0	16	5.00
	Seattle, PCL	13	19	0	1	.000	8	4	18	4.26

ED CEREGHINO

Seals 1951

In the late 1940s and early 1950s, the competition among major league clubs for young talent escalated to the point that unheard-of sums of money were being paid to prospects. It became such a concern that almost annually new rules were made to govern and attempt to control the spending. Eventually, a bonus rule was passed that required the signing club to carry the bonus player on its roster for two full seasons. This rule lasted from 1953 through 1957; it was a horrible rule and it did not control the situation.

Ed Cereghino was reportedly, at the time, given a $60,000 bonus by the New York Yankees in 1951. The true amount, we learn today, was $75,000, a whole lot of money in those days, but he was a hard-throwing righthander who had been courted by many teams. Two years later he would have had to remain on the Yankees roster, but not in 1951. The Yankees sent Cereghino, then 17 years old, to the Seals, with which they had a working agreement. This was basically his hometown team; he was from Daly City, only a stone's throw from San Francisco.

His was essentially a Triple-A career. He never made it to New York to pitch.

Ed Cereghino (courtesy Ed Cereghino).

BK: The Yankees signed you for a reported $60,000.

ED CEREGHINO: 75,000. In that era, you did not have to divulge what you got and it was all by guess and by golly.

BK: Where were you in school?

EC: Jefferson High School in Daly City. It was June of 1951. I went the following week to the Seals.

BK: Were you ready to play at that level?

EC: Yes. I thought I was at the time. You're young, you figure to take the challenge. I had not a bad season. I won 4 and I lost 6 for a last-place club. We had a lot of good ballplayers there, but it just didn't click. I was happy with the season I had with them.

BK: You say the team didn't click. What wasn't there?

EC: You know how the old Coast League was. The guys could come down from the majors and because of the weather out here and the Mondays off and all that, they could last another two or three years. We had a lot of guys on the ballclub that had been great ballplayers. We had Eddie Lake, we had Buster Adams; Joe Page had come down from the Yankees that year, we had Lou Burdette, Dario Lodigiani, Con Dempsey. It was a good ballclub, but we had younger guys and older guys and I only went half a season with them so I don't know. We just didn't click. In fact, we went into eighth place the last day of the season.

BK: Did you start or relieve?

EC: I was a starter and I relieved one time and it was the last game of the season and I lost the bloody thing. [Laughs] In fact, Lefty O'Doul told me, "Go home and get your shots. I'm taking you to Japan. I'm going to teach you how to pitch out," because that's how I screwed up. They had just put the rule in that the catcher had to jump out at the last minute if you're intentionally passing somebody. Well, I got the second pitch in a little closer to Joe Gordon. Fly ball, scored a run, error, and, boom!, we lost. [Laughs]

So here I am, age 17, taking the long walk up the tunnel, thinking, "Do I really want to go up there?" [Laughs] So O'Doul said, "I'll take you to Japan and teach you how to pitch out" and that's how I got to go over there.

BK: That must have been exciting at your age.

EC: Oh, God, that was fun. I pitched quite a bit. I pitched probably five or six games. We had a lot of great guys on that tour. Mel Parnell was on there, from Boston, and Bobby Shantz from Philadelphia and both DiMaggios, Joe and Dominic; and Joe Tipton. And then we had Johnny Price with us, the old baseball guy, the trickster.

It was a great tour and, of course, the Japanese people were just wonderful to us. I remember getting home and getting a call from the wharf in San Francisco saying some materials have been shipped. So I arranged to get a truck and have them shipped out and it was cases and cases of stuff that they had sent us. Noritake china, silk. You just couldn't believe it. In fact, I maintained a lot of friendships over the years in Tokyo and Osaka because of that tour.

BK: The Japanese loved Lefty O'Doul.

EC: He was next to the emperor. There was "O'Doul-san."

The fans used to get on him all the time, but he'd give it right back to them. As far as the ballplayers went, the guys that I knew respected him highly. And you had to. He was a feisty guy, but he was good to me.

He taught me a lot of things. He taught me how to dress. He said to me one day right after I walked in, he said, "Hey, kid, you gotta get some real clothes." So he said, "Meet me tomorrow morning at ten o'clock at MacIntosh's," which was a tailor across the street from his bar. So I met him there and he said, "Get one of those, get one of those ..." so I wound up buying three suits—tailor-made. I'd never had anything but off the shelf, you know. It cost me about $200 a suit. He said, "I order 'em a dozen at a time." Six hundred bucks, that was a lot of money.

That's how I got outfitted and that's how I learned to dress and conduct myself and so on.

BK: Lefty never went anywhere without a suit.

EC: Oh, no. And talk about a classy dresser.

That guy used to go around in San Francisco—he'd take me here and there in a cab to try to make me grow up in a hurry—and he'd always sit in the front seat with the cabbie with the window down. If we'd come to a traffic jam or something, Lefty would tell the cabbie, "Just move around there," and the cops would try to stop us and Lefty would wave and he'd wave us right through. [Laughs] Flamboyant guy.

BK: A $200 suit in 1951 was an uptown suit.

EC: Oh, yeah. It's Armani time today. [Laughs] I didn't know. I just followed his direction.

BK: You had the money to spend at that point.

EC: I did. Yeah.

BK: Did you use your money wisely?

EC: Oh, yeah. I had been investing before that as a kid and I plowed most of that away while I was earning my regular salary during the seasons and raising five kids and doing all that kind of stuff. I retired at age 55. I held on to it.

BK: What was your salary?

EC: The first year with the Seals it was $4,000 for half a season. That was a good salary. Then I went over to Kansas City — the old Blues — for a few years and then to Sacramento and Richmond, and I was at Denver, I was at Toronto. I was probably getting 8- to 900 bucks a month. 5400, 6,000. It was a 7200 minimum in the majors then.

BK: You had some decent seasons in the minors.

EC: I don't know. I had kind of average seasons, really. [In] '52 I went up to spring training with the Yankees and then I was assigned to Kansas City. That was a strange year. I won the first ten games — I was 10-and-zero — and then I lost the next eight, so I wound up 10-and-8. [Laughs]

We went to the [Little] World Series and we lost that one. Artie Schallock, myself, and Ed Erautt worked the rotation. They'd throw another guy in between.

Then '53 I went to spring training with the Yankees again, then I got sent back to Kansas City. About a third of the way through the season they said, "You better go up to Binghamton, New York. You gotta get more pitching in." I really had a good stretch for myself up there.

Then in '54 back to spring training with the Yankees and then back to Kansas City. I think I had a losing year there. In '55 back to spring training. They wanted me to go to Denver with Houk and I asked Casey to send me out to the Coast League, to Sacramento, because my wife was pregnant and about due, so he did. I stayed there — pitched Opening Day — less than half a season and was sent to Toronto because there was some guy on the shelf there. By the time I got there, he was off the shelf. I never pitched up there.

At the end of the season I wound up out in Denver with Houk and pitched just very little. From there, I went and played winter ball in Puebla, Mexico.

In '56 and '57, I was at Richmond with Eddie Lopat. International League. I don't think I had very good seasons there. I had an elbow problem in '57 and Lopat said, "You have to go down to New Orleans and work it out in the heat." I said, "It's just as warm here in Richmond. I'll stay here on the disabled list." "No, you won't."

So finally, I said, "I'm heading home." So I headed home and they suspended me for life, as they usually did. I went back to San Francisco—San Francisco State — and then come spring training they lifted the suspension and back I went. That was my last year. I think it was Denver in spring training and they assigned me with Charlie Silvera, who was managing for the first time, in New Orleans. That's where I finished.

At the end of that year, I told them, "This is the end of it for me. I'm just not doing what I should be doing for you guys." So they suspended me for life again.

The Commissioner's office called me one day and said to me, "We've noticed that you had requested voluntary retirement and you weren't granted it. Send a letter to Mr. Weiss," who was general manager of the Yankees at the time, "and request it again and the Commissioner will see that you get it."

So I did and they granted me voluntary retirement and to this day I'm on the roster of the Toledo Mud Hens. And, believe me, if I could get through spring training, I'd go just for the year because it was at a prior salary. [Laughs]

Jan and I took off last year and went to spring training in Arizona — we stayed there about a month and watched all the ballclubs— and, honest to God, the only people I saw sweating were the batboys. With all this aerobics, if aerobics are so good, how come there are so many injuries? It looks like a country club to me. I enjoyed it immensely, but it's nothing I knew. You busted your ass or you didn't feel like you did anything, but it's a different world. I understand.

I was just inducted into the San Mateo County Hall of Fame. I was asked, "What's the difference between today and yesterday?" I said, "Well, aside from the money, you still throw the ball, catch the ball, run the bases, slide, and swing the bat. It's the same damn game. The guys wear a little more colorful uniforms, the stadiums are larger and more beautiful, but it's still essentially the same game I loved."

BK: You were in spring training five times with the Yankees. Was there ever a chance of sticking?

EC: Yeah. In '55, or whenever Tom Sturdivant went up. Tom and I were old buds from Kansas City and we were rooming together. There was *one* slot on their pitching staff—every once in a while there was one slot open—and Tom and I were like brothers almost. We were pulling for one another; we said, "Whoever gets this deserves it," and he beat me on it, but I had a good spring. He had a better spring. That was about as close as I came.

BK: Eight years of professional baseball. Regrets?

EC: No, not really. That's a question that's asked quite a bit. I've always been a guy that's figured yesterday's in cement, today it's "I can still do something about it," but tomorrow the cement is very wet and I can do something about that, so at best I'm the future unfolding. That little career of mine for eight years—sure, I would've liked to have done a lot better, but I did my best and that's all I've ever done in my life. If it doesn't come out, okay, that's fine and dandy. I move along.

I had a grand time. I got to places all over the country. I got to Hawaii, I got to Japan, I got to Canada, I got to Mexico. I'd never been out of Daly City before that.

It took me ten years to finish college. I got my teaching credential and taught a few years. Then I got my administrative credential and I was principal of Jefferson High School, and also Rio Vista High School, for about 20 years. I was assistant superintendent for a couple of years. Then I retired.

I loved education as much as I loved baseball. Still do. Still love the teaching/learning thing. I did not like elementary, even though I've got eight grandchildren, but I loved high school. [Laughs] Elementary kids drive you nuts, but high school kids, I loved them.

BK: Seals Stadium was a good park to pitch in.

EC: Yeah, except that we had Paul's Porch. Paul Fagan, the owner, put some stands out there in left field and brought that in and it was a little tighter in '51 than it had been in the prior years. In the prior years, it took a blow and a half. The longest ball I've ever seen hit almost out of that place was by Joe Brovia, big lefthanded guy, hit the wall there in right field *way* up high, didn't quite go out. It took a cannon, really, except when they put the Paul's Porch in there for the righthanders. There was a few more home runs being hit.

It was a beautiful stadium. When I broke in there and then I went to New York for the World Series, I went down in the Yankee clubhouse and I thought to myself, "Geez, this is not much of a clubhouse." [Laughs] [At Seals Stadium] You parked your car, you smelled the Wonder Bread right away from the factory and in you'd go. It was a great old park. It was sad to see that bulldozed out of there.

BK: You mentioned Joe Brovia.

EC: Ah. Joe Brovia. Great guy. He lived in Santa Cruz. We had a reunion of San Francisco Seals a few years ago, anybody who was still around and all the fans in North Beach. It was a beautiful gala event. I ran into him there and he said to me, "You always figured I was a low ball hitter." I said, "Yeah. That's the way we pitched you, so we'd go up and in." He said, "You guys all had it wrong. I could hit with power anything up around my shoulders." I said, "You used to hit me like you owned me, I knew that." He said, "That's why. You were pitching me wrong." I just loved the guy.

BK: There were several Yankee farmhands there in '51.

EC: We had Brideweser and Lou Burdette, Bill Renna. Big Bill's still down the peninsula. Renna, for such a huge guy, he was such a gentle guy, unless you got him riled, and then he kicked the crap out of everybody and anybody. [Laughs] He and I roomed together for a few years and we remain close. Actually, I first hooked up with Bill in Kansas City in 1952.

Joe Page — I learned a lot from him. He used to tell me stories about when he was doing the relieving for the Yankees. He'd be cranking up and Houk was always the bullpen catcher — he and Charlie. Houk would rub the ball — there was always some black dirt out there — and Page got to believe that Houk was magic when they'd go in. Every time Page went in, Houk went with a little black dirt in his back pocket and he'd use it to rub the ball. [Laughs] And Page would not pitch to anybody else. He just believed that was the deal. He still threw pretty hard when he came out here. He wasn't the old Joe Page, but he still had a pretty good hummer for himself.

And there were guys like Dario Lodigiani and Nini Tornay. Lloyd Dickey passed away. Con Dempsey had one of the best damn curveballs I've ever seen. He could drop that right off the table.

When I went to the Seals, my first roomie was Joe Sprinz and Joe would teach you when you first went to a hotel room the first thing you'd do is you wash out the glasses 'cause they could be dirty and you'd get germs. [Laughs] I lasted about one road trip with Joe and O'Doul kept watching me and asking me, "How are things going?" I said, "I'm kind of a young punk here, but could I get waivers?" (Laughs) He said, "Sure," so I ended up rooming the rest of the year with Con Dempsey. We were both readers so we didn't mind with the lights on early in the morning reading. We had a good time for ourselves. We were a couple of good roomies.

Al Lien and Manny Perez. Inky [Lien] was a good guy and still throwing the ball pretty well. And Chet Johnson was there, too. Chesty Chet. He'd hit the ball on the ground and run to third base. Manny Perez was still doing pretty good, still getting them out. Good curveball, too, as I recall.

Ol' Bob Thurman, *good* lefthand hitter. Joe Orengo was general manager at the time. Burdette had good stuff, good hard sinker and he didn't mind blowing you back off the plate. Great, great career.

I have heard from guys that I played with more in the other leagues than I have out there. Wally Burnette and Steve Kraly, went up to the Yankees for a couple of cups of coffee. Sonny Dixon was my long-term roomie for years. Joe Soares, the trainer for the Yankees, just passed away. He was a good old guy. He followed Gus Mauch, who was the trainer for many, many years.

All in all, a lot of good guys and a lot of good times for me. Although I went to college and got all of my advanced degrees, my college was baseball really. That's where I learned to live a life and how to comport and conduct myself.

I remember the first time I signed with the Yankees and Joe Devine signed me. One night I got a call and he said, "You have to go over to Portola playground and talk to a few Boy Scouts." I said, "Sure," so he picked me up. I went over there and it was like *Patton*—the opening scene from *Patton*. He introduced me, put me on the stage by myself. There were about 400 Boy Scouts and their leaders out there and I never could put two words together. [Laughs]

But from that I learned I don't ever go anywhere unprepared. [Laughs] Stung once, never again.

BK: Was Sal Taormina there in '51?

EC: No. Sal had moved on. Old Hoggie. But he was playing for somebody. The last I ran into him was when he was coaching at Santa Clara and then he passed away some time ago. Heart attack. He was a good guy. We used to call him "Hoggie." Good hitter.

BK: Do you remember your first game?

EC: The first game I believe I lost to San Diego. There was a couple of runs differential. I remember going into that game and looking around at that big crowd and thinking, "Yeah, I can do this."

And then I remember my second game as well because I beat Seattle. In fact, I ran into their old catcher in the old Coast League get-together. I've forgotten his name now. I beat Al Lyons, who was having a great year that year. It was 3-to-2 or 2-to-1, I can't remember. I thought, "Yeah, I'm gonna settle on this deal. I can just feel it."

But I always got up for pitching. I had a bunch of guys with bats there, so let's get to it.

BK: What was your biggest thrill as a Seal?

EC: That would be the first time I walked in the clubhouse and met those guys whom I had pretty much idolized as a kid. That was awesome for me. Shake hands with guys that I'd been sitting in the stands watching and following their careers and keeping their stats and all. That was my biggest thing.

As far as the games go, I guess the first ballgame, stepping out there between 14- and 15,000 people, whatever it was. To me, that's kind of impressive, to be out there doing it.

ED CEREGHINO
Born November 24, 1933, San Francisco, CA
Ht. 6'2½" Wt. 200 Batted and Threw Right

Year	Team, Lg	G	IP	W	L	Pct	SO	BB	H	ERA
1951	SF, PCL	13	75	4	6	.400	35	49	79	5.64
1952	KC, AA	28	184	10	8	.556	85	80	165	4.16
1953	KC, AA	10	57	2	4	.333	29	39	48	3.47
	Bnghmtn, EL	19	139	11	3	.786	89	37	122	2.59
1954	KC, AA	35	188	11	14	.440	93	82	189	4.50
1955	Sac, PCL	25	79	2	5	.286	36	49	89	5.81
	Denver, AA	4		0	0	—				
1956	Richmond, IL	32	123	3	9	.250	72	90	111	4.39
1957				0	1	.000				
1958	N.O., SA	35	186	9	16	.360	95	109	215	5.06

◆ CHAPTER 8 ◆

1952:
Another New Regime

7th place: W 78 L 102 .433 31 GB

For the first time since 1934 a baseball season approached for the Seals without Lefty O'Doul as the manager. There was little difference in the final outcome. A total collapse by Sacramento allowed the Seals to finish seventh, but they were 31games behind champion Hollywood.

Paul Fagan and, for that matter, the entire league still wanted major league status. It was decided not to sign any more working agreements with major league clubs and not to accept players on option, beginning in 1953. But the Seals and a few others began this in '52. The agreement with the Yankees was ended.

A new manager was hired. He was Tommy Heath, a former major league catcher whose only West Coast baseball experience was in the service in World War II. Heath had a great sense of humor and became popular with the players almost immediately. Built much as Babe Ruth was, but without anything like Ruth's ability, he at first glance appeared to be fat, but it was a body like a barrel. He had been manager of Minneapolis in the American Association and among his players in 1951 was Willie Mays.

Last place in '51 gave the Seals the first pick in the draft. With it they chose pitcher Frank Biscan, who had been 16–9, 2.55 with Memphis in '51. He pitched poorly in spring training, didn't like the San Francisco weather, was a depressing clubhouse influence, and was soon on his way back to Memphis, where he had another good year (17–9, 3.20).

They also picked up first baseman Hank Biasatti from Buffalo. A reasonable power hitter in Triple-A, Seals Stadium was too much for him.

150

Manager Tommy Heath (author's collection).

His production was not unlike that of Jack Graham in '51. He was released less than a quarter of the way into the season with no home runs, only ten RBIs, and a .270 average and didn't reappear until 1954 with Drummondville in the Provincial League, where he also pitched.

Joe Grace (4-62-.299) took over at first, but his age was advanced and his production was weak despite his batting average. Jim Moran was back at second base after spending most of '51 in Oakland, but, although he was a slick fielder, he was far from a run producer (.258, but only 32 RBIs in 687 at bats).

Reno Cheso (3-57-.258) was also back after spending 1950 and '51 with Yakima and Vancouver in the Western International League and played well at third base. Lenny Ratto, acquired from Sacramento, replaced the departed Jim Brideweser, promoted to the Yankees, at shortstop, but his hitting was a liability (0-30-.223) and '52 was his last year in professional baseball.

In the outfield, Bill McCawley (4-78-.256) lost his power stroke with the removal of Paul's Porch, and Bob Thurman (9-52-.280) still could not consistently reach the far-away right field fences. Thirteen year veteran Frank Kalin (12-64-.294) was acquired from Indianapolis early in the season and turned out to be a pleasant surprise, and Sal Taormina (4-22-.286 in only 161 at bats) did well after being recalled from Yakima at mid-season.

Behind the plate, Ray Orteig also saw his home run production drop (to 3) with the departure of Paul's Porch, but he drove in 53 runs with a .266 batting average.

The pitching staff was not bad, especially when considering that there was so little offensive support. Elmer Singleton (17–15, 2.67, 170 strikeouts — second in the league) finally pitched like everyone thought he could. Rookie Bill Boemler (14–16, 3.21) came up from Yakima, where he had gone 14–13, 3.27 in 1951. Bill Bradford came from Binghamton, where he had been 17–14, 2.36. He went 15–11, 3.53, but veteran Al Lien had an off year (9–16, 4.30). Bob Muncrief, a mainstay for the St. Louis Browns' only pennant winner in 1944, was acquired from the Yankees and went 6–13, 2.69 out of the bullpen.

Veteran Bill Reeder, brought in from Rochester, pitched so well in spring training that he was the Opening Day starter. He shut out Portland with a one-hitter, but then lost his next nine decisions. He finally won another game, but it was too late. He was released with a 2–9, 5.93 record and 51 walks in 91 innings. It was his last year in professional baseball.

Singleton pitched the best game of the year in the PCL. On April 24, in a home game attended by fewer than 800 fans, he set the Sacramento Solons down without a hit for 12⅓ innings. Unfortunately, his anemic-hitting teammates couldn't score and he allowed three hits and a run in the 13th and lost the game, 1–0. It was the first no-hitter thrown by a Seals pitcher since May 14, 1930, when Jimmy Zinn set those same Solons down, 8–0, without a hit and it was the last ever thrown by a Seals pitcher.

There was another memorable incident in 1952 centered around Seals pitching. The PCL had integrated in 1948 when the San Diego Padres signed Negro leagues catcher John Ritchey and by '52 blacks were well represented on most teams in the league. The major exception was San Francisco. Yes, the Seals had had black players, but Thurman was the only one who had stuck around for long enough to contribute.

Across the Bay, however, Oakland had been among the leaders in signing Negroes. In 1952 the Oaks had Piper Davis and Rafael "Ray" Noble, both everyday players, although in Davis's case it was likely to be a different position each day. He once played all nine positions in a game for the Oaks.

Frequently the black players were the victims of taunts and jibes from many of the league's white players, but overall the feeling among the PCL players, especially those originally from the West Coast, was, "Let the better man play."

(The following incident is remembered slightly differently by Reno Cheso in his interview, but whichever way it occurred it was a heck of a fight.)

Some players, however, let their prejudices get in the way of their better judgment. Boemler, the Seals' very large (6'7", 225 pounds) rookie southpaw, had repeatedly pitched dangerously inside to the Oaks' Davis and Noble, hitting them or knocking them down several times.

On July 27 in Oakland in the first game of a double header, Boemler did it again. He knocked Davis down twice, but on the next pitch Davis singled. Johnny Ostrowski bunted, but Grace at first base couldn't handle

Cheso's throw and Davis went to third. Moran got to the ball and threw past third and Davis continued on toward home, where Boemler was covering the plate. Cheso's throw beat Davis, but the runner hit the waiting Boemler high and hard and a fierce brawl ensued. Both benches emptied and Oaks' veteran Augie Galan said later, "It was the biggest and wildest brawl I've ever seen in my 20 years of baseball."

The two initial combatants represented a mismatch. Davis was a good-sized man — 6'3", 185 pounds — but Boemler was huge, yet Davis held his own. Noble was a wild man, clobbering Seals and Oaks alike. Heath observed, "I think Noble would have decked the entire Oak team," if there had been no Seals present.

A group of Seals fans who identified themselves as the "Gang of 19" threatened harm to the Oaks the next time the two teams played in San Francisco, but it was an empty threat. Nothing more happened between the two teams.

Miraculously, no one was injured or ejected and Boemler went on to win the game by a 4–2 score, then Lien came back to win the nightcap by the same score. The Oaks had just taken over first place, but the sweep by the Seals knocked them out of the top spot.

The season was a financial loss for the Seals, who drew only 198,778 in paid attendance. Fagan again threatened to padlock Seals Stadium.

Hollywood, led by outfielder Carlos Bernier (9-79-.301, league-leading 65 stolen bases) and former Yankees outfielder Johnny Lindell (24-9, 2.52), the league's MVP, won the pennant. Oakland finished second with Tookie Gilbert, the league's RBI (118) leader. Third-place Seattle's Bob Boyd led the league in hitting (.320).

Around the league, former Seals prospered. Steve Nagy went 16–16, 3.04 for Seattle, Joe Brovia (21-85-.290) did well for Portland, Jackie Tobin (3-33-.287) was an outfield fixture for San Diego, and Dino Restelli (7-31-.357 in 249 at bats) continued his assault on PCL pitching, this time for Sacramento.

BILL BRADFORD

Seals 1952–1955

In 1949, the Seals signed Bill Bradford, a 27-year-old World War II veteran who was pitching semipro ball at the time. After three years of grooming, he finally joined San Francisco in 1952, where he became an important part of their pitching staff, winning 43 games over the next four seasons.

Bill Bradford (author's collection).

In 1952 he won 15 games and in '55 he won 12. He was the eventual ace of the bullpen and it was in that role that he was sold to the Kansas City Athletics for the 1956 season.

The A's were a bad team and a youth movement was in progress and there was no room for a 35-year-old rookie, so Bradford's time in the big leagues was short. Still, he got there, which is more than most former ballplayers can say.

BK: Where did you go when the Seals signed you?

BILL BRADFORD: They sent me to Yakima, Washington.

I came to the Seals in 1952. I went to Binghamton, New York, for a season [1951]. I was there with Moose Skowron and Bob Grim and those guys. They sent me out for a swap with Ed Cereghino. He was a bonus boy and never made it. He pitched there in Seals Stadium.

I had 13 wins and nine or 11 losses and I saved two or three for Bob Grim. I had the best earned run average there, 2.38. I believe the Yankees offered $75,000 for me after finishing that summer there. It was one of their teams and they hadn't seen me in San Francisco and they wouldn't sell me.

Before I came to the Seals I was pitching in the Sacramento Valley League [semipro]. I had won about 22 in a couple of years or so and lost two or three. There were a lot of ex–major leaguers playing in it. When I signed my first contract with the Seals, I walked into their training camp and asked 'em if they needed some pitching. They sent me down and Dr. Salmon gave me a uniform and dressed me out, brought me back up to the park there in Boyes Springs, California.

I warmed up and Lefty O'Doul, the manager of the team, said to go out there and throw nothing but fastballs. He put a lefthanded hitter up and I threw the fastball 18 pitches to him and he popped up six, I believe, to shortstop or second base and the rest of 'em he didn't touch. They called me off and I signed my first contract on the medicine chest over there on the third base line.

I was a starter in '52 and '53 and they moved me into the bullpen in '54. Bob Muncrief's arm had gone bad and he had to quit. They asked me if I could take his place and I said, "No, I don't believe anybody could take Bob's place, but I can give it a try." I had a good year coming out of the bullpen.

I went to spring training with the Athletics in '56. The Seals sold me at the end of the year in '55. I had pitched in 54 games; I had won 12 of 'em and lost 4 or 6 for myself and saved 29 for the other pitchers. I distinctly remember saving 13 of the lefthander Gene Bearden's 18 wins that year. He wouldn't let nobody else relieve him but me.

I went to spring training and they [Kansas City] took me right on with 'em on the team. I pitched 19 innings in spring training, gave up something like one run. Mickey Mantle hit a home run off of me in an exhibition game. That was about the extent of it and they took me on to Kansas City.

I only appeared in one ballgame. I don't really know why. I have a feeling that they knew that they had bought an older fellow when they bought me. I was 35.

There was no feeling of being present with [manager] Lou Boudreau. He never had a lot of time for me. I had a feeling they were looking at younger players and they sent me on to Minneapolis with the Millers. I'd been there about a month.

I think I had seven losses and five wins, or something of that nature [with Minneapolis]. Just relief work. But they were looking at younger pitching, I'm sure. Then I thought at that stage of the game it was about time for me. I only wanted to play the game of baseball because I had a desire to and before it was too late. That's why I walked into the first training camp with the Seals.

BK: The Coast League in those days was very close to major league quality.

BB: Oh, it was. Paul I. Fagan wanted to make a third major league out there. We were "Open" classification when I played. And we had a lot of good major league players come through our club. I think one year I had a real good third baseman in Reno Cheso, and Jimmy Moran, second base, Leo Righetti at short. Of course, his son became a lefthanded pitcher for the Yankees. I had a lot of respect for Leo.

BK: Do you remember Sal Taormina?

BB: Oh, yes. I was pitching a game one time. It was 0–0 against that knuckleballer from Hollywood, California. Lindell. Johnny Lindell. I believe it was the ninth or tenth inning and I was supposed to hit and he had two outs on us. I asked manager Tommy Heath if he thought about letting Sal hit. I said, "Send him up there and let him hit. Maybe he can hit one out of this ballpark." And he did. [Laughs] I liked Sal.

BK: You played in Mexico.

BB: One winter down in Mexico I had a super season at Obregon. They paid you well and were allowed seven American ballplayers. They treated us well. I told somebody down there I was more powerful than Pancho Villa. [Laughs] I beat the ace the first game I pitched for 'em down there.

See, they couldn't get Bob Lemon to fly down there and back and forth from Cleveland anymore and one of the outfielders— my outfielder in San Francisco, Bill McCawley — said, "If you want somebody to take Lemon's place, better go up there and get Bradford." They just sent him up there, car and all, to fasten me up and not come back without me.

BK: Who was the best player you saw?

BB: I had the privilege of having a guy like Spider Jorgenson from the Brooklyn Dodgers to play third base with us one year. He was coming down the slope from the big leagues, but he was good and he covered that ground like a spider.

BK: Who was the best hitter?

BB: I never had any problem with him, but Joe Brovia. Joe Brovia could rip the cover off that ball, but he never could hit me real well. He confronted me about it one time. He said, "You don't waste no time on me. Soon as I step up there, you throw me three about knee-high and I take my cuts and I'm outta there." [Laughs] But he could hit.

BK: Who was the best pitcher?

BB: I guess I would have to say probably because he was smart and was as good a pitcher as I've ever seen, it was Allen Gettel of Oakland. Allen didn't throw hard stuff but he knew right where it was going. I'll never forget what he said. The big leagues wanted him one time and he told them, he said, "I'd rather be a big duck in a little pond as a little duck in a big pond." [Laughs]

BK: How much money did you make in baseball?

BB: Oh, let me see. All of those years I put into baseball, along with a little bit of outside work, I guess I made between 90- and 96,000. We got paid well; I think $6,000 a season for baseball and more.

You would leave a place and they would give you a check. Binghamton, New York — they handed me a $3,000 check after all was said and done. I didn't think about it 'til I got over in Bradford, Pennsylvania, and I said, "Well, I've got to cash this check," and I went into a bank. The banker loved baseball and he talked to me 15 minutes. They sent me back to his office. I said, "I need to pick up my money and be on my way 'cause I'm headed for California." He said, "Oh, your money was ready right after you got in here." [Laughs] He was just a great baseball fan and wanted to talk baseball.

BK: I imagine baseball opened a lot of doors for you over the years.

BB: Well, it has been a great help.

I've never refused — I still get letters from young people wanting my autograph and sending me 3 by 5 cards. I never did try to sell it and I've been confronted with the sale of my autograph and I felt like that any youngster was entitled to my autograph, as small as it would be, and that they shouldn't have to pay for an autograph. The BAT people, the Upper Deck people, tried to get me interested in things, but when you start selling an autograph for $15 it loses some kind of value, it seems to me.

BK: Do you have any regrets from baseball?

BB: No, no. I got out what I put into it and I enjoyed it. I just enjoyed playing the game and pitting my wits against somebody's ability to hit the ball. They'd come and say, "I can't hit you." I said, "Not when I've got everything working." I had about between a 95 and 100 mph fastball and anybody rips one of those is putting the bat on the horsehide pretty good because there's only about a one-half an inch of that bat down through the dead heart of it, about 12 inches long, that's gonna jerk that ball out of the park, otherwise it's a popup or a groundball. [Laughs] If you hit that ball at 95 mph, you're really jumping on something.

BK: Would you be a professional ballplayer again?

BB: Oh, yeah. I'd try to get into it a little quicker. A pitcher reaches his peak about 28 or 30 years of age and then he has about five years of the best pitching in him and everything works, unless he gets hurt. Barring all of that, it's just a good time. And I was in my peak when I walked into spring training camp at Boyes Springs at the beginning, at 27 years of age, so I didn't have far to go. All I had to do was just strengthen my arm up a little and it worked. I never had arm trouble. It seems like it was a rubber arm.

WILLIAM D BRADFORD
Born August 28, 1921, Choctaw, AR
Ht. 6'2" Wt. 180 Batted and Threw Right

Year	Team. Lg	G	IP	W	L	Pct	SO	BB	H	ERA
1949	Yakima, WI	29	191	13	9	.591	98	66	215	3.96
1950		34	221	14	9	.609	143	79	237	4.07
1951	Bghmtn, EL	30	198	14	11	.560	74	70	191	2.36

Year	Team. Lg	G	IP	W	L	Pct	SO	BB	H	ERA
1952	SF, PCL	44	206	15	11	.577	96	75	209	3.58
1953		39	191	10	8	.556	69	74	188	3.35
1954		33	104	6	2	.750	55	36	98	3.39
1955		51	149	12	5	.706	63	42	141	3.13
1956	KC, AL	1	2	0	0	—	0	1	2	9.00
	Mnpls, AA	51	92	5	7	.417	41	38	111	5.17
1957	Buff, IL	10		0	1	.000				
	LtlRk, Tx	11	41	1	6	.143	19	23	58	6.59
1958	LtlRk, Tx	2		0	1	.000				
	Amrlo, Wst	9		0	2	.000				

RENO CHESO
Seals 1949–1950, 1952–1955

In the early and mid 1950s I saw dozens of Seals games, as many as I could convince my stepfather or brother to take me to see. In most of these from '52 through '55 Reno Cheso was the third baseman, but I was young so I really don't remember many individual performances.

Reno Cheso (author's collection).

I do recall two games, however, in which Reno did something outstanding. One must have been in 1954. The opponent was Hollywood. Carlos Bernier, who probably could have bunted .300 with his speed, laid one down the third base line. Cheso dashed in, made a fine barehanded pickup, and fired the ball toward first base. I use the word "toward" because that's what it was. It went in that direction, but it was easily 15 feet over the head of first sacker George Vico. Vico was 6'4" or -5" so this was no mean feat. The ball ended up well down the right field line and well up in the stands.

The other instance I recall

was more favorable. The San Diego Padres were leading the Seals by two runs in the eighth. Reno came up with men on second and third. I had never seen him hit a home run, but I thought this was it. He drove the ball to deep left-center, but it was a long way out there and instead of going over for a three-run homer, it hit high on the fence for a two-run double to tie the score. The next batter singled to score Cheso and the Seals held on in the top of the ninth for a one-run win.

Reno Cheso was one of the many San Francisco natives who were signed by the Seals. Originally a second baseman, he moved to third and was the regular there from 1952 until the Red Sox took over the franchise in 1956. His best season was 1953, when he batted .297 with 11 home runs and 80 RBIs.

BK: Were you always Seals property?

RENO CHESO: I signed with the Seals but I was traded to Seattle. Rogers Hornsby was the manager — great guy — and I went to Vancouver [in 1951]. I was there all year and in 1952 I was signed by San Francisco again.

BK: When were you originally signed and how old were you?

RC: In 1948; I was 19. I was on the club. Lefty O'Doul was the manager. I was like a player that was inserted when we were way ahead or way behind as a rookie. I pinch hit. Finally I went up to Frank [O'Doul] and said, "Why don't you send me someplace where I can play every day?" and they did. They sent me to Salt Lake City in the Pioneer League.

BK: Were you always a third baseman?

RC: Second base. After awhile when I was with San Francisco they put me in left field for a while, but mainly I played third base.

BK: You rejoined the Seals to stay in 1952 until the team became Boston property.

RC: Right. My last year was 1955. Boston came out in '56. Formerly the Red Sox organization had the farm club in the American Association. Minneapolis. They sent 12 of our players there and I was one of eight players that were sent to Louisville, Kentucky. I declined to go; I hung 'em up. I was 26.

Normally in baseball your prime, at that time, was 28 to 32, 33. Now I guess there's players out there that are 40, so things have changed, but in your prime years you had those five years. You're bigger, stronger, and more knowledgeable.

BK: Did you regret leaving the game at that time?

RC: Sort of, especially when spring training came around. I got antsy.

During the off-season when I was playing I worked for a garbage company. I stayed in shape and stuff like that. After I did leave the game I became a partner in the garbage business. It was called the San Mateo County Scavenger Company and then we eventually — in '73 — sold out to BFI. I ended up being a general manager for them.

BK: Talk about your days with the Seals.

RC: We were an independent club. Charlie Graham was the owner that I signed with and then his son took over and we weren't affiliated with any big league club like most of the other clubs were, like Los Angeles was with the Chicago Cubs and the Hollywood Stars with the Pirates. If they sold anybody from San Francisco, it didn't make any difference which team they were sold to.

At one point Jimmy Westlake and I were sold to the Pittsburgh Pirates. As a matter of fact, Bing Crosby wined and dined us up at his big home in Hayden Lake, Idaho. For some reason, the deal fell through.

I've always said I played with players and against players that were actually better than some of the people that were up in the major leagues. It was a good league. We were first class, instituted by Paul Fagan when he bought it.

We had to ride the train once a year. Suppose there was a strike of some kind; at least we supported the train. The train trip would probably be the one that went to Portland and Seattle. We flew all the time outside of that one time. We were allowed to drive over to Oakland except when we played those morning and afternoon doubleheaders. Then we'd take the bus.

I was lucky to have the managers I played with and against. Lefty O'Doul was my manager and Casey Stengel was at Oakland. Then he left to go manage in the big leagues and then Charlie Dressen came and he went up to the Dodgers and then Mel Ott. Tommy Heath was very good. Great guy.

Frank O'Doul could've managed in the big leagues but he wouldn't want to go. San Francisco paid him more money. I know for sure he was making 25[,000] and then they escalated him. How high I don't know. Then he ended up going to San Diego when Tommy Heath took over.

I played against Freddie Hutchinson at Seattle and Bobby Bragan at Hollywood Stars.

A lot of friends say, "Hey, Reno, do you know how many home runs you'd've hit if you were playing today?" I say, "I know. I wasn't strong enough to get it over the wall in Seals Stadium." I led the club, I think, four years in doubles. I was averaging like 38 to 42 doubles a year.

They had a sign out there — Roos Atkins, advertising sign on the wall. Down the line it was 365. They had this billboard out there with a guy laying in a lounge in a suit and any Seal ballplayer that would hit one over that sign would receive a free suit from Roos Atkins Men's Store. One year I hit five over it. [Laughs] The fifth time, instead of getting a suit I got an overcoat. I was getting too many suits. It was about 380 and I just barely cleared the wall.

BK: It was a tough ballpark for home runs. Rarely did a Seals player have more than 15 or 18.

RC: Very seldom 25 home runs. You'd hardly ever see it. The right field line was 380.

BK: What was your biggest thrill as a Seal?

RC: Oh, I don't know. When you hit a game-winning home run; I was fortunate to do that numerous times. My first year as a rookie in Salt Lake City, I think I still have the record there: five grand slams in a year.

Oh, I don't know. I've struck out with the bases loaded. I can remember one game. We played 23 innings in San Francisco and my first four times up I knocked in runs; I was 4-for-4. In the later innings—15, 16, 17—I got up four more times; popped up with men in scoring position, struck out with men in scoring position. It was just the reverse.

In '49—Opening Day—I was a rookie. Mickey Rocco played first; Cliff Melton was the pitcher. I got the winning hit in the ninth inning. My first game I played with San Francisco.

I was having a good year. I was batting .319, second on the club, and made the sports pages in *The Sporting News*. Then they received a couple of players from the big leagues and I kinda sat down, but I was there all year.

And you remember the exciting things—making a good play defensively, or booting one. [Laughs] The fewest errors I ever made was by throwing. I had a pretty good arm. I had a few [errors]; I'd get knocked on my shins. I've got scars to show for it still today.

BK: Talk about some of your teammates. Sal Taormina.

RC: He was one of my best friends. As a matter of fact, he coached my son at Santa Clara University. He always had great teams down there. The unfortunate thing is, the guy was in good shape; he was jogging every day and he had a heart attack jogging.

BK: Leo Righetti and Jim Moran, the double play combination.

RC: They were great.

The best one when I played second base was Roy Nicely, the shortstop. Somebody hit a shot in the hole. I'm starting to run to second base—there's a man on first. It looked like a base hit. It wasn't. He catches it and he comes up throwing and he couldn't throw 'cause I wasn't there. He comes up to me after and says, "Okay, rookie Reno, let me tell you something now. Anything hit on the left side I can catch and you better be there where you're supposed to be." [Laughs]

And the guy was, I would say, one of the best shortstops ever. If he reached .200 he was lucky, but he was such a great shortstop that his hitting didn't bother the managers. He was unbelievable. The reason he didn't make the majors was because of his hitting.

BK: The infield there at Seals Stadium was great,

RC: Yes, it was. As a matter of fact, they had one of the best ballparks in the United States, the way it was and the construction. And then Paul Fagan came in and he did all the clubhouses—refurbished them all. And the men's room and the ladies' room for the fans. He was great. He was aiming for the majors.

BK: The Seals had great defense with Nini Tornay behind the plate, Moran at second, and you at third.

RC: I only led the league one year, but I know Tornay led the catching quite a few times, and so did Jimmy.

BK: Moran was a .260–.270 hitter, but he had no power.

RC: No. He was basically like a right field hitter. He'd hit line drives to right field more than left field for a righthand hitter.

BK: Al Lien.

RC: Lefthander. Great guy. I thought he was a really good pitcher. His buddy was a real good pitcher. Elmer Singleton. They were great guys. I was a rookie and I got treated so well by all the guys on the team. They were like 10 to 15 years older than me. And Bill Werle. He was a good pitcher.

All these guys we're talking about, they all went nine innings. [Laughs] We had two relievers that were really great at one time: Bob Muncrief and Adrian Zabala. When the Seals picked up Muncrief he'd been with the Yankees. And the St. Louis Browns. I think Zabala led the league in games and maybe earned run average. They were both so much alike. Zabala was lefthanded and Muncrief was righthanded and they could throw the biggest curve you ever wanted to see. You'd think they were brothers.

BK: The only year the Seals went to the playoffs while you were there was 1954.

RC: We were down around fifth place and we ended up winning like ten in a row and we went on a string of like 25 out of 30 and moved into second place. In my day that was our only playoff.

I think they did well in 1947. I was still in high school. In '46 they won the whole thing.

BK: In 1954 there was the Kiddie Car Express.

RC: I was the oldest one. [Laughs] At 24. I know there was Jimmy Westlake playing first. Mike Baxes could've been playing shortstop. Jimmy Moran was older than I was. Tony Ponce was one of our pitchers. I probably had more years in at that time. I already had six years in.

We won like ten in a row or something, then we lost one and then we won another eight or nine. It was something like winning 25 out of 30 games. That's when we moved up from about fifth place to tie for first or second, if I remember correctly. It put us in the race.

BK: How did the Little Corporation affect the players? Were there concerns over pay?

RC: That was the problem when the Little Corporation was formed. I think it was with young Charlie Graham and Damon Miller. I think he was vice president or general manager of the club. They just didn't have the funds; they didn't have the money.

It didn't affect us. [Laughs] Actually, I was fortunate to be kind of a high-salaried player for that era in that league, but we never even thought of it. I know the old adage, "We played for the love of the game." Actually, it was different then and that's what we did. We just wanted to play. That was basically the deal. And then I think after the Little Corporation that's when the Red Sox finally come out. That bailed 'em out.

BK: In 1952 there was a tremendous brawl between the Oaks and the Seals and you were involved.

RC: Piper Davis for Oakland — he was a good ballplayer, a colored fella — and our pitcher was Bill Boemler, lefthanded pitcher. I was playing third base that day. Mel Ott was the manager for Oakland.

Boemler threw at Piper Davis. Piper Davis gets on base and then he gets to second base on a bunt, I think. Then somebody got a basehit and Davis is coming home and the ball got away from the catcher before Davis got there and Boemler's standing at home plate. The catcher threw the ball to Boemler to tag him out and Piper Davis went up high with his spikes and cut him in the leg and the brawl started.

It was a pretty good one. Rafael Noble was catching for Oakland at that time and our outfielder, Sal Taormina, came in and he rocked him in the nose. I think he got a broken nose out of it — the catcher, Noble. I think I threw a punch in there at Piper Davis. [Laughs] It's in a picture at the [*San Francisco*] *Chronicle*. The next day he saw it and said, "So *you're* the guy that got me. [Laughs]

Some of the fans came on the field. In those days there wasn't that much security, but there was a few cops out there — guards— and they came out and broke it up. It was probably one of the biggest [brawls] in baseball.

I was in two of 'em. I was in another one in Salt Lake City. That was even worse than the one in Oakland. It was against Twin Falls. Twin Falls was in the Yankee chain and they had a really good ballplayer — outfielder, could run, hit, everything, he was destined to get up there — but he was pretty bad on the bases. He'd try to hurt people and this one time he came into second base — tried to steal second — caught our second baseman and cut him pretty bad on the forearm with his spikes. He just threw 'em up there.

And unbeknownst to a lot of people, the pitcher that we had then was John Bilbrey and actually he was an older guy. At that time I was— what?— 19; he was about 27, 28 and he was already in the service and he was light-heavyweight champion of boxing in the Navy. He took this guy on and I'll tell you, man, he kicked the hell out of him. Then Charlie Metro, who was manager for Twin Falls, he tried to break something up and he got rocked in the nose — broken nose — and a couple other guys *really* got hit pretty hard. That was worse than the one in Oakland.

These beefs that they have today, they don't even come close to those two that I've seen. [Laughs] They're just shoving and today they wear rubber spikes, so nobody gets cut too bad. Once in awhile somebody may throw a punch, but they normally miss. They'll go out and tackle a guy.

BK: Did you enjoy your playing days?

RC: Loved it. It's an experience that's pretty hard to even think about. I felt fortunate that I was able to do it. I played eight years and it's an experience that most people don't have a chance to do.

BK: Would you do it again?

RC: Yeah. Tomorrow. [Laughs]

One of the highlights, I was on that trip to Japan. The Goodwill Tour in '49. A great trip. Lefty O'Doul was a hero over there. They just loved him to death.

We played against the Armed Forces on our way over. We even played a game in Manila and Wake Island. And then we played the Japanese people. We won every game.

I became a hero there. Our fifth game, I guess, it was pouring rain. There were 55,000 people in the stands, all under black umbrellas. They were ahead, 4-to-1, and they wouldn't call the game because they wanted to beat us. It was the fourth inning and they wanted to get to the fifth. I hit a grand slam to put us ahead and we ended up winning the game. It kept going in pouring rain. They wouldn't call it. I think the final score was 16-to-4.

Then I was treated like a king over there. It was unbelievable. They treated us so great. It was an experience I'll never forget.

We played in Osaka one day. You'll have like 50,000 people there in the stands watching batting practice and infield. In Osaka for that one game: 105,000. That's how big that stadium is. They love baseball.

BK: What's the one big difference today from your time?

RC: The salaries have gotten out of hand. I can't see how anybody could possibly be worth more than one million dollars. See, when we played you went on the year that you had and all contracts were only one year. You had a good year, you'd get a raise. You had a bad year, they'd probably lower your salary. We had no agents. We did our contracts all on our own. Times have changed. The fans are paying for it. It's frustrating that the owners let it get away so bad.

BK: Any regrets?

RC: The only thing, when I was gonna be sent to Louisville I was gonna go and then decided not to. Then I was offered a job from San Francisco to be a playing manager for San Jose in the California League. That's the only thing I regret — not trying that. I was still young and I could've learned how to manage and maybe something else would've come of it.

When I signed, I signed with San Francisco and the Yankees wanted me bad. I've never known what would have happened if I'd signed with the Yankees. I played against their farm teams. I played against my two buddies at Mission High School: Gus Triandos and the shortstop, Joe Polich. We all played in high school together and Gus and Joe signed with the Yankees and they wanted me, also. They went to Twin Falls when I was at Salt Lake City. Gus finally got up there.

RENO ANTHONY CHESO
Born August 2, 1929, San Francisco, CA
Ht. 5'10" Wt. 175 Batted and Threw Right
Third baseman

Year	Team, Lg	G	AB	R	H	2B	3B	HR	RBI	BA
1948	SLC, Pio	122	486	102	173	22	5	13	133	.356
1949	SF, PCL	123	395	43	98	20	1	6	46	.248
1950	SF, PCL	10	31	5	6	3	0	0	2	.194
	Yakima, WI	140	521	109	163	41	6	4	107	.313
1951	Vanc'ver, WI	139	528	72	152	31	4	1	87	.286
1952	SF, PCL	111	400	27	111	21	0	3	57	.278
1953		155	529	80	157	33	5	11	92	.296
1954		116	395	55	99	19	2	4	41	.251
1955		109	307	36	70	17	1	4	35	.228

CHAPTER 9

1953:
Good-Bye, Paul Fagan

5th place: W 91 L 89 .506 15 GB

Tommy Heath's team put forth a surprisingly good offense in 1953 and almost made it to the first division, but missed it by one game. Still, the club finished above .500 and gained 16 games in the standings.

But even with the good play on the field, the fans continued to stay away. Attendance dropped to just over 170,000, or an average of fewer than 2,000 a home game. That and other events represented the last straw for Paul Fagan. More on that below.

The offensive resurgence was led by several new faces. First baseman George Vico, a major league veteran, was acquired from Seattle and led the team with 93 RBIs. Shortstop Leo Righetti came from Charleston in the American Association. His defense had always been outstanding and in '53 he had the best offensive stats (3-61-.258) of his career.

Outfielder Al Lyons (22-77-.269) was also acquired from Seattle and outfielder Jerry Zuvela (16-50-.273) was brought up from Yakima. Catcher Nini Tornay finally took over as the number one receiver. He gave the Seals the best defense behind the plate since the days of Jarvis and Partee in 1949.

Jim Moran (3-44-.266) was back at second base and had his best offensive numbers to date. Reno Cheso (11-80-.297) had the best year of his career. Sal Taormina (8-62-.297), who had been up and down with the Seals since 1942, finally earned an everyday job and looked as if he should have been there all along. Frank Kalin (16-55-.293) continued to be a bargain, and Bill McCawley (3-45-.251) was a solid contributor.

This offensive display benefited the pitching staff, which was again

166

Indians and Seals ballplayers gather around Seals outfielder Sal Taormina (on ground), who was hit by a throw while rounding second base. Indians pitcher Bob Lemon is on the right with his glove on his hip (author's collection).

led by ace and workhorse Elmer Singleton (15–17, 3.23). Al Lien (12–8, 4.07) was another year older, but was still a pitcher to be reckoned with.

The trio of new hurlers from 1952 met with mixed results in their second years as Seals. Bill Bradford (10–8, 3.35) and Bob Muncrief (10–12, 2.67) held their own, but Bill Boemler fell to 8–17, 4.60 and found himself dealt to Portland in '54.

The offense generated by the team in 1953 was lacking on August 25. The Oaks swept a double header from the Seals and in the seven-inning game Jim Atkins tossed a no-hitter at them. A few days later Atkins came back with a seven-inning, no-hit relief stint against the Los Angeles Angels.

Three newcomers to the staff were important contributors. Veteran John "Windy" McCall was picked up from Birmingham in the Southern Association, went 12–7, 3.08, and found himself back in the majors in 1954 with the world champion New York Giants. Ted Shandor (9–9, 4.16) was another Yakima graduate and was used as both a starter and reliever.

McCall and Righetti were both native San Franciscans who took scenic routes to their hometown team. McCall took seven years as a professional to reach San Francisco and Righetti took ten.

The third newcomer wasn't acquired until the last of August when he was purchased from Ventura in the Class C California League and he was undoubtedly the reason for the fifth place and .500+ finish.

Heath was looking for help late in the season and former Seals infielder Dario Lodigiani suggested he look at two players on the Ventura roster, catcher Jose Perez, the California League's leading hitter at .373, and pitcher Tony Ponce. Ventura was the last place team, 50-some games out of first, and Ponce was the ace. During that season, the 32-year-old minor league veteran had won 15 and lost 20 with a 4.42 ERA. The 20 losses tied the California League record, and he gave up 320 hits and 186 runs, both new records, in 289 innings. But Heath took a chance and bought the two players.

Perez found little playing time and was back in the California League in 1954, where he continued to hit. In a 12-year career spent mostly in Class C, he compiled a .323 batting average.

Ponce, though, found a home in San Francisco for a few years. He had a mediocre fastball, a so-so slider, and a decent forkball, but a killer knuckleball that he threw in the low 80s. He once said, "I could give a batter three balls, then give him three knuckleballs to get him out." The constant wind in Seals Stadium was ideal for his knuckler and he made full use of it.

Ponce pitched the last inning against the Oaks on August 27, the day he joined the Seals, and the next day he started. He beat the Oaks, 15–2. The next week he defeated the league champion Hollywood Stars three times, then he downed the L.A. Angels four times in the final week of the season.

The last two came on the final day when he pitched and won a double-header. He won the opener, 4–2, and then shut out the Angels, 1–0, in the nightcap.

For the time he was with the Seals in 1953 he pitched in ten games, had six starts and six complete games, won eight, lost none, and posted a 1.31 ERA. All this in just 16 days.

Hollywood won the championship by eight games over Seattle, with third place Los Angeles another five games back, a game ahead of fourth place Portland, which was a game ahead of the Seals. The Stars were led by former Seal Dale Long (35-118-.272), who led the league in home runs and RBIs. Other ex–Seals did well, also. Jackie Tobin batted .296 and Steve Nagy went 13-8 for Seattle, Dino Restelli went 12-41-.340 in 256 at bats for Portland, Joe Brovia went 20-97-.314 for Sacramento, and Lloyd Dickey was 7-9, 3.01 for sixth-place San Diego.

The Pacific Coast League directors voted to do away with the no-option clause for 1954 and Fagan took the vote personally. That, along with repeatedly losing money due to poor attendance, caused him to put the team up for sale at the end of the season.

Eddie Mulligan, the president of the Sacramento Solons, was named by the league to settle with Fagan. The outcome was Fagan selling the Seals to the league for $100,000 (Fagan had asked a million dollars two years before) and leasing Seals Stadium to the league for five years. There was also a stipulation that Fagan could buy the team back for $100,000 if San Francisco was given a major league franchise.

On September 23, Damon Miller, the Seals general manager under Fagan, was named president-conservator of the team. The franchise was transferred to Miller's name and he agreed to raise the money needed to run the club the next season. Paul Fagan's run in the PCL was over after only eight years.

NINI TORNAY
Seals 1951–1957

Nini Tornay was a true Seal. He was signed by the team and remained their property until the very end, even when the Red Sox moved in. It was not until after there was no longer a Seals franchise that he finally played for someone else.

He was a good field, decent hit catcher who never got a shot with a major league team. With the expansion that has occurred since he retired as an active player there may well have been a spot somewhere on a big league roster for a man of his skills.

BK: When did you join the Seals?
NINI TORNAY: [In] 1951. I started my career three years before that. I played down in Martinez [California League] and then I went to Yakima. Always a catcher.

Nini Tornay (author's collection).

BK: How did the Seals find you?

NT: I played high school baseball for three years and a lot of semipro in the city. They had a C league and a B league and an A league. I played with Ralph's 622 Club, and a lot of baseball players in San Francisco remember the 622 Club because we had a fantastic outfit.

Moffit Mantega had a great team, too. We're talking about Pieretti and all the guys from the big leagues; they used to play with Moffit because they used to get jobs at Moffit.

This is where I really learned a lot of baseball. Pope Elia was my coach in high school and he was a catcher and he taught me quite a bit, but playing in the semipro leagues I learned a lot.

BK: In all your years with the Seals, you always seemed to share the catching job.

NT: When I signed up, Will Tiesiera was one of the other catchers, and Harry Eastwood. We always did carry two catchers all season. I used to go to spring training every year and we had the same catchers fighting out for the job. We'd go down about three weeks, maybe four weeks, of spring training and it was always Harry Eastwood and Will Tiesiera — and Brocker was another guy — and we four people fought each other for the job three or four years in a row.

When I was playing my second year, I was playing in [Class] B ball up in Yakima, they broke in Ray Orteig. Ray was a third baseman, as you know, and they sent him up to Yakima to make him a catcher because he was a pretty good hitter and he and I caught for Yakima that one year. Then in time he came on down and tried to make it as a catcher, but it always ended up that San Francisco always had a second catcher and they put Ray back at third base. I guess they never had a really good third baseman other than Ted Jennings. He passed away recently. But Ray Orteig ended up being a catcher.

He started out late being a catcher. I'm not saying I was the best catcher in the world, but you had to have something behind the plate. And there was a lot of guys that didn't have it. I'm talking about remembering the hitters— you know, what they can hit, what pitch they can hit with their power, and things like that. Orteig did a pretty good job, but he still ended up at third base each year.

BK: Reno Cheso played third base there quite a while.

NT: Reno was my roommate eight or nine years. Boy, he was something else. He'd give you the shirt off his back.

BK: When the Red Sox took over the Seals in 1956, they kept you.

NT: There was me and Sal Taormina and Bob DiPietro. We were the only three from San Francisco to stay.

BK: I heard they kept you because they had no experienced catcher in their system to help develop their young pitchers.

NT: That was one of the reasons, but the Red Sox brought their own ballplayers from their minor leagues. One of the reasons I think was because of my experience at that time. They had Haywood Sullivan; he was later president of the Red Sox. He was one of the catchers, and Eddie Sadowski was a catcher. They kept me only for that year for my experience. Bob and Sal and I, we didn't play much that year. Like I said, they had their own players.

BK: Where did you go after you left the Seals?

NT: I went to Portland, Oregon. They bought my contract and I had one of the best years I ever had. I did most of the catching. Lenny Neal had been the Oakland catcher and he was the second catcher in the two years I played with Portland.

I hit some home runs. I hit 27 with Portland. I went down to the Dominican Republic and I hit close to 30. I think when I got older I started to learn how to hit. [Laughs]

From there I went to Kansas City for one year and then Pittsburgh [systems] for a year, but I didn't do very much catching. I retired in1960.

BK: In 14 years of professional baseball, is there a game that stands out?

NT: I think the best I can remember — and I can remember like it was yesterday — is when I was in spring training with the Boston organization, playing in San Francisco. Boston came in to play us three ballgames. That was a Friday, a Saturday, and a Sunday. We had Sullivan and Sadowski, so Sullivan caught the first game on Friday night. The second game — Saturday afternoon — Sadowski caught. I caught the Sunday game and I went 4-for-5 and I hit three doubles that day. I think it was the best day I ever had.

We were playing against some pretty good pitching. I know Mel Parnell pitched one of the games. A couple hit off the wall and in Seals Stadium that's a pretty good poke: 365 [feet].

With the Seals, every year we played two or three, maybe four, big league teams. The Indians we played three games, the Yankees we played a couple of games, the Cubs came through, Pittsburgh came through. This was on the swing from spring training. It was spring training, but they were ready. When they came to play us, their whole ballclub was ready to play big league baseball. They didn't want to lose.

When we played the Yankees, they beat us, 18 to 3. Mickey Mantle got up and hit one lefthanded and one righthanded and they didn't even want us to get the three runs.

BK: You caught some pretty good pitchers. Who were the best ones?

NT: Ewell Blackwell. And then I caught Fireman Joe Page. I think Ralph Buxton, too; he was another big leaguer that came on down. These people were just out of the prime, but they could still throw the ball.

I played ball with the all-star team going to Japan. I think in 1951 we had one heck of a ball team. We had Parnell pitching and Cereghino was another one. We had Al Lyons, a pitcher, and then we had Bobby Shantz from the Philadelphia Athletics. At third base we had Lou Stringer and at shortstop was Strickland. At second base we had Billy Martin and Ferris Fain at first. Then we had Dino Restelli in left field, we had Dominic DiMaggio in center and Joe in right. That's not too bad; they could go get 'em. And the catchers were Joe Perry, Joe Tipton, and myself. Joe Perry was a utility man, but he was also a catcher. Joe Tipton played for Philadelphia [Athletics]. We had a pretty good ballclub. It was a lot of fun and a trip that you don't think of making again.

BK: Do you remember Jerry Casale?

NT: Oh, yeah. He came on down with the young Boston Red Sox. He threw the ball pretty darn good, too.

BK: He was a heck of a hitting pitcher.

NT: Good power for a pitcher. He was never built like a pitcher. You know, you usually get a pitcher long and lean. He was close to six foot, but built firm. Stocky.

BK: I remember one home run he hit. It went over the center field scoreboard and landed on the embankment across the street.

NT: That was against Marino Pieretti with Sacramento. In fact, Pieretti was born in San Francisco.

BK: Who was the best player you saw?

NT: I saw three you'd have to go a long way to beat. I've seen Snider and I've seen McCovey and I've seen Mays, but I think the three best ones I've ever seen was Musial, DiMaggio, and Ted Williams. That's the best three I've ever seen. I'll put 'em in the lineup and you can shuffle 'em any way you want to.

Here's a fella that doesn't strike out too much — Musial; he always got a piece of the ball somewhere along the line. Williams was the kind of a guy who hits the ball a long way. He had the home runs to prove that. And then the other guy — my God, what can you say?

Joe DiMaggio. I get together with him once in a while when he gets into San Francisco. When he was back east he'd send me some [auto-graphed] baseballs. I wanted certain baseballs, like 500 home run hitters and the ones that have made the Hall of Fame. I have 15 and the 15 I have I cherish. One of 'em is Pete Rose. He's not in the Hall of Fame, but he should be there. Another one is Nolan Ryan and he'll be in there. And I got Williams and DiMaggio and Musial, Yogi Berra, Hank Aaron, Willie Mays, [Al] Kaline, Bob Feller, Mickey Mantle. That's a pretty good selection right there. There are a few more. He kept on sending 'em for a while and then all of a sudden they just stopped.

When he comes into town, sometime he thinks of me and other times he's pretty busy. He gives me a holler and we get on the phone and we talk about '51 and a few little details. He stays out of the limelight. He's always been that way, even in 1951 when I got to know him real well.

You remember when he married Marilyn Monroe? The whole United States remembers that. He came on in to Seals Stadium. We were playing a ballgame and they introduced him over the PA system. He got up — Marilyn was sitting right there alongside of him — and all of a sudden they want him on the field to say a few words. So he came on down with his wife and walked across. We were all in line — I guess it was Opening Day or closing day — and when he went on down the line saying hello, he stopped and he looked at me and he said, "Hi, little Dage." I'll never forget that. "How ya doin'? Call me; we'll get together." And he introduced his wife and went on. That was a big thrill.

In Japan he was more private 'cause the sportswriters would come around for an interview and he would be interviewed for ten or 15 minutes, then there was something about him that said, "This is enough." He wouldn't tell them, but he'd get up and walk away or walk back in the club-house. It gets tiresome when people are in your face all the time.

BK: You played under several managers.

NT: We had a good manager [in 1957] — Joe Gordon. He was one hell of a guy. Wright was one of his coaches and he got cancer in his throat and I wasn't doing very much catching so he put me as one of his coaches. I used to write the lineup every day and here are all the young guys — Jim Mahoney and Ken Aspromonte. Joe would say, "We have the same lineup as yesterday and the day before. If you want to switch this guy around, you do it." And if it worked that day, we did it the next day. Anything that works, you stay with it. [Laughs]

Tommy Heath was very sincere. He was the type of a manager that was more or less easygoing, *but* he got his point across. He could get kind of upset. Now I'm not talking about knocking over drinking fountains and stuff like that. I'm talking about coming in and having a meeting; firm at the meeting, and saying this is what we *have* to do.

I think the best one I ever played for was O'Doul. Frank O'Doul was the best one, and yet I came in the latter part of his life. He was managing already and he'd had quite a few years in the Pacific Coast League. He came out to the ballpark a little later than he did when he was younger, but he got his point across. He led the National League two years [in hitting].

BK: I remember when he was managing the Seattle Rainiers in the late '50s. He must have been close to 60 and he batted in a late-season game and hit a bullet. If he still had legs he probably could have still been playing.

NT: [Laughs] I remember. Not only the bat control he had, the legs were his biggest asset. He could really run. He'd beat the ball into the dirt and run like heck. He's got to be in the Hall of Fame sometime.

He had one big thing. When you were a hitter and he was the manager, he'd come out early and watch you hit and he'd say, "Now the main thing is, you wanna pull the ball. You can't pull *every* pitch because some pitchers pitch outside and things like this, but from the middle of the plate inside you should be able to pull that ball." One of the reasons why he used to say that all the time is because there was your power. Your power was pulling — a righthanded hitter to left field and left-center. He said when you hit a lot of balls to right field, even if they're down the middle of the plate, he says you're *behind* on the ball itself.

BK: Any regrets in 14 years?

NT: Not a one! Never! I think it was so fantastic; I met so many people — good people. Like going to Japan, we went to Ridgeway's house. General Ridgeway was the head of the Pacific at the time.

And I met Danny Kaye and Joe Louis. I can go on and on. I had a wonderful time. In Hollywood the stars would be sitting in their boxes. George Raft — *big* fan. Frank Lovejoy was another one.

You meet so many. The door was there and it opened. I had a few contacts and could have gone into a lot of other businesses than I did. I went into sporting goods with my brother Frank and I'm retired now. Frank played for 16 years.

BK: Would you go back and do it again?

NT: Yes, I would. Tomorrow.

ANTHONY "NINI" TORNAY
Born October 6, 1929, San Francisco, CA
Ht. 6' Wt. 185 Batted and Threw Right
Catcher

Year	Team, Lg	G	AB	R	H	2B	3B	HR	RBI	BA
1948	Rosev'le, FW	13	37	9	14	3	1	1	11	.378
	Yakima, WI							1	4	.219
1949	Yakima, WI	77	257	57	82	13	6	4	39	.319
1950		91	292	53	98	28	3	1	45	.336
1951	SF, PCL	80	208	17	50	4	1	0	23	.240
1952		51	109	7	26	3	1	0	8	.239
1953		136	396	28	91	21	0	2	34	.230
1954		101	264	24	68	17	0	1	30	.258
1955		68	161	12	34	9	0	2	13	.211
1956		25	43	1	7	3	0	0	6	.163
1957		44	133	8	32	6	1	0	9	.241
1958	Port., PCL	90	250	24	75	14	0	10	39	.300
1959		95	299	36	80	13	2	6	35	.268
1960	Columbus, IL	49	127	8	24	5	0	1	6	.189

JERRY ZUVELA
Seals 1953–1954

Jerry Zuvela played professional baseball for seven years, two of them with the Seals. His rookie year with San Francisco was perhaps his best season. In 385 at bats, he batted .273 and clubbed 16 home runs. For his career he batted .292, including three seasons over .300, and had an excellent .392 on base average.

BK: How did you begin playing professional baseball?

JERRY ZUVELA: In 1950 Lefty O'Doul was the manager of the Seals. Three of us from down here in San Pedro went down to El Centro and one injured himself while he was down there and two of us signed. Francis Xavier "Lefty" O'Doul — God rest his soul, hell of a man. We signed in 1950 with the Seals, but we went to Yakima. There were two farm clubs: Yakima in the Western International League and Salt Lake City in the Pioneer League. Several of the Coast League teams had similar affiliations.

Pat Monahan signed with me. He was with the Seals for a short time, as was I. I wasn't exactly a spectacular thing myself. Pat was a pitcher.

Jerry Zuvela (courtesy Robert Zwissig).

My first year at Yakima I hit over .300 and I was rather pleased. I had a shaky start as rookies do occasionally, but as it turned out I lucked out in a couple phases of the game — got a couple basehits that gave me my confidence. Then I went from there. I thought I had a fairly decent season. I hit .314 my first year.

BK: Were you through with college at that point?

JZ: No, I had not graduated. I graduated later on. I went back to school during the off-season when I could. I eventually did get my degree. It took me ten years to get my BS [from Loyola University].

It was kinda funny. When I went in for my final semester, Father Martin was the dean. I go into his office and he looks up at me and puts his hand to his head and says, "Are you back again?" I said, "Yes, Father, but this should be it." He said, "Well, look," and he writes things and says, "Take this, that, this," and then he hands me my schedule and says, "Now, Jerry, do me a favor." I said, "What's that, Father? I'd be more than happy to, if I can." He says, "Do this and get the hell out of here!" The Jesuits had a good sense of humor.

My degree is Bachelor of Science in Liberal Arts. I did various jobs during the off-seasons, but I eventually ended up working on the docks and I also substitute taught in the L. A. City School System.

BK: You played with the Seals in 1953 and 1954.

JZ: I was there for a cup of coffee in '52. I didn't even get the cream and sugar, just the coffee. In '51 I was up in Yakima. [In] '50, '51, and then in '52 a cup of coffee with the Seals and then they sent me back to Yakima and then in '53 I was with the mother club. I have fond memories of the gentlemen I had the privilege of playing with. They were good men.

BK: In 1953 I was 12 years old and Harlond Clift was a coach with the Seals. One day I went down to the Seals' dressing room to try to get some autographs and the guard at the door told me to go away. Just then,

Clift came by and said, "Let the kid in." That was one of the most exciting things that had ever happened to me. I got ten or 12 autographs from you fellows.

JZ: You know, it's amazing. I've had similar experiences. Sometimes you do not feel that you've touched people. My sister-in-law was down in Mazatlan and she strikes up a conversation with some people — husband and wife — and they exchange names and "what-do-you-do" and stuff. This man said he had some sort of franchise, but, he said, "Prior to getting the franchise, I worked on the docks in San Francisco." And she said, "What a small world. My brother-in-law also worked on the docks." He said, "What's his name?" "Jerry Zuvela."

And immediately he says, "He played for the Seals!" He wanted some pictures and I sent some to her, which she in turn sent to him. And he told me, "When I was 12 years old, you gave me your autograph and I just never forgot that."

You think you don't touch youngsters and you do. When somebody comes up and asks for your autograph, I feel it's a special thing that someone would want my autograph.

One of the funny things— and this is the humbling thing about it — we were playing up in Portland and we came out and this youngster comes up. "Oh, gee, Gimme your autograph." And I gave him the autograph and he says, "Zuvela! Who are you?"

But I appreciate it. Somebody wants your autograph, I think that's nice of them to even think that much of you.

I don't understand why there's this fascination with the old Pacific Coast League. A friend told me it wasn't the same with the American Association and the International League.

BK: The Coast League was major league to a great portion of the country. In the East, where the American Association and the International League were, within a few miles, or at least in the same time zone, there were major league teams, but out on the coast there was not.

JZ: They changed it from Triple-A to Open classification because they were thinking of making it the third major league, but the Dodgers and Giants came out.

It was great "growing up" in the system. We all matured and then played with the major club — the Seals. The sad part is there aren't many of us left.

I heard Joe Brovia passed away. He was quite a guy. At the end of his career they told him he was gonna go up to Cincinnati and they were gonna use him as a pinch hitter. He sat at his locker and cried. It was all over for him, but he finally got a chance to go up. He was something else.

Jerry Zuvela (courtesy Doug McWilliams).

I remember when Bobby Bragan managed the Hollywood Stars. Joe used to hold his bat damn near upright, right at his waistline and the bat was straight up. Bragan said, "Hell, we can pitch this guy inside." They kept telling Bragan, "No, he'll wear you out!" And he did; he beat 'em to death! But Joe was so damn strong; he could get that bat up and around.

You know, he was so slow. I remember Jimmy Moran, he'd play Joe off the dirt part of the infield. Jimmy was on the grass in right field and poor Joe'd hit the [devil] put of the ball and Jimmy'd scoop it up and throw him out. The guy clobbered the ball, but it was an out.

As I say, we've lost so many, many of 'em. George Vico died in 1994, right before the big earthquake down here. Inky Lien is dead, God rest his soul. Old One Ton — Elmer Singleton — he was in Utah somewhere, but he's gone, too.

BK: Where did you go after 1954?

JZ: I was traded to Seattle, then I went down to Nashville and then to Wenatchee and then back to Seattle. I ended the season at Seattle. We won the — "we" [laughs] — pennant in 1955.

Then they wanted to send me down to the Texas League and I didn't want to go down there, so I stayed out of baseball. I went back to Loyola to finish up and I coached the baseball team there for that one year. That was in '56. Then in '57 I went back into professional baseball. When I contacted the minor league officials back in Columbus, Ohio, they thought I was gonna stay out of baseball completely. That gave me my free agency.

Tommy Heath was managing Sacramento and they were spring training in the Pasadena area, so I contacted him and he allowed me to try out and they wanted to sign me. I said, "If I can help your ballclub, fine. If I can't help your ballclub, just let me go."

So I come home and then I get a call from the guys from Fresno. I guess it was a Sacramento farm club. They said, "How about coming up and playing with us?" I explained to 'em I wanted my free agency at the end of the season and they agreed. So, anyway, I went to Fresno and played and I had a good time.

That was it. The following year another club contacted me and wanted me to go up and play in Lewiston, Idaho, in the Western International League. So I said, "That'll be fine," and we were expecting a child, so I asked my wife, "What do you think? Should I go or do you want me to stay?" And she asked me if I would stay, so I said, "That's fine. I'll stay."

So after the child was born I contacted Lewiston, but I guess by that time it was a little too late for them. That was kinda the end of it, although I did work out and try out later on.

I sum up my career, I tell 'em I was a prospect for a while and then I became a suspect.

BK: Is there one game that stands out?

JZ: In those days, over the right field fence [at Seals Stadium] was 355 feet to the wall and then you had stands and then you had the back wall. If you hit one all the way out of the ballpark — over the right field fence all the way out onto the street — 16th and Bryant, where the intersection was — they put a star up there. One of the guys that hit one out was the Rifleman, Chuck Connors.

After I started playing there, they painted them [the stars] over. One night we were playing Oakland and Ernie Broglio was pitching. He was just a youngster coming up. I hit one over the back wall. I wanted to go out there the next day and put a star up there myself. At night in San Francisco the air was kinda heavy with the fog, so it made it a little more difficult. And then the wind blew across right field and over the left field fence.

The one thing that really touched my heart was Joe DiMaggio. We were playing in San Francisco and Joe was standing in our dugout. He had retired, barely, and he had his suit on. The guy comes over the intercom and asks if Joe would come out and take a few swings. I'm standing right by him. He looks around and says, "I don't have anybody to hold my jacket." I said, "Hey, Joe, let me hold that thing." I could rub that baby and get another hundred basehits out of that. I was in awe of the guy. What a ballplayer!

But the time that really made me feel great — he had played in an old-timers game or something and he's up in the clubhouse. I says I gotta get this guy's autograph. I'm like a kid! He's seated in one of the cubicles and a pitcher on our ballclub — I can't recall his name now — played with the New York Yankees and they're there together. I go over and get a ball and I'm walking over there like a little kid with the ball in my hand and I'm standing there and I don't wanna interrupt the conversation. In a little while, the pitcher looks at me and says, "Oh, Joe, by the way. You've never met Jerry Zuvela." And do you know what Joe said? He says, "No, I've never met Jerry, but I've heard of him." I just melted. He probably didn't know me from anything, but what a *great* thing to say! I'm speechless.

I've still got the ball. I've got some of the balls from the Seals and I've got autographed balls from Seattle, too. The guy who has a great collection of memorabilia from the big leagues and the Coast League is George Vico. He had foresight. He got all that stuff when he was in the big leagues. He wanted it for himself. He had just wonderful stuff. His wife still has it.

BK: Most of the guys from those days say they didn't think anything about it.

JZ: Yeah. Who knew that some of this stuff — baseball cards — would go crazy?

BK: Who was the best player you saw?

JZ: There were several. For instance, when I was playing in the California League with Fresno, there was Vada Pinson in the league, Johnny Callison was just coming up, and Chuck Estrada was pitching in Salinas. The guy I thought was a hell of a ballplayer, to tell you the truth, was from here in my hometown. Bobby Balcena.

That's a tough question. There was big Luke Easter at San Diego. There were several I thought were all damn good ballplayers. I was lucky to be there.

The one guy that impressed me a lot was Lefty O'Doul. For one thing, in1950 when we were down in spring training he got in the batting cage and he was hitting the [devil] out of the ball! I saw Earl Averill, Sr., at an old-timers game up in Seattle, also, and I looked at him. He got in the batter's box and, boy, I tell you, he hit a rope! I talked to him. I said, "Mr. Averill, you're swinging that bat quite well," and he said, "I can still do that, but the legs go."

BK: It seems those guys who can swing the bat can swing it forever.

JZ: It seems like it. It's a God-given thing. You can polish the stone up a little bit, but they've got the ingredients. The great ones, they just have it. The Lord blessed 'em.

That's one thing I didn't do. I didn't get those guys' autographs.

BK: Who were the best pitchers you saw?

JZ: They were all tough to me. [Laughs] I had the privilege of facing

Bob Feller. We had an exhibition game against Cleveland in San Francisco and I got to face him and Lloyd Dickey, who was on our ballclub. Now Lloyd could bring it; he went to Cleveland at the time. So I got to face Feller, Lloyd Dickey, and Bob Lemon; I faced the three of 'em in that particular game. Of course, that was a spring training exhibition game.

There were guys that gave me trouble, but that doesn't apply. A lot of guys gave me trouble. Even with our ballclub in Seattle, we had Larry Jansen, Ewell Blackwell, Lou Kretlow, Vic Lombardi. We had guys on that ballclub that had all kinds of major league experience, you know.

BK: Was it fun?

JZ: Oh, yeah! I loved it.

JERRY MIKE ZUVELA
Born September 21, 1929, San Pedro, CA
Died July 28, 1995, San Pedro, CA
Ht. 6' Wt. 190 Batted and Threw Left
Outfielder

Year	Team, Lg	G	AB	R	H	2B	3B	HR	RBI	BA
1950	Yakima, WI	100	331	66	104	25	9	4	61	.314
1951		139	528	69	151	25	11	9	77	.286
1952		147	528	87	141	23	10	12	83	.267
1953	SF, PCL	135	385	69	105	16	6	16	50	.273
1954		44	96	7	24	4	1	1	12	.250
1955	Seattle, PCL	52	138	17	35	9	1	3	22	.252
	Nashville, SA	22	70	6	20	3	1	2	17	.286
	Wntchee, NW	51	186	54	66	13	3	8	45	.355
1956	did not play									
1957	Fresno, Cal	133	503	91	163	31	9	14	102	.324

♦ CHAPTER 10 ♦

1954:
The Little Corporation and
the Kiddie Car Express

4th place: W 84 L 84 .500 18 GB
Governor's Cup
First round: San Francisco 2, Holly wood 1
Second round: Oakland 3, San Francisco 0

Damon Miller had to raise money so the Seals could operate in 1954 or the team would revert to the league. He approached the club's employees— those who were still there — and offered them shares in the club. In this manner he raised $20,000 and incorporated as San Francisco Seals, Inc., but his group became known as the "Little Corporation."

But $20,000 was nowhere near enough to begin operations. On December 2, 1954, Miller was given until December 11 to raise further sums or the league would take over. The goal was $100,000 and he did it within a week. Stock was offered to the public for as little as ten dollars a share. Pitcher Al Lien invested $1,000. Manager Tommy Heath also invested. By the target date, Miller had raised $91,000.

A $50,000 indemnity bond on Seals Stadium was covered by Earle H. LeMasters of the Pacific National Bank. Another large chunk of money came in when KSAN television paid $75,000 for the TV rights to the night games. With this the team was a go, but in developing a budget it was calculated that there had to be at least 300,000 attendance to break even. This was a scary number; the Seals had not drawn that many fans for several years.

Beginning the season, the roster was quite similar to that of 1953. The biggest missing name was Windy McCall, who was sold to the New York

Giants for cash and two pitchers, Frank Hiller and Adrian Zabala. It was a great deal for San Francisco; Hiller both started and relieved and went 11–8, 2.92, and Zabala led the league in games and also had an 11–8 record, with a 3.22 ERA.

Also gone early in the season was Al Lyons, to San Diego where he pitched as well as played the outfield. More on him later. Soon to follow was first baseman George Vico, who started very poorly and was sold to Hollywood. Frank Kalin also never got going and retired. Al Lien, who had spent a lifetime as a Seal, finally showed his age and although he was still there, his contributions were minimal (2–4, 4.76). It was his final season. Jerry Zuvela (1-12-.250) could not reproduce his rookie year, played sparingly, and was gone after the season was over.

The season began slowly. The Seals fell to last, but Heath shook up his lineup using youngsters from the lower classifications and new arrivals from the higher classifications to replace the departed and/or unproductive.

Taking over at first base was 23-year-old Jim Westlake, who had been Seals property since signing in 1948. He batted .285 and led the team with 70 RBIs. Mike Baxes (2-54-.248), also 23 years old, became the utility infielder. Bob DiPietro (7-49-.269), a San Francisco native who signed with the Red Sox eight years before, became one of the all-time favorite Seals. He and Dave Melton (9-54-.301), 25, who had signed with the Seals our of Stanford University in 1950, divided playing time in the outfield with Sal Taormina (5-46-.272), who had his second straight good year.

Veteran Ted Beard was purchased for $10,000 from Hollywood early in the season. It was questionable if the Seals could afford that large an expenditure, but he settled in center field and led the team in home runs (11), batting average (.300), and stolen bases (30) and was second to Westlake in RBIs (62).

Also from Hollywood, veteran first baseman Chuck Stevens was claimed off waivers and was the number one pinch hitter on the team. Nini Tornay (1-30-.258) was back behind the plate, dividing time there with Will Tiesiera (1-18-.259).

Rounding out the everyday lineup were the three returning infielders from 1953: Jim Moran (0-34-.292) at second base, Reno Cheso (4-41-.251) at third base, and Leo Righetti (2-34-.255) at shortstop.

Once Heath made the changes in his lineup, the Seals took off. They rose from the cellar and climbed into the first division in a short time. This group of youthful players was dubbed the Kiddie Car Express and their quality play generated fan interest and attendance was up.

The pitching staff was very different. Tony Ponce was back from his

✿ Makes a Hit Every Time! – *Borden's* Ice Cream

1954 SEALS

two-week dominance of September of 1953 and went 14–16, 3.41. Elmer Singleton (13–13, 3.00) pitched solidly again. Major league veteran Ken Holcombe was picked up from the Red Sox's discard pile to go 10–10, 3.07, then retired after the season. Eddie Chandler was taken off waivers from the Los Angeles Angels to go 12–12, 3.32.

Again, the Seals had a superb bullpen. In addition to Hiller and Zabala, who led the PCL in games (59), returnees Bob Muncrief (3–3, 2.95) and Bill Bradford (6–2, 3.39), moved to the pen full time, were there in the mid to late innings to hold off opponents' rallies. Zabala was reunited with Heath; he had pitched for him in Minneapolis in 1950 and '51 and considered him to be an excellent manager.

The 1954 Seals were an excellent defensive team, finishing second in the league in fielding.

Three Seals—catcher Nini Tornay (.989), first baseman Jim Westlake (.992), and second baseman Jim Moran (.982)—led the league. The sure-handed Moran led the league four years in a row (1952–55) and in '55 he set the all-time PCL record for fielding percentage by a second sacker (.992).

Also, in '54 Tornay led the PCL in assists for the second straight year, center fielder Ted Beard had the most outfield chances, and Moran led in double plays (and again in '55). The '54 team also led the league in double plays.

As the season entered the final week, Oakland was solidly in third place and San Francisco and Seattle were in a close race for fourth. Due to rainouts that were not made up, Seattle had played six fewer games than the Seals but a Seals victory on the final Thursday clinched the fourth spot.

Even with fourth clinched, the club kept on winning and almost caught the Oaks in third. They ended up one game behind their cross–Bay rivals.

As in 1947, there was a tie for the top spot in the standings. This time it was San Diego and Hollywood that tied, each at 101–67. Ironically, Lefty O'Doul managed the Padres, but this time he won the playoff game to break the tie. Former National League MVP Bob Elliott, a reserve most of

Opposite: 1954 San Francisco Seals. *Back row (left to right)*: Don Rode (batboy), Leo Righetti, Al Lyons, Bill Bradford, Gordon Brunswick, Tommy Heath, Al Lien, Elmer Singleton, Ken Holcombe, Leo Hughes (trainer). *Second row:* Jim Moran, Adrian Zabala, Jim Westlake, Jerry Zuvela, Chuck Stevens, Tony Ponce, Bob Muncrief, Mike McCormick, Merv Donahue, Frank Hiller. *Front row:* Will Tiesiera, Sal Taormina, Ted Beard, Mike Baxes, Billy Heath (batboy), Reno Cheso, Bob DiPietro, Eddie Chandler, Nini Tornay, Bobby Muncrief, Jr. (batboy) (author's collection).

Second baseman Jim Moran (author's collection).

the season, played third base for San Diego in this game, hit two home runs, and drove in five runs to give the Padres and O'Doul a 7–2 win. The next season Elliott would manage the team.

For the first time since 1951— and the last time ever — there was a Governor's Cup playoff. First place San Diego played third place Oakland and second place Hollywood played fourth place San Francisco and both series were won by the lower finishing team.

Oakland took the first game, 4–1, over San Diego behind catcher Lenny Neal's two-run home run and three RBIs and George Bamberger's five-hitter. The second game went 11 innings and in the top of the 11th former American League All-Star Sam Chapman belted a grand slam to give Oakland the 7–3 win. Former Negro leagues all-star Theolic Smith started for San Diego and had allowed only two hits and one run through seven innings, but he was relieved by Al Lyons, who came in from center field to pitch. The Padres had a 3–1 lead at this point, but the Oaks got to Lyons for two runs in the ninth to send the game into extra innings.

Lyons had a good year for San Diego. Platooned in the outfield, he went 10-42-.265 and used out of the bullpen, he was 8–2, 2.30. His only start of the season came in the second game of the double header on the final day. He won, 7–3, to give the Padres the tie with Hollywood. Roger Bowman, pitching the second game of the final double header for Hollywood, hurled a perfect game.

In the San Francisco–Hollywood series, the Stars took game one, 5–3, on three unearned runs, thanks to errors by Baxes and Righetti. Taormina and pinch hitter Stevens homered for the losing cause. Singleton won game two, 7–0, with a seven-hitter. Westlake drove in three runs with a double and a home run, and Tornay went 4-for-5 with a double and thee RBIs.

The third game was won by the Seals, 4–3, on the strength of an eighth- inning, three-run rally, aided by the Stars center fielder Tommy Saffell's error. Holcombe pitched seven strong innings of one-run ball for the win.

In the champion series, there were two one-run games and a two-run game, but the Seals came up short in all three. Allen Gettel, the Oaks' ace, won game one, 4–3. Game two was a slugfest with the Oaks coming out on top, 8–7. Beard, Melton, and Westlake homered for San Francisco, and Spider Jorgenson, Piper Davis, and Jim Marshall did the same for Oakland. Jorgenson's blast was a three-run shot off of Zabala in the seventh to tie the game at 7-all, then the next batter, Marshall, homered to end the scoring.

Don Ferrarese pitched a five-hitter in game three to beat Singleton, 2–0, to give the Oaks their second ever Governor's Cup championship. On this final day a double header was scheduled, so the two teams played a meaningless second game. The Seals won it, 5–4, but it was too late.

But the Seals and the Little Corporation made money on the season. They led the league in attendance with 298,908, just short of their 300,000 goal. Playoff attendance raised them above 300,000 and the club made a profit of $464 for six months of baseball.

Besides Lyons, other former Seals did well around the PCL in 1954. Lloyd Dickey was 14–11, 2.68 for San Diego, Dale Long was 23-68-.280 for Hollywood, Ray Orteig went 14-65-.254 for Seattle, old reliable Joe Brovia was 13-91-.302 for Sacramento, and Dino Restelli went 12-44-.261 for tail-end Portland.

LEO RIGHETTI

Seals 1953–1955

Leo Righetti will always be remembered as the father of Dave Righetti, a top major league pitcher, but Leo was more than that. He was a short-stop — a *good* shortstop — who peaked a half-step below the major leagues. In fact, if the money had been right, he would have been a major leaguer but he, like many other PCL ballplayers, would not take a pay cut to go up.

His professional career began at the age of 17 when he was signed by the New York Yankees out of Bellarmine College Preparatory School in San Jose, California. Bellarmine has produced many outstanding baseball players over the years. It was after his junior year and the worry was World War II; the Yankees told his parents that they could keep him out of the war.

He was sent to Newark, New Jersey, to play that first year (1944). In another year he may well have been signed to play closer to home because there was a team right there in San Jose and there were the PCL teams a few miles up the road in San Francisco and Oakland. As it was, it took him nine years to play near his home. He finally became a member of the Seals in 1953 and in his two plus-years he batted .259 with solid defense.

BK: When were you originally signed?

LEO RIGHETTI: [In] 1944, with the Yankees. They sent me to Newark — International League. I was a junior in high school. There was a war on and

Leo Righetti (author's collection).

there was a lot of guys missin' then and I should've never done it, but I did it. I signed with the Yankees in June of '44. After school ended I went to Newark.

BK: You were only 17. The Yankees farm system was massive in those days.

LR: Unbelievable! I went in the service after that and came out and I had to join Kansas City. Oh my lord, the ballplayers!

BK: What chance were you given?

LR: I didn't get any. In 1944, I played with Binghamton in the Eastern League and we won the playoff — the Governor's Cup — that year. Then I went in the Coast Guard and I got out May tenth, 1946. They sent me to Kansas City and there must have been 50 guys there. I mean, they're older because they were in the service. I was still only 19.

I had no chance. I don't even know what I reported for. I *had* to because the Yankees told me I had to report. Otherwise, what the hell, in those days you're suspended if you don't. I hadn't played ball in a year-and-a-half. I had no chance when I got there. They didn't give me a chance.

Then they sent me to Binghamton again. That's when I played ball with Vic Raschi and Jerry Coleman and Dick Kryhoski, Hank Bauer; we had a load of ballplayers there, too. We came in *last* in the Eastern League. I wish Lefty Gomez was still alive because I always used to tell Lefty before he died, I said, "You were such a great manager; you brought us in last with a ballclub like that!"

But, geez, everybody had great ballplayers. The Cleveland organization and the Red Sox — they had ballplayers. I couldn't believe where they all came from. But four years a lot of 'em were out. They were in the service. Everybody got out at once.

Phil Rizzuto was still with the Yankees. He come out of the Navy; he was playin' shortstop. And they had Billy Johnson and Joe Gordon. Jerry Coleman got a chance, then Billy Martin took his place because Jerry had to go in the Korean War. That's how Billy got his chance and then Gil McDougald got a chance. Gil was a hell of a ballplayer anyway. I was with him, too, and Andy Carey.

And the Yankees had farm clubs. Eight years I put in that farm system. They finally let me go 'cause I wouldn't report. I was with Rogers Hornsby in Beaumont, Texas, and I told him what he could do with his ballclub and he told me what I could do with myself and he put me on a Greyhound bus and sent me home and I got suspended. Then the Yankees finally let me go and Sacramento bought me in '51.

BK: The Solons were independent.

LR: Yeah. Most of the Coast League was, except Hollywood was Pirates and L. A. was Cubs. They were gonna make the third big league out here in the Coast League until Stoneham and O'Malley got ahold of it and then the Dodgers and Giants moved out here.

BK: You were in the Coast League for several years.

LR: Yeah. I was with Sacramento in '51, then the Seals in '53 and '4, then Seattle in '55, '56, and '57.

They were makin' more money in the Coast League than guys in the big leagues were. Roy McMillan busted his leg in Cincinnati and they wanted me to go to Cincinnati while he was healin' and I had to take a cut in pay. I should've done it, but I was makin' as much in the Coast League. And I was [living] at home, too. When I played with the Seals I lived here in San Jose — Sal Taormina and myself and Reno Cheso and a couple of other guys.

They've had a couple reunions. One for the 1955 Seattle team, when we won the championship, but nobody invited me. John Oldham didn't get one; George Schmees was with us then. Carmen Mauro told me about it. My number's in the book. I never took it out or went unlisted, not even when my son was playin'. Oh my God, the phone rang all the time!

BK: There weren't player strikes when you played.

LR: Oh, the players are strong [today]. Back when I played you took what they gave you. Like Mantle. Mickey goes in there and he was so scared of George Weiss he took anything that George gave him. Weiss was terrible. He was a *bad* man.

I got ten grand from the Yankees. I was the first guy from around this area — northern California — to ever get that kind of money from the Yankees and I made 300 a month the first year. And then Bill Sarni came along and then Wayne Belardi with the Dodgers got 17,000 right after that and then another kid from Bellarmine, Jim Small, got 35,000 [from Detroit], then it started escalating.

I never played my senior year at Bellarmine at all. I lost my senior year because I had played pro ball with the Yankees.

But the Coast League, that was it. That was the greatest league of all time. There was no horsin' around; they paid good meal money and we had airplanes. I don't ever remember travelin' on a train; I did in the American Association and at Newark, but I never did in the Coast League.

They would play seven games a week. David, my son, says, "You did what?!" and I says, "Yeah, we played seven games a week. We played a doubleheader on Sunday and Monday we had off. Every Monday was off unless it was Labor Day or a holiday, then we had to play a doubleheader. We didn't play no one-sixty-two, we played a hundred-eighty-somethin'." Then I said, "The next year they cut it down to a hundred and seventy-some." He said, "You played in all those?" and I said, "Yeah, and I never pulled a hamstring." As long as I could walk I was out there because I didn't want anybody takin' my place.

When they took Hollywood and Oakland and San Francisco and Los Angeles and San Diego later, the Coast League just died. Seals Stadium was beautiful — you remember that? It was one of the best diamonds I ever played on in my life. Shorty had that infield dirt and that outfield was immaculate. They took all that sod over to Candlestick and then they decided to put that Astroturf in; they lost all that and then Shorty died and that was the end of that. I don't remember Shorty's last name.

BK: Did you go to spring training with a major league club?

LR: Yes. Boston Braves in '52. Sacramento sold me to the Braves after '51. Eddie Mathews was there that year, and Johnny Logan was with me. Roy Hartsfield, Jack Dittmer, George Crowe, Earl Torgeson, Warren Spahn, [Lou] Burdette. Walker Cooper, I think, was catchin', with Ebba St. Clair. Del Crandall and Johnny Antonelli were in the Army.

Jack Cusick was the shortstop that Logan and I were behind. They had Sibby Sisti as the utility infielder, so [general manager] John Quinn said, "We gotta use Cusick 'cause we traded Bob Addis for him and Bob

Addis hit almost .300 for us and we needed a shortstop." Tommy Holmes, the manager, tells me that, too. He tells Logan and I that we're gonna go down to Milwaukee, which was American Association at the time.

Well, Logan goes. I took a plane when I got to Chicago and came home. I didn't report. I wound up a month later in Toledo, playin' in the American Association. Then I went to Charleston, West Virginia, that year.

Cusick was terrible. He was with the Yankee organization. I knew him at Beaumont in '50. He had good hands, [but] he couldn't get to anything. But Logan turned out to be a hell of a ballplayer. Tough kid, too; he'd fight at the drop of a hat. And Mathews—just as tough.

BK: After that year, you joined the Seals. How did they acquire you?

LR: They traded Bob Thurman for me. I played the rest of my career in the Coast League. I was only 30 when I quit.

BK: Is there one game that stands out?

LR: I guess winnin' the pennant in Seattle [in 1955]. We won, 3-to-1, and I drove all the runs in. The whole week stood out, really, 'cause I was about 11-for-21 that week against Los Angeles.

Playin' for Fred Hutchinson — I'm so happy that happened. He wasn't pattin' you on the back every five minutes, but he said, "I'll make the lineup out — I don't want no questions asked — and that's the way it's gonna be." He said hello to me when I joined the club and goodbye at the end of the year, but he thanked you. He would wait for you at the clubhouse — whoever did good that night — and he'd pat you on the back and go his own way. He didn't make a big deal out of it, but he knew what he was doin'. He knew pitching and I always said that's the main thing. You gotta get a manager that knows the pitching staff and when to pull 'em and when to put 'em in.

But, geez, he had some throwers at Seattle. We had [Lou] Kretlow and Elmer Singleton. Do you remember Elmer? What a tough pitcher he was. He refused to go to the big leagues, you know. He was makin' so much in the Coast League, he *refused* to go to the big leagues. When Elmer said no, that's all there was to it. There was no debating it.

He'd call me to the mound and say, ""What do you want up here?" I'd say, "Well, you called me up here," and he'd say, "No, I didn't. I just wanted to see what the hell you were lookin' at in the stands." "I wasn't lookin' at anything." "Just go back and play shortstop and I'll do the pitchin'." It was a way for him to break whatever was goin' on in his mind, so he used me all the time 'cause I had played with him two years with the Seals and then another three years at Seattle. The man confused me all the time, but I never made an error behind him. Elmer would say, "I'm out here bustin' my tail and you better do the same thing behind me."

He'd win 18, 19 like it was nothing, but he didn't wanna win 20. If he won 20, he said they'd want him to win 22. But he was like Don Drysdale — every four days he was there.

BK: Who was the best player you saw?

LR: Oh God. I know the best pitcher. It was Koufax. No, I really can't say that because Koufax couldn't hit the backstop when I saw him.

Warren Spahn, I guess. He was the most fantastic, I think. He went about his business. He would throw so hard in battin' practice, he'd be so sore he couldn't move the next two days. But that's the way he did it. They didn't baby their arms like they do today.

And Herb Score. Mudcat Grant when he was with San Diego. Elmer Singleton. Lou Kretlow, when I faced him when he was with Williamsport. He'd get up to about a hundred [mph], I think. They talk about Nolan Ryan; this guy's ball looked like it *exploded* when it came to home plate. Herb Score — I knew he threw the ball. It's right there and I'm swingin' and all of a sudden the catcher's mitt goes "POP!"

Sad Sam Jones. I faced him when he was with San Diego and I was with Sacramento. He could bring it up there, too. Toothpick Sam. A great guy.

I played with blacks then, like Artie Wilson, Joe Taylor, Milt Smith. I never gave it a thought. I don't think anybody from California gave it a thought. Jackie Robinson was actually my hero when he was at UCLA.

BK: What about Emmett Ashford, the first black umpire?

LR: He had a rough time in the beginning. Those dirty boogers, you know what they would do to him? They used to throw watermelon out there at him. Some of the guys from the South, boy, they were rough! Earl Robinson used to play third base for Baltimore. They did the same thing to him, too, when he was with Hollywood. Curt Roberts was with Hollywood. They'd do it to him.

Emmett would come over and run your ass right now, though. I liked Emmett. I thought he was great. At least he woke the umpires up. He put on a show when he was out there.

I never turned around in my life and hollered at an umpire. I did on the infield but never at home plate. I could holler at 'em or whatever I wanted, as long as I didn't turn around and look at 'em. And they'd say, "What did you say?" and I said, "I'm not talkin' to you," which I was.

I could see the pitches better at shortstop than the guy behind the plate could see 'em. Paul Runge's father was an umpire — Ed Runge; he'd wink at me. He'd be standin' out there in the infield. I'd look at him and say, "Where in the hell was that pitch, Ed?" and he'd wink at me. I'd know it was a wrong call.

We knew where each umpire's strike zone was, like Hal Summers. We knew where Pelekoudas's was. Pelekoudas was a friend of mine anyway, from the peninsula here. I got along good with Chris. But they never blew plays on purpose. They'd call the play and say, "Hey, gimme a little better tag next time," or "That was a little bit *too* much phantom." They never hollered back in your face like they do today. They come right back at you today! They excite you more. They didn't do that in my day.

Ron Luciano blew the whole thing for 'em. I can't believe what he said in his book about Earl Weaver; any chance he got to stick Weaver, he stuck him. So finally he couldn't do a Baltimore game anymore. I know he's not the only umpire like that.

BK: Were you a collector in your playing days?

LR: I could've got autographs along the way — Jackie, Snider, Furillo. What a collection I would've had. Never gave it a thought. Talked to Ted Williams, never even *thought* of gettin' an autograph.

My son, I told him, "Get Rickey [Henderson] for me." He says, "Why would you want those, Dad?" And I say, "David, you don't realize it, but when you get to be 50, 60, you're gonna wish you had 'em."

He's played with Don Mattingly, he's played with Rickey, he's played with [Dave] Winfield. I told him to get [Dennis] Eckersley for me, but I got Eckersley myself because I played in a golf tournament with him. And Barry. I said, "Get Barry Bonds for me." He never got it.

BK: What a rotten kid.

LR: Yeah. [Laughs] It finally dawned on him: he better start doin' this. And he is now.

BK: Any regrets?

LR: I played 13 years. I got suspended in '50, but it counted as a year, I guess.

Yeah. I should've never signed with the Yankees. Really. I did it at the time because they saved my butt from goin' in the Army in World War II. They got me in the Coast Guard and my mother and father went along with that. I had no say; I'm 17 years old. They said, "You're signin' with the Yankees 'cause we want you to be safe." I understand now, but at the time I didn't. I should've never done it because I could foresee what was gonna happen to me, too — how many ballplayers those Yankees had. I had no choice.

You know, with Henrich, DiMaggio, and Keller in the outfield, there wasn't too many guys breakin' into that outfield. And there was a *lot* of guys wound up in Kansas City or wound up in St. Louis [Browns] and they were doormats for the Yankees. That's all they were 'cause they sure as hell never won anything. At that time it was Cleveland, Boston, and the Yankees winnin' in the American League.

I should've went even with the Red Sox with [scout] Charlie Walgren or Philadelphia Phillies. *Any*body but the Yankees. Not Detroit or St. Louis [Cardinals] at the time because they had just as many ballplayers. I think the commissioner cut loose a lot of guys on Detroit and the Cardinals. They had to cut 'em loose; they had so many guys in the farm system. I'm tellin' you, you weren't goin' anyplace.

They never took care of you, either. You hear about, aw, "They're gonna take care of you, they're gonna do this, they're gonna do that." Like my two boys went with Texas [Rangers] — to Ashville, North Carolina — in 1977 and they said there'll be somebody there waitin' for you to show you where the hotel and everything is and I said, "Don't you two believe that. There isn't gonna be *anybody* waitin' for you. You're on your own the minute you signed." And I told 'em what to do.

They said, "Dad, you were right," when they called. There wasn't anybody there.

And I said, "Now don't think your new teammates are gonna welcome you, either, 'cause that means two guys gotta leave when you get there. And sure enough, David said it took 'em a while before they came around. He started winnin' right away, otherwise, he says, "I don't know what the hell would've happened."

And I told 'em, "The more money you get [to sign], the better chance you have to stick with the ballclub." If you get a hundred thousand to sign, they're gonna look at you before they look at the guy that got 10,000. I don't care who's the better ballplayer, they're gonna give *you* the chance.

David got a chance. They gave him 25 [thousand], I think. My other son, Steve, didn't get nothin'. Wayne Terwilliger was the manager there when Steve was playin' the next year after David went to Tulsa. He stayed there with Wayne Terwilliger. Mark Davis is pitchin' for a Phillie team at the time. He goes 4-for-5, drives in about eight runs that night, hits two home runs off of him, and he's so happy when he calls home and then three days later he calls back, he says, "Dad, you know I haven't played a game since." He says, "He [Terwilliger] told me in the office he's gotta play [Dave] Hibner. He got 80,000 to sign and we gotta play him." And he never played.

BK: The 1955 Seattle Rainiers were Seattle's last championship team in the original Pacific Coast League, before the Dodgers and Giants moved west and changed everything.

LR: It was a great team, great players. I was lookin' at my '55 [team] picture and it's gettin' scary. Bobby Balcena's gone, and Freddie Hutchinson and Vern Stephens, Gerry Priddy, Bob Swift, Don Rudolph — he got killed, Ray Orteig. They're all gone.

LEO RIGHETTI
Born March 3, 1927, San Francisco, CA
Died February 19, 1998, San Jose, CA
Ht. 6' Wt. 170 Batted and Threw Right
Shortstop

Year	Team, Lg	G	AB	R	H	2B	3B	HR	RBI	BA
1944	Newark, IL	4	7	0	1	0	0	0	0	.143
	Bghmptn, EL	67	237	27	55	13	3	1	31	.232
1945	military service									
1946	Bghmptn, EL	57	187	17	31	3	0	0	17	.166
1947	Victoria, WI	140	487	66	122	21	4	19	81	.251
1948	Bghmptn, EL							0	3	.162
	Augusta, SA	79	270	35	64	13	1	3	35	.237
1949	Augusta, SA	141	521	66	117	20	1	4	46	.225
	did not play									
1951	Sac., PCL	122	352	48	71	14	0	3	27	.202
1952	Tol/Chstn, AA	113	371	24	74	16	1	3	26	.199
1953	SF, PCL	150	532	50	137	21	1	3	61	.258
1954		139	455	48	116	17	4	2	34	.255
1955	SF/Sea, PCL	121	405	42	107	10	6	3	38	.264
1956	Seattle, PCL	158	578	61	162	23	0	0	49	.280
1957	Sea/Sac,PCL	154	594	56	144	18	0	2	32	.242

JIM WESTLAKE
Seals 1949, 1950, 1954

"I planned on playing for the Seals when I was about 10 or 12 years old." Jim Westlake's early plans came to pass. I planned the same thing, but I had roadblocks: there were no longer any Seals when I was finally old enough, and I didn't have the talent.

But Jim Westlake did. His older brother, Wally, had shown what ability lay in the Westlake genes as a slugging outfielder for the Pittsburgh Pirates in the late 1940s and there was great interest in the younger Westlake during his senior year in high school. Obviously, as can be seen from the above quote, the Seals had the inside track.

He only played one full year (1954) in San Francisco, but he was one of the leaders of the offense that season. He led the club in RBIs.

BK: You were originally signed by the Seals.
JIM WESTLAKE: Yeah, in 1948, out of high school.

Jim Westlake with the Philadelphia Phillies in 1955 (author's collection).

BK: You went to Salt Lake City. How did you find the adjustment from high school to professional baseball?

JW: In professional, they're all pretty good. In high school you've got maybe two stars on a team. There's quite a difference.

I hit around .300 my first year out, .298 or something like that. Then I went to the Seals at the end of the season just to work out with them. And then when 1949 came around I was supposed to go back to Salt Lake but the first baseman had a broken cheekbone, so they kept me there for six weeks, the first six weeks of the season. Then I went back to Salt Lake again. I hit .340–something that year.

BK: You spent most of 1950 in Yakima and hit well again.

JW: Yeah. I had a pretty good year. I joined the Coast Guard and went in in '51, '52, and '53. In 1954 I was with the Seals the whole year.

There were several of us who were pretty young and the ballclub started out *real, real* bad, sort of like 5-and-28 or something like that. So they released all the veterans, let all the veterans go, and started playing what they called the kids. I was 23 years old at that time. Myself and Mike Baxes and Dave Melton. We went from last place to first place in about six or eight weeks. We got on a tear.

That year I think we finished third or fourth; I think it was fourth. Then they sold me to Philadelphia at the end of the year.

BK: Your major league career was brief.

JW: Very brief. [Laughs] I got sold to the Phillies and [manager] Mayo Smith wasn't too enamored with anybody that came from the Coast

League and I never really got a shot with 'em. He had me pinch hit one day in the Polo Grounds. There were two outs in the ninth inning and the score was 10-to-nothing Giants. He made me take two balls and no strikes and three balls and one strike, until I got 3-and-2, so I only got one swing.

BK: Tony Ponce was the Seals big winner in '54.

JW: He was a real character. Knuckleball pitcher. He pitched a double header in Seals Stadium one day. I think he won both games. I ran into him at a reunion in southern California. He'd been around quite a few years when he came to the Seals.

Dave Melton, he had a real good year for us. Teddy Beard was the center fielder and Jim Moran was playing second. Leo Righetti, that's the father of Dave who's now the pitching coach with the Giants, was a good shortstop. Reno Cheso was the third baseman. Reno was young; Reno was a real good hitter, not a very good infielder. Restelli was there for a while, too.

I ran into Nini Tornay and Will Tiesiera at a reunion at Candlestick Park. It's funny; I was walking out of a Raiders game one day — this was probably 20 years ago or so — and I look up and here standing next to me is Will and his wife. Gene Brocker was a catcher, too; he was with us for a while.

We had a pretty good year in 1954. We drew *real* well after we started winning and we had big crowds on the weekends, especially Sundays and holidays.

Bob DiPietro — God, there was a character. He was really a funny guy. I haven't seen him since I played with him in Portland in '59. That was my last year. He could put on a show just like any nightclub act. He's just funnier'n heck. God, I'd like to see him.

BK: Your offense was probably better than your pitching.

JW: Bill Bradford was one of 'em. Al Lien was on that staff. Al Lyons was a relief pitcher, a pretty good pitcher. Kenny Holcombe was a pretty good pitcher, too. Bob Muncrief was a pretty good pitcher. He had to be in his mid 30s, maybe a little older.

BK: Does a game stand out?

JW: I think the whole year, the way we turned around. We had gotten off to such a poor start. The one thing that really stands out was a two-week road trip we made to Seattle and Portland. We played 15 games, we won 13 of 'em. That really started us.

When we got back to San Francisco, my God, the crowd was waiting for us. We spent the night and flew back the next morning 'cause we had to play a game. It had to be a holiday; it had to be Memorial Day, I think. When we finally got there, the stadium was already filled before we even took batting practice. Seals Stadium held about 25,000 people.

That was a lot of fun playing there. It was a little cold at night. The days were beautiful, just beautiful for the players. At night it was wet as hell. The grass was awful wet and it was cold.

It's funny. The new ballpark in San Francisco's not too far away from there. It's only three or four miles away. I've been there a couple of times during the day, but I haven't been there at night, but people say just a light jacket is all you need at nighttime.

BK: You led the Seals in RBIs in '54, but power in Seals Stadium was rare.

JW: No, it was a big park. You could hit a ball a ton, especially to right field because the wind blew over the right field fence over to the left field fence. You could really put a charge in one and it was a big a-b. It would be a home run in a lot of parks. For a lefthanded hitter, especially. For righthanded hitters, it was a big park for them, too, but if you got it up in the air it'd go out.

BK: Did you have any days in '54 that you recall?

JW: I broke my finger and I was out for a few days and I went back in actually too soon 'cause my finger's never been the same since. I think I got four hits the day I came back against Oakland.

I was hitting over .300 most of the year and toward the end I just ran out of gas playing every day. I went from over .300 and I think I finished .285. Playing every day was tough and even though we had Mondays off we'd be traveling on Mondays.

And San Francisco was perfect for the league. You didn't have long trips because we were right dead in the middle of the league. Usually we'd go to San Diego and then from San Diego to Sacramento and another time we'd play Hollywood and L. A., and then Oakland, of course, right across the bay. As far as for traveling, ourselves and Oakland probably had the better deal than anybody.

BK: You played in Syracuse for a year.

JW: I hated it. Oh, God, your road trips were from Montreal to Havana and we never had any scheduled days off. I think the whole year we had like three or four.

I was looking at Sacramento's new Triple-A club. They've only got five scheduled days off for the whole year. That's not a lot of time off and a lot of that time you're traveling.

But, God, it was just terrible playing there. I'd never been in a place where it was real humid and places like Syracuse and Buffalo and Rochester, too, was just humid as hell. Richmond, Virginia, was in the league and it would get awful hot down there. I had a hard time getting used to things like that. It wasn't bad in Cuba, except I had a hard time eating the food down there.

Then I went from there to Sacramento. I got sold to Sacramento and played here for two years, through '58. Then I went to Portland and that was my last year, '59.

BK: Tommy Heath was your manager twice, at San Francisco and at Portland.

JW: I liked playing for Tom. He was real easy to get along with. He just went out and he let you play.

O'Doul — I played for Lefty, too. Earlier in San Francisco and also in '56 up in Vancouver. Lefty was easy to play for.

Actually I played for Heath three times: San Francisco and Sacramento and Portland. He was a funny guy, great sense of humor.

They didn't try to get fancy. They just went out and played the game the way it's supposed to be played. You're supposed to hit-and-run when you're supposed to hit-and-run, bunt when you're supposed to bunt. I think the biggest trick of managing is when to change the pitcher.

Tommy, he hated to fly. God, he *hated* to fly. The top of his head would just bead up in sweat. He was bald, you know, and his head would actually just bead up and there'd be little balls of sweat all over his head. [Laughs] And then every time we'd land he'd clap. Applause for the pilot. [Laughs]

A lot of the teams when I was still in the Coast League were still taking trains, like from up north into San Francisco. But then it got to the point where I think by the time — maybe that year, in '54 — I think everybody was flying then. In 1949 when I was there, a lot of the clubs were taking trains. We always flew; we were flying in '49. We didn't take the train when we played. The only thing we'd do, we'd take a bus to Sacramento and then for Oakland we just drove over the bridge ourselves. We got to the ballpark ourselves.

BK: Was there a pitcher in the Coast League who was tough on you?

JW: Oh, Tommy Byrne. He was a mean son of a buck, too.

BK: Was there one who was easy?

JW: [Laughs] There wasn't none of 'em. There was a guy that pitched down in San Diego. He couldn't throw hard enough to break a pane of glass. Bob Kerrigan. He used to drive me *nuts.*

BK: Who was the best player you saw?

JW: God, there were some good ones. A couple of the better hitters in the Coast League were Max West and Earl Rapp. They were good hitters. Veterans. Those guys had been around.

Joe Brovia was a good hitter. Joe wasn't a very good outfielder, couldn't run very well, but he could swing the bat. He could pull anybody.

BK: Do you receive fan mail?

JW: It's amazing. I still get people writing for an autograph even though I only got up one time in the big leagues. I'll get maybe 30–40 a year. My brother gets 6- or 700 of 'em.

JAMES PATRICK WESTLAKE
Born July 3, 1930, Sacramento, CA
Ht. 6'1" Wt. 190 Batted and Threw Left
First baseman

Year	Team. Lg	G	AB	R	H	2B	3B	HR	RBI	BA
1948	SLC, Pio	79	294	60	87	15	5	1	39	.296
1949	SF, PCL	40	121	16	26	2	1	1	10	.215
	SLC, Pio	113	416	111	143	18	13	4	74	.344
1950	SF, PCL							0	4	.308
	Yakima, WI	151	563	97	164	31	7	5	122	.291
1951–53		military service								
1954	SF, PCL	142	459	63	131	17	5	5	70	.285
1955	Phi., NL	1	1	0	0	0	0	0	0	.000
	Syracuse, IL	144	447	64	117	30	1	4	41	.262
1956	Miami, IL	7	20		5			0	0	.250
	Van/Sac.PCL	125	362	40	89	7	5	10	59	.246
1957	Sac, PCL	131	477	62	136	16	2	5	44	.285
1958		130	387	49	103	18	2	3	56	.266
1959	Port., PCL	110	305	30	75	13	2	1	24	.246

CHAPTER 11

1955:
Where Did Everyone Go?

6th place: W 80 L 92 .465 15 GB

The Seals' lineup underwent great changes before the 1955 season began and even more early in the season. Tommy Heath and the Little Corporation were optimistic, but that optimistic bubble was soon burst as the Seals fell into the lower reaches of the second division and stayed there.

Of the regular eight position players from 1954, only two retained their jobs: Jim Moran at second base, who turned in a typical Jim Moran season (2-34-268), and Ted Beard in center field, who also turned in a typical Jim Moran season (8-34-.245). The problem was Beard needed to turn in a typical Ted Beard season: double figure home runs, a productive level of RBIs, a batting average in the high .200s, and 20+ stolen bases.

First baseman Jim Westlake went to the Philadelphia Phillies and outfielder Bob DiPietro was converted to a first baseman. This was a great move, until midseason. At that point DiPietro was the league's leading hitter (.372), but then he broke his ankle and his season was over. Veteran Chuck Stevens (5-29-.234) took over for a while and he may have been the best fielding first sacker in the PCL, but his best years with the bat were behind him. Shortly after midseason the Seals acquired Wayne Belardi from Detroit, via Buffalo, and in the second half of the season he put up 13-43-.269 numbers. Coupled with his Buffalo stats, he was 23 –72-.250 for the year.

Reno Cheso (4-35-.228) also had an offensive drop at third base, so veteran Bill Serena (18-71-.270) was brought over from Oakland. Leo Righetti, Elmer Singleton, and the newly acquired Ewell Blackwell went to

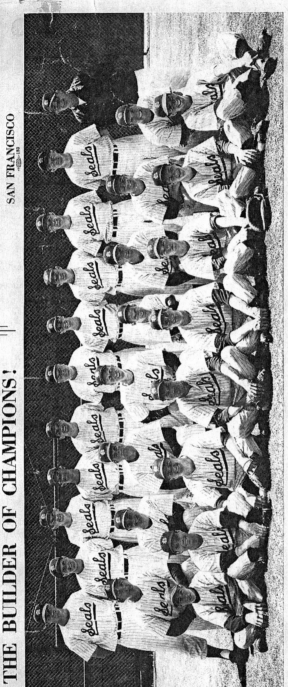

Compliments of

CHRISTOPHER MILK ‖ CHRISTOPHER DAIRY FARMS
THE BUILDER OF CHAMPIONS!

SAN FRANCISCO

1955 SEALS

Infielder Dave Melton (courtesy Robert Zwissig).

the Seattle Rainiers for Gene Bearden and Steve Nagy. The departure of Righetti opened the way for young Mike Baxes to play shortstop and he took advantage of it. His .323 batting average was tops on the team among qualifiers and the best for a Seals' shortstop in modern memory.

Beard was flanked in the outfield by Dave Melton (19-116-.299), who made the most of the opportunity to play every day, and former major leaguer Walt Judnich (9-60-.279), who came from Portland after the season began for his second stint with San Francisco. It was his last season as a professional. Sal Taormina (10-45-.261) became a productive part-timer and Joe Kirrene (3-52-.257) also came over from Oakland and divided his time between third base and the outfield.

John Ritchey took over as the number one catcher. Back in 1948 he had been the first black in the PCL and annually produced solid offense, which he also did with the Seas (6-41-.285). He was also sound, if not spectacular, defensively, but there were questions about his arm so he never advanced to the major leagues. Nini Tornay, whose arm and defense were never questioned, was a solid backup (2-13-.211).

Opposite: 1955 San Francisco Seals. *Back row (left to right):* Bob Greenwood, Steve Nagy, Walt Judnich, John Ritchey, Sal Taormina, Tommy Heath, Mike Baxes, Dave Melton, Don Fracchia, Jim Moran, Leo Hughes (trainer). *Second row:* Tony Ponce, Bill Serena, Maurice Fisher, Chuck Stevens, Ted Beard, Bill Bradford, Reno Cheso, Nini Tornay. *Front row:* Damon Miller, Jr. (batboy) Bob DiPietro, Lowell Creighton, Gene Bearden, Jim Walsh, Jim Stoll, Johnny McCormick (batboy), Ed Orrante (batboy) (author's collection).

The Seals had a no-hitter pitched against them on July 25. George Pik-tuzas of Los Angeles battled control problems, but no Seal could hit safely against him and he won, 2–1. It was the first of three no-hitters in the league that week. On July 24, Singleton no-hit San Diego in a seven-inning game and two days later Chris Van Cuyk of Oakland also tossed a seven-inning no-hitter against Los Angeles. Both of these games were by the score of 2–0.

But usually the Seals hit. The new lineup led the PCL in hitting with a .268 batting average.

Bearden (18–12, 3.52) was a good acquisition for the Seals and was acknowledged as the staff ace, but Singleton (19–12, 2.20) was a better acquisition for the Rainiers. In fact, the trade helped Seattle to win the pennant. Blackwell (5–5, 4.09) gave the team some help out of the bullpen and Righetti (3-38-.264) gave them a shortstop, a position that had been woefully weak in 1954. With the three former Seals, and a completely revamped roster, including a new manager (Fred Hutchinson replaced Jerry Priddy after the '54 season), Seattle climbed from fifth to first.

The other former Rainier, Nagy, was not the pitcher he had been. He finished at 6–12, 4.04. Tony Ponce (10–12, 4.26) was shaky. Newcomer Jim Walsh, from Hollywood, went 8–10, 4.45. He had been 10–7, 3.21 for the Stars in '54. Bill Bradford (12–5, 3.13) turned in another solid year and was used both as a starter and reliever.

A pleasant surprise was Don Fracchia (14–12, 3.28), who came up from Tulsa. Another surprising newcomer was Bob Greenwood (5–15, 4.83). The Seals had expected more from him when they got him from the Phillies as part payment for Westlake. Maurice Fisher (1–6, 3.36) pitched better out of the bullpen than his record would indicate.

Late in the season the Seals signed local high school hurler Lowell Creighton, but professional baseball was too much for the kid. He won one and lost one for the '55 Seals, went 0–3 with Salinas in the California League in '56, and was gone from the scene.

The *San Francisco Chronicle*'s headline on the last day of the season read, "Little Corp now Little Corpse." The season killed the Little Corporation as attendance fell drastically to 158,476, only slightly more than half of 1954's figure. The only team with poorer attendance was Oakland (141,397), now managed by Lefty O'Doul, and the Oaks fled the Bay Area for Vancouver, British Columbia, where they became the Mounties, in 1956.

Damon Miller and his group were broke. A few dollars came in when the Kansas City Athletics bought Melton, Baxes, and Bradford for $75,000 and a player, but it was just a drop in the bucket. The league took the franchise over and the fate of the ballclub was uncertain, but then the Boston

Red Sox stepped in and bought the franchise, assuring that there would still be San Francisco Seals in1956. Also, the action by the Red Sox was supposedly to protect San Francisco for the American League in the case of expansion or relocation.

To recap the 1955 season, Seattle won the pennant by three games over San Diego, with Hollywood and Los Angeles another game back, tied for third. If there was any consolation for the Seals, they finished three games ahead of their rival Oaks, who were seventh in their last season in the Bay Area.

In addition to Singleton and Righetti, other former Seals around the league included Bill Werle (17–8, 3.54), who came back from the major leagues to be Portland's ace; Joe Brovia (19-73-.325), at Oakland, who finally made it to the major leagues briefly with Cincinnati; Jackie Tobin (.270) with Sacramento; George Vico (.282) with Hollywood; 1946 hero Larry Jansen (7–7, 3.34) with Seattle; and Ray Orteig (.296), also with Seattle. And Al Lyons, still with San Diego, hit poorly but was primarily a pitcher, winning 10 and losing only 5.

TED BEARD
Seals 1954–1955

At 5'8" and 165 pounds, one would not expect much power from Ted Beard, but he could hit a ball as far as anybody could. An excellent center fielder and exceptional base runner, he provided the Seals with a lot of their home run production in his two years with the club. In 1954, he led the team with 11 round-trippers.

Acquired from the Hollywood Stars early in the 1954 season, Beard had been around for several years and he provided a veteran influence for the "Kiddie Car Express," as the youthful Seals were called that year. Earlier in his Coast League career, he hit four consecutive home runs in a game and in 1953 had 12 consecutive hits over a five-game period, tying the PCL record set in 1930 by Mickey Heath. These feats were done when he was with the Stars.

Today he is remembered as an Indianapolis Indian more than anything else. He spent all or parts of 13 seasons with that team, and he spent parts of seven years in the major leagues.

BK: You had been around for a number of years before joining the Seals. How did they acquire you?

TED BEARD: I was with Hollywood and they had an extra outfielder and San Francisco wanted an outfielder and they made a deal. They just sold me outright. I was there two years.

BK: Talk about Seals Stadium.

TB: It was a wet place, cold and wet at night. But otherwise, it was a nice playing field. They kept the grounds up good. I enjoyed the park.

BK: How were you originally signed and by whom?

TB: I went to a baseball school in Frederick, Maryland. The Pittsburgh Pirates had one. I went in there and they signed me up out of that school. That was in 1942.

BK: You split several seasons between Pittsburgh and Indianapolis. What was going on there?

Ted Beard (courtesy Doug McWilliams).

TB: Pittsburgh had the old-time ballplayers and they wanted those, like Dixie Walker and Wally Westlake and Ralph Kiner and Johnny Hopp. They were more interested in the old-timers.

BK: Were you still Pittsburgh property when you went to the Coast League?

TB: Yes. I went to Hollywood, California, and I liked that. We had a good ballclub; we won the pennant both years I was there. I was owned by Hollywood at the time of my sale to San Francisco.

BK: You were not a big man. Where did you get your power?

TB: [Laughs] I don't have any idea.

Talking about power, Ralph Kiner used a heavy bat — 42 ounces — and I liked those bats because you'd stick that bat out there and that ball'd jump off of that heavy bat. They put me in to pinch hit in Brooklyn one day against Don Newcombe. Newcombe could throw hard. I took Kiner's 42-ounce bat up and the first one he fired by me I didn't get the bat started in time. The next one I got my bat out there and hung a line drive off the right field wall. That ball really jumped off that Kiner bat.

BK: When you left the Seals you went back to Indianapolis again. Were you Pittsburgh property?

TB: No. I was Indianapolis property then.

BK: You were up and down with the White Sox for a couple of years.

TB: I was too damn dumb. When I went to the White Sox I tried to hit the ball so hard that I'd take my eye off when I started to swing and I was too dumb to know it at that time. It was nothing but my fault, nobody else's. It's important to watch that ball. You can't hit it if you don't see it.

BK: In your first year in San Francisco the team got off to a horrid start and then you guys turned it around.

TB: Things just started clicking a little bit. I think we finished fourth. San Francisco didn't have their good quality players when I was there, any top-notch ones.

BK: Tommy Heath was your manager.

TB: I liked him real well. Tommy managed Minneapolis when I was playing in Indianapolis for a while. I knew him before I went out there.

I'd like to tell you a little story about Tommy Heath. Tommy was the manager. We were playing in Portland and a black umpire — not Emmett Ashford — throwed him out of the game one night. When Tom took the lineup to the plate the next day, this black umpire said, "Now, this is a new day. Let bygones be bygones."

Tom said, "I'm not mad at you. I'm mad at those other two guys."

The umpire said, "What other two guys?"

Tom said, "Branch Rickey and Abraham Lincoln." [Laughs]

That Tommy was quite comical.

BK: Gene Bearden was the Seals' top pitcher in 1955.

TB: Yeah. Gene was a nice guy. I liked Gene.

Moran was second base and then we had Righetti at short, Cheso at third. Righetti did a good job at short, I thought. Chuck Stevens come up from Hollywood, too, that year. It was a separate deal. He was a good pinch hitter. Whenever they'd put him in to pinch it, he got a basehit, seemed like.

John Ritchey was a nice-looking ballplayer. I liked him. He was a nice little ballplayer. Nini Tornay was the other catcher. Sal Taormina was there quite a while. I guess he just didn't have the ability to go any higher.

Elmer Singleton done a good job. Adrian Zabala and Bob Muncrief relieved. Al Lyons was getting over the hill at that time. I remember Lowell Creighton was there, but I can't remember much about him. Ewell

Blackwell could still bring it pretty good. I liked him. [Laughs] Bill Bradford, I liked him.

BK: The Seals always had a reputation for paying well. Were you paid well?

TB: Yes. They paid me a little better than Hollywood.

BK: Why did you leave the Seals?

TB: I had a bad year in '55 and the Red Sox took over and they didn't want me because I was up in years so Indianapolis took me back.

BK: Is there a game that stands out in your career?

TB: In Pittsburgh I hit the ball over the roof in Forbes Field. [Laughs] I was the second man to do it. Babe Ruth done it in the last game he played there. The pitcher was Bob Hall, Boston Braves.

In San Diego I hit four home runs the first four times at bat in a game. I was with Hollywood.

BK: Did you enjoy your baseball career?

TB: *AB*-solutely! I remember one time it was so hot. The clubhouse had no air conditioning. We were just sweating and we needed to take a shower. The guy sitting next to me said, "Boy, I'll be glad when this season is over, won't you?" I said, "No. I hope it never ends." [Laughs]

BK: You played a long time.

TB: 1942 to '63, but then I lost three years to the military, 1943, '44, and '45. I played ball in Hawaii, Philippines.

In Hawaii I played against Joe DiMaggio. In the outfield they didn't have any fences and DiMaggio hit three balls so far back and I went back and caught all three of 'em. [Laughs] The guys told me after the game, "DiMaggio's so mad he won't even talk to anybody." [Laughs] He really clobbered those balls.

BK: Who was the best player you saw?

TB: Hitters—my favorite was Ted Williams. DiMaggio was next, I believe.

I'll tell you what, I don't like a fielder who wins the Gold Glove. Usually they can't cover any ground. I'll take the guy that makes errors and beats you every time. He beats the Gold Glove guys.

I don't call it baseball anymore. I call it "diveball." If you can't dive, you can't play. Infielders won't move over in front of a ball; they just stand there and dive. Too much diving.

BK: Talk about pitching.

TB: Back then they had to go nine innings.

You talk about stretching your arms, there for years I played with a bad shoulder. My shoulder ached winter and summer. One day I went out there and I throwed batting practice for two hours—didn't quit. And you know, the shoulder hasn't ached since.

BK: What do you think of today's salaries?

TB: That's unbelievable. My top salary was 10,000 with the White Sox. But I loved it, even without a million dollars

CRAMER THEODORE BEARD
Born January 7, 1921, Woodsboro, MD
Ht. 5'8" Wt. 165 Batted and Threw Left
Outfielder

Year	Team, Lg	G	AB	R	H	2B	3B	HR	RBI	BA
1942	Hrrsbrg, InSt	20	54	9	14	2	1	1	4	.259
	Hrnell, PONY							9	43	.240
1943–45					military service					
1946	York, InSt	125	403	127	132	24	13	12	75	.328
1947	York, InSt	123	423	99	138	27	12	14	81	.326
	Albany, EL							0	3	.143
	Indnpls, AA							0	0	.000
1948	Indnpls, AA	142	511	131	154	31	17	7	63	.301
	Pitts., NL	25	81	15	16	1	3	0	7	.198
1949	Indnpls, AA	127	426	108	118	17	16	5	40	.277
	Pitts., NL	14	24	1	2	0	0	0	1	.083
1950	Indnpls, AA	29	107	15	25	7	1	0	2	.234
	Pitts., NL	61	177	32	41	6	2	4	12	.232
1951	Indnpls, AA	117	396	101	108	17	9	8	30	.273
	Pitts., NL	22	48	7	9	1	0	1	3	.188
1952	Pitts., NL	15	44	5	8	2	1	0	3	.182
	Hwd., PCL	127	390	75	105	17	8	11	53	.269
1953	Hwd., PCL	134	402	91	115	13	13	17	60	.286
1954	Hwd/SF,PCL	160	563	104	169	35	5	11	62	.300
1955	SF, PCL	159	522	91	128	15	8	8	34	.245
1956	Indnpls, AA	116	256	56	70	11	5	7	36	.270
1957	Indnpls, AA	96	349	91	121	20	12	10	50	.347
	Chicago, AL	39	78	15	16	1	0	0	7	.205
1958	Indnpls, AA	123	414	81	120	18	5	5	31	.290
	Chicago, AL	19	22	5	2	0	0	1	2	.091
1959	Indnpls, AA	102	290	44	73	7	4	2	22	.252
1960		115	348	55	90	11	7	1	24	.259
1961		4	6	0	1	0	0	0	0	.167
1962		2	2	0	0	0	0	0	0	.000
1963		2	4	0	0	0	0	0	0	.000

Stolen bases (totals for all teams each year): 1942—1, 1946—17, 1947—33, 1948—14, 1949—23, 1950—4, 1951—17, 1952—26, 1953—21, 1954—30, 1955—13, 1956—11, 1957—13, 1958—21, 1959—9, 1960—12, 1961—0, 1962—0, 1963—0.

CHUCK STEVENS
Seals 1954–1955

It must have been late in the 1954 season, but I won't swear to it. My stepfather and I were at Seals Stadium watching the Seals play the San Diego Padres. We were sitting a few rows behind the first base — the visitors' — dugout. My stepfather pointed to the Seals' first baseman, a new guy whom I didn't recognize. "Watch him," he told me. "Why?" I asked. "Because he can really field," he replied.

So I watched him. Even to a kid's eye, he was graceful and agile. The most impressive play of the day occurred somewhere in the middle of the game. Dick Sisler, hero of the 1950 Phillies' Whiz Kids who, in '54, was San Diego's first baseman, singled off the Seals' pitcher. I think it was Elmer Singleton.

Chuck Stevens with the St. Louis Browns in the mid 1940s (author's collection).

Sisler was on first. The Seals' first sacker moved to the bag to hold him on. Sisler took a modest lead. The pitcher threw over to first and Dick got back easily.

He took his lead again. The pitcher threw over once more, but turning much more quickly and throwing much harder this time. The impressive part was the move by the first baseman. He caught the ball in his glove hand — his right — about waist high and slapped it down on the bag so fast that you almost thought he had to be moving it before the ball got to him. Sisler moved quickly, too, but when his extended, diving right hand reached for the base, the ball and glove were already there.

I can still see Sisler to this day standing up, brushing himself off, and walking back to the first base dugout. No argument, but he wasn't happy. "Son of a bitch!" was how he expressed his displeasure.

The Seals' first baseman was Chuck Stevens. He had just been acquired from the Hollywood Stars. I saw him several more times over the next year or so and he really was a magician around the bag. I don't remember his hitting, but almost every time I went to a game he did something great in the field.

I didn't know it then, but that was nearing the end of Stevens' career. A few years later, he began another career: he worked for the Association of Professional Ball Players of America, aiding retired players—major or minor league—in times of need.

BK: You played professionally for 18 seasons. Who signed you and when?

CHUCK STEVENS: I signed in 1937 out of Long Beach, California, and was signed by a scout named Willis Butler. He lived in northern California, around San Francisco, but at that time very few organizations had more than one or two scouts in an area, so he covered the entire coast.

From there, I signed a contract and went to spring training with the San Antonio Missions, which was a member of the Texas League, saw spring training there, and then was sent to North Carolina to the Coastal Plains League. That was my first year. Each year I'd move up a classification or so.

BK: By 1941 you were playing for the Browns. Do you recall your first game [September 16, 1941]?

CS: As I remember, I think the first ballgame I played was in Washington against the old Senators and it seems to me I was batting third in the lineup and I hit a ball up against the right field fence. As I remember, it was off Early Wynn. At that time, Early was just beginning to get established, too. It ended up a triple, only I missed second base. I never will forget Cal Hubbard—later we'd become good friends—and when they called me out, old Cal said to me, "Son, up here you have to touch all the bases." I thought that was funny. I think that was the first ballgame. It was either there or Cleveland against Feller. If that was my first ballgame, I walked up there and, as I remember, looked at three straight.

BK: Where were you in 1942?

CS: I was with Toledo in the American Association. That was the Browns' Triple-A ballclub. Then I was in the service for three years. I played ball, but you don't play that much.

BK: When you came out, you stepped right into the Browns' starting lineup.

CS: That's right. I played for the Browns who didn't have a really good year. I don't know that any of the guys coming back had real good years. Not good enough to stay, really, because the next year I think I was back in Toledo, then in '48 I was back with the Browns.

BK: Your reputation was as an outstanding defensive first baseman.

CS: Right. I led every league I ever played in in fielding.

BK: In 1948 with the Browns, you were as good a hitter as Hank Arft and a better fielder, yet you guys split the time at first. What was going on?

CS: As I remember, when I was waived out of the American League, I think I was leading first basemen in hitting. Maybe one other guy was hitting more than I was. They just wanted to make a change. There was no explanation. They brought Hank Arft up there and he lasted that summer and that was it, I think, with him.

You've got a bad ballclub and you've got to satisfy a lot of people and I guess they felt I wasn't getting the job done. At that time, you've gotta remember that they expected power from first and third base and, say, one of the outfielders — guys that had to really furnish the sock. Well, you know, in my best years I only hit 10 or 12 home runs and it just wasn't enough, I suspect. They probably figured Hank Arft had more power than I did. He did not.

As a matter of fact, I left the ballclub. They wanted me to go to San Antonio. They had a chance to win a pennant down there and they thought if I'd go down there and join the club for the last month, or whatever it was, of the season that they could win it. I refused to go. I came home. I loaded my wife and daughter up in our car and I drove back to Long Beach.

They were on the phone continually and I said, "I won't go. Sell me." So they sold me to the Hollywood Stars. I joined the Hollywood ballclub the last month of the 1948 season. I guess it was a month; it may have been less. I played two or three series and ended up hitting well — .300 or .320 or something like that — for the time that I played there.

In the meantime, in '49 they signed Fred Haney to manage the ballclub. Well, I'd played several years for Fred in Toledo. He knew what I could do; as a matter of fact, he used to call me "Across the Boards." I'd hit .290, .295, drive in 70, 80, 90 runs — that kind of thing. That was his nickname for me.

I was there until '54. I went to San Francisco mid-year or a little later and I was in San Francisco '54 and '55. I was a player-coach at San Francisco in '55 for Tommy Heath, then in '56 they wanted me to manage so I managed in the Western League. I managed Amarillo, Texas; won the pennant down there and then Heath contacted me. He left San Francisco and went to Sacramento and wanted me to come over there as a player-coach, which I did. And that was my last year.

BK: I vaguely remember you with the Solons. How did you do?

CS: I didn't play too much and didn't hit much. I don't think I had 30 appearances. We didn't have a real good ballclub.

I considered in many ways that Tommy Heath was the best manager I ever saw. In many areas. He was a great handler of pitching and I figured he could teach me a lot because it doesn't take a Fullbright candidate to realize that Sacramento wasn't gonna be in the thick of things. You don't voluntarily join a ballclub like that knowing it's not going anyplace, but it was worth a gamble for me because I wanted to be around Heath and see what I could learn there.

BK: Were there management opportunities?

CS: Yeah. As a matter of fact, I had agreed, verbally, to manage a Coast League ballclub when the majors moved out there. I was gonna manage the San Francisco ballclub.

There were several of us on that roster that, when they moved — remember, Boston moved in there with a working agreement — and there were several of us that apparently others wanted. I know they wanted me to report to Louisville, Kentucky, and I refused to go and ended up buying my contract from Louisville so I could manage. They would not release me.

I guess that was the end of the '56 year I had to buy that contract to manage. In '56, Joe Gordon came in with Boston. During the winter ['55–'56], I received notification that I was sold, I guess, to Louisville in the American Association. They owned my contract. I said that I would not report and in the meantime, the opportunity to manage presented itself. Buck Fausett — do you remember that name? — contacted me and, to take that manager's job, I had to buy my contract. *Very* unfair.

There were some longtime friends of mine — that I *thought* were friends of mine — that hung me out to dry in that area and I've never forgiven 'em for that.

I left [professional baseball] at the end of the '57 season, the year that I was with Sacramento.

BK: What did you go into at that time?

CS: I went for a couple of years into private industry. We were industrial acidizers; in other words, we acidized oil wells and power plants and that kind of thing. I worked for 'em for a year and the general manager died of a heart attack and I was appointed as the general manager. In the meantime, he left a widow and a couple of kids. We were the only licensee with Dow Chemical in the western part of the United States, so we engineered a sale and we got out of that business.

While we were negotiating that sale — it was finalized, but we were still operating — I got a phone call from Chicago wanting to know if I'd be interested in this job. That call was from Clarence Rowland, who then was the vice-president with the Chicago Cubs. It came on a Sunday night and I remember we had a whole house full of people — we had had a dinner — and this phone call came and they wanted to know if I was interested. The job had been vacant for a year, year-and-a-half.

BK: So you've been working for old ballplayers ever since. It's a good cause.

CS: Yeah. I felt that it was then and I still do. It was badly needed in our day. In another ten years it will not be as important as it has been in the past because of the money that they're making. There will always be a need because, I suspect, of the minor league structure. They haven't done anything about protecting them.

BK: Back to your playing days. What was your best game or biggest thrill?

CS: I had a lot of 'em. 'Course, my first five-hit ballgame — it seems to me it was in Philadelphia against the A's — that was a big day. But I think the one that stands out in my mind was, we're playing Los Angeles in Hollywood and I got hot during the week and I drove in a whole bunch of runs and was in a big hitting streak. We ended that series and went to Oakland and I got a couple of basehits there for 12 straight basehits. I'd driven in a lot of runs. I'd hit two home runs with the bases loaded and that kind of thing. That was 1951 maybe.

BK: Who was the best player you saw?

CS: I think the all-around best player that I played against was [Joe] DiMaggio. Williams was certainly in the league, but Williams defensively was not the same ballplayer that Joe was and Joe could outrun him and out-throw him.

Let's turn this around a little bit and put DiMaggio in that Boston ballpark. Wonder what would have happened?

BK: But if you do that, you're putting Williams in Yankee Stadium with a shorter right field.

CS: That could be, but how much did Williams hit in that ballpark, that's the thing. It might have been awesome; you don't know. It's all supposition on our part, but Joe still hit .340, .345 and he's hitting in an airport. *Plus* the fact that he's winning — that's the important thing. The other guy's having great years and not taking anything away from him, but you've gotta go with a guy that's on the constant winners. That's what I go by — who's winning and who's losing.

BK: The Yankees always had the better pitching, but, as you say, winning is what pays the bills.

CS: That's right. And I think it's important when you look at a guy, say, is he a winning ballplayer or is he not a winning ballplayer? I'm not inferring that Ted Williams was a losing ballplayer. I don't mean that at all, but you gotta look at New York and look at what that club did while he [DiMaggio] was there. Man, it's *awesome!*

BK: You mentioned Joe Gordon earlier. Talk about winning ballplayers; the Yankees won when he was there and when he was traded to Cleveland, all of a sudden the Indians were winners.

CS: That's exactly right. Joe and I were close friends. We ended up in the service together and we were buddy-buddies and stayed in close touch after the war. He was the kinda guy that you loved. He was loosey-goosey and he knew how to play. He could make plays that were unbelievable and could get you out of a jam defensively and you make a mistake on him and he's gonna take you out in the parking lot. He's the kinda guy that really knew how to win and was great for the morale of a ballclub.

BK: I don't recall who told me, but it was a pitcher. He said he knew Gordon was batting .270 or .280, but he'd rather have anyone else in the league up in a crucial situation because with the game on the line, Gordon was a .400 hitter.

CS: Yeah, that's right. He may have been only hitting .270, but it was the stoutest .270 you ever saw because he hit a lot of home runs, he drove in a lot of runs, and just think what he could do with a glove.

One time we were playing in the service and Joe was playing second base and I was playing first base. Somebody — a pretty good ballplayer, but I don't know who it was now — said, "When you two guys are playing out there, you need a license to hit one through the hole." You know, if he's not diving getting it I am. It was interesting. I had never thought about it, but we pretty well had that side covered.

Joe was not a gazelle. Joe was *not* real, real fast and he made up for that by being in the right spot and diving and doing everything in the world to beat you. He was a great infielder.

BK: Hall of Fame?

CS: In my mind, if there are some guys that are in that Hall of Fame, Joe belongs in. Joe Cronin once told me that, in his mind, it would be important, when you look at a candidate for the Hall of Fame, that they be four-dimensional. I thought, Man, that makes a lot of sense. These are the qualities Joe said that for those voting — and Joe was in the Hall of Fame at the time — that it would be important to look at the ability to run and to field, throw, and hit.

BK: There are a lot of bats in there with nothing else attached.

CS: Yeah. I guess that's what he was talking about. It made a lot of sense to me.

I look back at guys I played with, there was a kid and we went to high school together. We were good friends, we roomed together. Vern Stephens. Vern was a shortstop that drove in 150 runs. I questioned somebody one time about it; I said, "You know, you're evaluating guys," and they said, "Well, he wasn't around long enough." Well, I think he was there 12 or 13 years. What the hell do you have to do? Over 200 home runs, nearly 1200 RBIs—as a shortstop! And he's never even been considered.

One time a fellow said to me, "Yeah, but he didn't take care of himself." And I said, "Yeah, that's right. So he liked to have a toddy once in a while. That would not be acceptable in the Hall of Fame because Babe Ruth and all those guys were from the health camp." That was the *dumbest* statement I ever heard. I'm not saying it because I knew Vern, but I just look at some of the figures, some of the stats that are in there and a guy like this should be there.

BK: And he was a good fielder. Not an Ozzie Smith, but good nonetheless.

CS: He had a hell of an arm and he covered a lot of ground. That's just my personal feeling.

BK: Who was the best pitcher?

CS: There were so many. I personally felt that Spud Chandler was virtually impossible for me. Bob Lemon was real tough. Hal Newhouser. Jim Wilson had great stuff, I thought. Later he was with Baltimore. He pitched against us in the minor leagues. He had some good years. And Early was a hell of a pitcher. There were a lot of 'em. Mel Parnell. These guys were all good pitchers. Some of 'em you hit a little dab and others were virtually impossible.

BK: Someone said you can count the good pitchers of today on one hand, but back in your day every team had two or three top ones.

CS: You want a nightmare? Get off the train in Cleveland for a four-game series or three-game series. Holy smoke, these guys'd dazzle you to death! You get a Gene Bearden or somebody like that, it was like a day off. And then you'd go to Detroit and you could get some b-b tossers over there and then you'd go to New York.

The most interesting thing; I was talking to a guy that works as a special assignment fellow on the major league level, and it doesn't do any good to use his name 'cause he might not care for that. He said, talking about the rabbit ball today, he said, "There's no rabbit ball. There's just no pitching." And I thought that's probably the truth. This is a guy that every night he's looking at big league ballclubs. I thought that was a heck of an observation. I'd certainly go along with it 'cause he sees a million ballgames a year.

BK: Did you save souvenirs from your career?

CS: Very few. It wasn't a big deal. Unless early on you had a house, you kinda kept things in trunks and then somebody'd come along and want something and you'd give it to him or her, if they happened to be fans. That happened to me a lot. I do have three grandsons and they have some great things that I've managed to save over the years.

BK: Today the guys save everything.

CS: Of course. They are *aware* of them. We were not aware of the potential. I get phone calls often, wanting to know if I have a St. Louis Browns uniform and I guess you could name your own price. But I don't have and doubt whether I'd sell it even if I did have.

BK: Do you get much fan mail?

CS: Yeah. You're not a high-profile ballplayer, but again, we're talking about autograph people. Today, I got two pictures of me in a Browns uniform in Shibe Park in Philadelphia. I've never seen the pictures before. They're press pictures. On the back, it says a guy named Connolly was the photographer, Shibe Park, and it was 4-30-46, and it says, "Chuck Stevens, new first baseman," but I have never seen the pictures before. As a matter of fact, I put 'em in my briefcase to take 'em home to show Mrs. Stevens how I looked when I was young. [Laughs]

I sign 'em the day I get 'em and send 'em back. Incidentally, a lot of guys get criticized for charging for autographs. I think I oughtta tell you now, Bob Lemon, Early Wynn, Johnny Vander Meer, *Dominic*—and I emphasize Dominic — DiMaggio — all of the money that they got for autographs they sent to the Association.

BK: A modest charge for a good cause is reasonable. Some of the high-profile players are probably overwhelmed with autograph requests.

CS: Oh, they are! I know that for a fact. Where we get, say, a couple hundred a year, they get probably a couple thousand. They're liable to get a request from one guy for ten. You know damn well he's selling 'em.

When I was involved with the national old-timers game, that Cracker Jacks series, the [hotel] lobby was just full of people. You couldn't get across the lobby 'cause we had all the old stars there. If I signed one for some guys, I signed ten different things. They'd come back like they never saw you before, "Would you sign this?" Hell, you're signing for some guys to sell. It doesn't bother me 'cause I don't get that many, but some of these Hall of Famers, they drive 'em crazy.

BK: Regrets?

CS: My regret — that I wasn't able to play in the major leagues another five or six years. I was privileged to have played there and *knew* I could play in the major leagues, but just happened to be on a ballclub that could afford not to have me furnishing 15 or 20 home runs. I'm sure I could've played in the major leagues for years.

BK: That's a fair and honest regret and appraisal. The Browns had to get everything they could.

CS: Yeah, that's right. I'm certainly not bad-mouthing the Browns 'cause that's who gave me the opportunity, but they couldn't afford the luxury of a guy who could hit .275, .280 in the major leagues and drive in some runs, but I couldn't hit the home runs. I was not what they needed at that time.

BK: Would you go back and play ball again?

CS: Yeah, I would. I enjoyed every minute of it. There were disappointments. That was one of 'em. I was lucky. I was never injured badly — you know, hit with pitches and stuff like that. I have nothing but the greatest thankfulness of being involved with baseball. I don't think baseball owes me a living. Never have.

CHARLES AUGUSTUS STEVENS
Born July 10,1918, Van Houten, NM
Ht. 6'1" Wt. 180 Batted Both, Threw Left
First baseman

Year	Team, Lg	G	AB	R	H	2B	3B	HR	RBI	BA
1937	Wmstn, CP	97	358	16	103	9	8	10	51	.288
1938	Jhnstwn, MA	128	469	69	136	30	5	7	56	.290
	Sprngfld, III		no record listed							
1939	Sprngfld, III	119	443	79	140	24	6	5	74	.316
1940	SanAntno, Tx	158	576	71	158	30	6	5	67	.264
1941	Toledo, AA	145	558	74	162	19	6	5	72	.290
	StL, AL	4	13	2	2	0	0	0	2	.154
1942	Toledo, AA	147	532	69	133	16	11	8	84	.250
1943–45		military service								
1946	StL, AL	122	432	53	107	17	4	3	27	.248
1947	Toledo, AA	141	434	78	135	21	5	7	55	.279
1948	StL, AL	85	288	34	75	12	4	1	26	.260
	Hwd, PCL	38	140	13	45	10	2	1	19	.321
1949	Hwd, PCL	183	679	121	202	41	4	10	82	.297
1950		171	605	103	174	28	3	12	82	.288
1951		144	489	81	143	26	6	10	67	.292
1952		142	490	63	136	31	7	2	57	.278
1953		108	274	36	63	11	3	5	35	.230

Year	Team, Lg	G	AB	R	H	2B	3B	HR	RBI	BA
1954	Hwd/SF, PCL	78	132	15	32	5	2	2	23	.242
1955	SF, PCL	83	252	25	59	11	1	5	29	.234
1956	Amarillo, WL	98	305	71	102	18	1	12	67	.335
1957	Sac, PCL	25	21	0	3	0	0	0	2	.143

♦ CHAPTER 12 ♦

1956:
The Red Sox Move In

6th place: W 77 L 88 .467 28½ GB

The old saying "A new broom sweeps clean" was never more applicable. The parent Boston Red Sox fielded a new Seals team in 1956.

There were strong San Francisco ties in the new front office. Joe Cronin, the Red Sox general manager, was a native San Franciscan and he named Jerry Donovan, another native of the city who had most recently been president of the California League, president of the Seals. And the man chosen to manage in 1956 was another San Francisco product: Eddie Joost, who was also still able to play.

But the players from 1955 were scattered to the four winds. Mike Baxes, Dave Melton, and Bill Bradford were in Kansas City, but only briefly for Melton and Bradford. Don Fracchia and Jim Moran went to Seattle. Manager Tommy Heath took over in Sacramento and with him went Gene Bearden and Maurice Fisher. Buffalo ended up with Steve Nagy, Jim Walsh, and Bill Serena. Walt Judnich and Reno Cheso, only 26 years old, retired. Cheso had been assigned to Louisville before deciding to call it quits, but Tony Ponce accepted his Louisville assignment.

Only three 1955 Seals were still 1956 Seals: Sal Taormina, Bob DiPietro, and Nini Tornay.

Except for the couple of years on Maui at Paul Fagan's ranch, the Seals had never had spring training out of California. In 1956 they trained with the Red Sox in Florida. The team didn't appear in San Francisco until April 8, two days before Opening Day.

Opening Day attendance was excellent, in excess of 14,000, as the fans were eager to see the new faces. Somehow it seemed to fit: the Opening

1956 Opening Day lineup. *Left to right:* Albie Pearson, rf; Harry Malmberg, ss; Grady Hatton, 3b; Bill Renna, lf; Frank Kellert, 1b; Pumpsie Green, cf; Haywood Sullivan, lf; Ed Sadowksi, c; Earl Wilson, p.

Day opponents were the Vancouver Mounties, nee Oakland Oaks, managed by Lefty O'Doul. These were not the same old Oaks; housecleaning, although not as extensive as in San Francisco, had occurred there, too. Instead of young Red Sox, there were fledging Baltimore Orioles.

The "new look" Seals had DiPietro (11-60-.268) at first base, and Sal Taormina (13-56-.298) had arguably his best season in the outfield. Nothing else was even remotely similar to the Seals of 1955. Larry DiPippo (10-45-.250), a young slugger who had trouble making contact, backed up DiPietro.

Taking over for Moran at second base was Ken Aspromonte (3-42-.281), one of Boston's prize youngsters. Replacing Baxes and Cheso at third base was Joe Tanner (8-37-.281) initially, then Frank Malzone (6-42-.296), who had a family loss, came down and replaced Tanner, who became the utility infielder. Malzone tells what happened: "That winter my daughter, our first child, passed away ... and I was just all fouled up that spring ... when I got out to California, it took us almost a week before I got to playing the way I was capable of playing. I finished strong ... Joe Gordon was the manager at the time and he was a good man to play for. He kind of stayed with me...." The shortstop was Jim Mahoney (3-37-.228), an outstanding fielder who never hit.

Beyond Taormina in the outfield were a couple of veterans and a couple of prospects. Five-year major league veteran Don Lenhardt opened in left field and was leading the team in home runs (16) and RBIs (49) with a .299 average at midseason when his leg was broken. It ended his season and he retired at the end of the year. Defensive gem Tommy Umphlett (5-61-.285) played center field and had one of the best years of his career with the bat. Speedy Gordie Windhorn (8-45-.307) and super prospect Marty Keough (9-30-.315), who missed much of the season with injuries, filled out the outer defense.

Another top prospect, Haywood Sullivan (11-77-.296), started the season in Boston but was sent down and became the number one catcher. He was backed by Eddie Sadowski (7-24-.235), leaving little playing time for Tornay (0-6-.163 in only 43 at bats).

The pitching staff contained no familiar faces. Hard-throwing and hard-hitting Jerry Casale (19–11, 4.10) was the ace. He hit one of the longest home runs ever seen in Seals Stadium. The ball went out just to the right of dead center, cleared the street, and landed on the embankment on the other side of the street.

The rest of the staff was iffy. Russ Kemmerer (12–14, 3.48) was the most effective of the others. The unrelated southpaw Smith boys (Robert W. "Riverboat" and Robert G.) were 9–10, 4.44 and 8–11m 4.38, respectively. The bullpen contained Bill Henry (4–5, 4.23), Eli Grba (7–4, 4.82), and old-timer Max Surkont (4–6, 2.38). All of these would pitch or had pitched in the majors with varying degrees of success.

The Seals played decently, hovering around .500 well into June, but then embarked on a nine-game losing streak. Joost had been having trouble with his fiery temperament. He had been ejected several times, and suspended, and Johnny Murphy, the farm director of the Red Sox, was unhappy with both him and the way the team was playing and the losing streak didn't help.

The uneasiness between Joost and Murphy came to a head early in July. Joost was playing third base and thought he had tagged a runner out, but the umpire saw it differently. After an argument, Joost was ejected. He took the ball he still held and threw it completely out of Seals Stadium.

Murphy fired him and replaced him with Joe Gordon, who guided the club home in sixth place.

All in all, it was not a successful PCL debut for the Red Sox. They had not been aware of the strength of the league and failed to man the club properly. As the team continued to play uninspired ball late into the season, the attendance tailed off. The final count was slightly over 183,000, up from 1955 but not up enough to show a profit. It was a losing season both at the gate and on the field.

The 1956 season belonged to the Los Angeles Angels, who walked home 16 games ahead of second place Seattle. MVP Steve Bilko (55-164-.360) won the Triple Crown and five other Angels belted 20 or more home runs. Portland finished third, 21 games back and two games ahead of fourth place Hollywood. Tommy Heath brought his Sacramento Solons in fifth, five and a half games ahead of San Francisco, followed by San Diego in seventh and O'Doul's Vancouver Mounties in eighth, 38½ games behind Los Angeles.

Manager Joe Gordon, who took over in mid-season (courtesy Robert Zwissig).

Seattle was well represented by ex–Seals. Elmer Singleton was 18–8, 2.58; Don Fracchia won 10, Larry Jansen won 11, and Leo Righetti (0-40-.280) had another good year at short, as did Ray Orteig (9-53-.278) behind the plate. Bill Werle won 16 for Portland, Bearden won 15 and Jackie Tobin batted .283 for Sacramento, and Jim Westlake went 10-59-.246 for Vancouver.

BOB DIPIETRO

Seals 1954–1957

Bob DiPietro was a native San Franciscan who did not sign originally with the Seals. The Boston Red Sox laid claim to his talents first and he had seven professional seasons, including a cup of coffee with Boston, before he became a member of his hometown team. When he did, he was owned by the Seals and no longer a member of the Boston organization, but after two years the Red Sox took over the operation of the Seals and he was right back where he started from: a Boston farmhand.

In his three full seasons as a Seal, he was one of the most popular members of the team, due in part to his San Francisco roots; in part, he claims, to the fact that he comes from a large family; and in largest part to his hustling play and great attitude. In 1955 he was on his way to a season that would have put him back in the major leagues when a broken leg ended his year early. He was leading the PCL in batting with a .371 average when the injury laid him up.

BK: How were you originally signed and by whom?

BOB DiPIETRO: I was signed by Charlie Walgren, who was a scout for the Boston Red Sox. He was a great guy, a

Bob DiPietro (courtesy Richard T. Dobbins collection).

wonderful guy. I had some great moments with Charlie, who loved to sing. He and I got to know each other and we used to sing as we drove around prior to when I signed with him. I went in the service in 1946 and then my dad died in 1947. The war was over at that point, so I got out on a dependency discharge and signed right after that and went to the Boston affiliate in San Jose. That was in '47. I played there a year and then went to Scranton and played there. Then Birmingham for a year, then Louisville, and then in '52, I believe it was, I went to spring training with the Red Sox under Lou Boudreau. They brought me up at the end of '51.

They sold me to Shreveport, which was *not* a Boston affiliate, and I got a penicillin reaction. The deal evidently hinged on my making that ball-club and I couldn't play and they sent me back to the Red Sox. I went back to Birmingham then for the balance of that season.

I lived in San Francisco—I was born and raised there — and it was in

'53 they sold me to San Francisco [for 1954], then I was out of the Red Sox organization, which was a blessing. If I was ever gonna make it, I had to be out of there. They were playing with just no room on that ballclub. They had, individually, the best team in baseball, I think. Collectively, they couldn't beat the Yankees, but they also had a heck of a time gelling as a ballclub. But they had Vern Stephens, Pesky, Doerr, DiMaggio, Williams—all those guys. At that time, Yawkey paid very good salaries because each one individually had some pretty good stats, but as a ballclub they just never could beat the Yankees.

One of the highlights of my time there that year that I went up at the end of the season was when we played the Yankees in Yankee Stadium and I was allowed to play. I'm in the Hall of Fame, I guess you know that. They figured as long as I was up there they might as well let the kid play. Allie Reynolds pitched a no-hitter and they took the pitching rubber from Yankee Stadium and had everybody that had played — everybody on both ballclubs—sign that, then they put that in the Hall of Fame. [Laughs]

It was great. You talk about thrills. Here's this wide-eyed, open-mouthed kid in Yankee Stadium, of all places, and Reynolds had to get Williams out for the final out. He pops him up right behind home plate, not where Yogi had to flip his mask off and run back to the screen, but he's *right there.* Reynolds comes roaring off the mound and is standing almost right at home plate when Berra drops the ball in foul territory. So he's gotta go back out there and get Williams out again, which is tough enough the first time but two times in five minutes is kind of a heroic request. He popped him up again and Berra made a hell of a catch over by the dugout — a one-handed, sliding catch — which vindicated his having dropped the first one. I thought Reynolds was gonna kill him. That was the highlight of being there.

In one of the games, I played right field in Yankee Stadium. My claim to fame is that I threw out Mickey Mantle at home plate. Hence, the Italian-based moniker "The Rigatoni Rifle."

On my first and only trip to Fenway Park to join the Red Sox, I was sitting in the dugout watching, along with the other rookies as the game against the Yankees progressed. The then manager of the Sox, McCarthy, called out a name which nobody recognized and told that person to pinch hit for Dominic DiMaggio. Since we didn't know to whom he was referring, we all just sat. Al Richter, another rook who had come up with me, said, "Hey, I think he means you!" The fact that he didn't know who I was seemed to be a pretty good indication that I was not going to be a permanent fixture on his team.

Needless to say, I was pretty excited and after having corrected his pronunciation of a fine old Italian name, I went to get a bat and suddenly realized I didn't bring one with me. Fortunately, some fella shoved a bat at me and said, "Here, kid, take my bat." It was Ted Williams. I could just barely squeak out a thanks and took off for the batter's box. I was about halfway there when it came to me. *What if I break his bat!?* It's at a time like that when prayers are a first and last resort. Evidently He was listening because Vic Raschi walked me on four pitches and I started breathing again.

Then when I got out on the coast, it was great. I just loved San Francisco, playing at home and all. I broke my ankle in '55. I was leading the league at that time, but that finished that year. In '57 I went to San Diego and came back to Portland in '58. In the meantime, I went to South America, to Venezuela, and played winter ball there in '57.

BK: The Red Sox reacquired you in '56.

BD: Yeah. Here I thought I was out from under; I could celebrate, I'm having a great year. I'm really looking forward. Then the rumor at that point was I was going to be sold to Kansas City in the biggies. I was very excited and that's when I broke my leg. And I'll be damned if the Red Sox didn't come in and put together a working arrangement with San Francisco and I was right back where I was.

BK: You were a fan favorite with the Seals.

BD: I had a big family. [Laughs]

BK: What stands out in your time with the Seals?

BD: The Little Corporation. That was great. That was a *wonderful* era. I can recall flying in to the San Francisco airport and the ballclub getting an escort into the stadium. When we got to 16th and Bryant the entire area — streets, sidewalks, the whole thing — was jammed with people cheering and yelling. I can recall the stands being jam-packed. I think that was the highlight of my San Francisco sojourn. It was super. We had a good bunch of guys.

What is fascinating for me is to see young men now who are offspring of the guys that I played with. Leo Righetti was our shortstop and his son was a pitcher with the Yankees. *He's* since retired. That adds a few miles.

Jimmy Moran was the second baseman. Reno Cheso was the third baseman. Nini Tornay was one catcher. Sounds like it was the Sons of Italy playing. [Laughs] Will Tiesera was a catcher. Jim Westlake was the first baseman. Sal Taormina was my roommate for five years. Absolutely the greatest guy in the world. Jerry Zuvela was also an outfielder. Albie Pearson was an outfielder for a couple of seasons. Al Lyons pitched for a while, and Al Lien.

I thought that the Coast League was an absolutely *great* league. If you couldn't play in the bigs and get that $7500 contract for being a major league ballplayer, then the Coast League was the place to play. I was making more than the 7500, which was the minimum major league contract at that time.

It was a great league. You went for a week and, for instance, if you had a series with Hollywood and then you played Los Angeles you stayed in the same hotel for two weeks. It was great in that respect. You weren't in three days and gone and on the road.

They had a lot of good, seasoned ballplayers. A young guy could learn a lot in a relatively short period of time.

At the time that I was playing I would hear the older ballplayers saying, "Well, the guy could hit, but he couldn't hit like ol' Dusty-baby," or somebody. I find myself in the same situation, making a lot of the same remarks. Fortunately, they're mostly to myself. I see these guys that are in the biggies now and I know that some of the guys that I played with could really swing the bat and never really got a chance.

Sal Taormina was beyond all others in terms of being a competitive guy. He loved the game and loved every aspect of it. He was a guy that could've played anywhere. Cream of the crop. When I heard that he had died, it didn't surprise me when I found out how it happened because that's the way he was with me. He was out jogging, from what I understand, and was out at the park and got in his car and had a heart attack and died. What I believe happened, knowing him, in spring training he would drive me into the ground. "Come on! One more! Come on, rooms! We gotta go! We gotta push ourselves! One more! Keep going! Keep going!" And it was that kinda thing *all* the time. That's the way he drove himself. And I'll bet you a dollar to a doughnut he was out of gas and he

Outfielder Sal Taormina (photograph by the author).

said I'll go one more, maybe two. That was just typical of him. He was some kinda character; he was a wonderful guy.

My son went down and pitched at Stanford. My wife and I went down and had lunch with Sal and talked to him and he wanted my son to go there [Santa Clara University, where Taormina coached], but he had this opportunity to go to Stanford and we just plain couldn't pass it up so we took it. We tried to explain it to him, and you know you can't explain to that rockhead.

When Bob was pitching and pitched against Santa Clara, he called me and said, "Geez, Dad, your buddy was *all over* my case and never let up for nine innings." That's typical of Hog. That's what we called him. The Hog was just so competitive and if you weren't with him, you were against him. And there was no grey area in between.

Jerry Zuvela was a guy who was a *great* hitter, but they'd have to find a place for him to play. Ken Aspromonte did get a shot, went up with Cleveland. Mahoney was the shortstop. Malzone was the biggest name off those teams. Tommy Umphlett was a center fielder there for a while.

Leo Kiely was a very good friend of mine. We were together in the Red Sox chain. In fact, Leo lived with us one summer. He stayed at our home. He was just a wonderful, wonderful guy. When he died, I just couldn't believe it.

When I was with Louisville, one of the highlights of any of our visits to any of the towns was the fact that we had two All-American quarterbacks on that team: Larry Isbell, who was a quarterback and All-American from Baylor, and Harry Agganis, who was a first baseman with us and an All-American from Boston College. We had both on the same team. Larry was a catcher. I don't know what ever happened to him; I know that Harry Agganis died. That was a tragedy. Absolutely the most beautiful-looking guy you'd ever see, one of those sculptured physical specimens. Great guy, loved life.

Al Richter was the shortstop. Close friend and a roommate of mine. We correspond every Christmas; he's still going. I get this *BAT* piece in the mail every once in a while and they've got this obituary section and, my Lord, it's terrific. These are guys I played with; we're the same age. It just shakes you right to your shoes. As I look back and remember these guys, they were young and full of life.

You know what it's like to be on a professional team where you're living together and earning a living together. It's a *great* experience, one that I don't think you can duplicate in any other field. I've often been asked by folks, "You didn't make it to the majors. If you had it to do over again knowing what you do now and what your expectancy would be, would you do it again?" In a minute. My wife and I both *loved* the life. It's a great way of life.

BK: Seals Stadium was a beautiful ballpark, but a heck of a park in which to hit a home run.

BD: Oh, boy, I'll tell you it was. It was a *big* ballpark and as I recall, I think it was either 335 or 350 down the [left field] line and 385 to the power alley and over 400 to center field. And the big scoreboard in center field, so you'd have to be Hercules or start at second base. And right field was the same dimensions. And it was a tough place to play at night once that sun went down; this was before batting gloves. I remember Jim Moran one time brought a pair of gardening gloves — you now, those canvas type — and wore those to take batting practice. Everybody was laughing at him. [Laughs] He was just ahead of his time. Same in Seattle. We'd go there and sometimes the air would be so damp you couldn't get that ball out of there with a Howitzer. It was *really* tough to get a ball to carry in the heavy air.

But it [Seals Stadium] was a great place to play. It was a good hitters' park if you're not looking to hit a home run. You know, you have a lot of space out there to hit in. I just loved to play in Seals Stadium. I understand it's no longer there.

BK: Tommy Heath was the manager when you joined the Seals.

BD: One of the funniest guys that I have known in baseball. [Laughs] A *good* manager. I enjoyed being around him. He was no stranger to John Barleycorn; in fact, everybody thought he was the most innovative manager in the world because he was the one who came up with dragging the infield after the fifth inning, which had not been done before in the Coast League that I was aware of. That gave him an opportunity to go back in the clubhouse and get a couple of snorts. [Laughs]

He was a very comedic guy with a wry sense of humor. You'd have spring training and you'd have to go to the must-do functions, like the Rotary and Lions' Club and Chamber of Commerce, and he'd get up and introduce the club and he'd say, "Now, you have to understand that I'm gonna have trouble with some of these names because I don't recognize a lot of 'em. I've been coaching third base all spring and I haven't seen many of these guys." [Laughs] That was typical of his kind of humor. He was great to play for. He was fair; he was a good baseball man.

Eddie Joost followed him. I don't think Eddie was cut out for management. He was such a volatile guy. He was a good guy to play for — there's no problem there — but he was *so* volatile. I've seen him get upset with a call and throw the ball out of the stadium. He was still able to play so he played part of the time and I think managing was difficult for him.

Had he stayed with it a little longer he could've become a good one because he certainly knew baseball and knew how it should be played, but he had a temperament problem that I think needed some help.

BK: Joe Gordon.

BD: Great, wonderful guy. I just loved the guy. He was so much fun to play for and never really put any pressure on anybody. He taught you the game and he brought people in that knew the game and have 'em work with you. He was one of the first guys that really brought in solid help. He didn't bring old baseball cronies that were looking for a job. He brought in guys that could help you with fielding, hitting, and specialty parts of the game that he didn't feel capable of doing. I always admired him for that. He had hitting theories that were very solid. Lord knows, he knew how to play the game.

I wish he'd been around because the Red Sox had told me in '52, I guess, "We're gonna send you down to Scranton"—this was the second year I'd been there and I'd had a good year; this was also a ballpark I think was modeled after Seals Stadium, it was a *big* park and tough to hit the ball out—but, "Bobby Doerr is gonna retire and we want to make a second baseman out of you." I think that was the only reason they could think of to get me to go to Scranton. [Laughs] So, like a dummy, I went. I would loved to have been able to do that with Joe Gordon 'cause I think he could've taught me how to play that position and maybe I could've. I don't know. I never did feel that I could've cut it at the major league level as a second baseman, but I didn't get hurt in the year that I played there.

BK: Second base is a tougher position that many people give it credit for.

BD: Yeah. I made third base pretty tough, too. [Laughs] I think I still may hold the record in Scranton for six errors in a double header. I'm not sure I'm in the record books. I know my manager was Mike Ryba; he was one of those old iron horses that pitched the first game of a double header and caught the second one. You talk about rawhide, this guy was tough, didn't brook *any* fooling around. He was just a different cat. Finally, after my fourth error with a throw that bounced at the pitcher's mound, I was tight and this time I was praying, "Oh, please don't let them hit the ball to me."

Mike was kind of low key, said, "Bobby, I don't give a damn what you do, but if you get another'n, throw that damn ball as hard as you can throw the son of a bitch and don't, for cryin' out loud, bounce it on the pitcher's mound." Damned if I didn't go out and the very first shot—and I made a hell of a play, a backhand stab over the bag—and I remembered what Mike said and I reared back and I can still see those fans behind first base up in the stands— one group went left and the other group went right and the ball went into the seats. [Laughs] Mike said, "Bobby, come in and sit with me. I think you've had enough for this day." [Laughs] He's another guy that's passed on.

Pinky Higgins was a great guy to play for. He and I got along just great. I think Pink had occasion to have a snort or two, which was not unusual in that era. A lot of guys had more than their share of booze, but I loved the guy. He was an awfully good guy to play for.

When all is said and done, that's really the highlight of my baseball career — the years spent with the Seals. I just enjoyed them so much. Of course, it helps when you're having a good year. The year I broke my leg I couldn't do anything wrong. If I swung the bat I had a damn good chance of getting a basehit. It was just one of those years.

And the team was good. We had good chemistry and everything was great.

I sure didn't enjoy San Diego, and when Tommy Heath went to Portland he had a problem with the guy who was playing first base for him. By this time, after I broke my leg and came back they made a first baseman out of me. I was one of those kind of guys that could play any position for about five minutes. I'd take infield and they'd say, "Geez, listen, you could play this position." And the game started and they'd say, "Hey, listen, you can't play this position." [Laughs]

He went to Portland to manage and he had trouble with a drinking problem with the first baseman and I was gonna retire in '57 and he called me in San Francisco and said, "Why don't you come up and play for me. I got a problem with this guy." And I did; I came out of retirement and played through '59.

BK: What did you do when you retired?

BD: I was working with Bob Blackburn. Bob was the announcer for the Portland ballclub and had put together a little network — a radio network — and he sold his broadcasting of the Portland Beavers baseball games through this network. He had a guy working color with him and toward the end of '59 I had been hurt so I sat in with him and he and I kinda liked it and he said, "Why don't you come and do this next year? The guy that's working with me is gonna retire. I could really use you."

I thought that sounded great. I loved to do that. So I met a guy who knew a guy who said come up to Yakima and I'll give you a job up there. I thought I was gonna be a sportscaster, become a great talent, and be discovered and go back to Portland and make a million dollars and all these things that go through a dumb guy's head.

I came up to Yakima. I had heard of Yakima in San Francisco in 1953,

I think. They had a guy that Tommy Heath had brought in to work with us on hitting instruction. He was a third baseman with the Browns, a *great* hitter. Harlond Clift. One day in spring training we came out to the ballpark and everybody asked for Harlond and he said, "Harlond had to go back to his home." "Where's that?" "Yakima." "Where the hell is Yakima?" They had a big snowstorm there and he had some cattle and they froze. And a few years later, some guy's telling me to go to Yakima and get some experience. I figured I'm gonna go up there and freeze.

But I came up here. At the time there was no position for me on the sportscasting, but I had a chance to get into sales. That's what this guy really hired me for, and I came and said I'd go into sales, knowing full-well I'd get a shot with the sports department and be discovered and be a great star in a matter of time.

After I found out there was no sports department and no chance of getting in there, I decided to get serious about sales. I really enjoyed selling time. It was the first time I had done that. Two years later I'd become sales manager at the station. We had four television stations and three radio stations in the group — Cascade Broadcasting Company.

I got a call from Bob, who said, "Come on. It's open. The job is now." I said, "God, Bob, I hate to do this, but I'm really enjoying what I'm doing. I think I better stay with this." As it worked out, it was a good move by me because a year later Bob got the job announcing the Sonics basketball and became an icon up there in the Seattle market, so I would have been down there by myself and no telling what the hell would've happened to me.

I stayed nine years with the television station and then decided to open my own advertising agency, which I did in '67 and just retired in 1999. It was very successful.

I just love Yakima. I thought it was just going to be a matter of time before I'd get back in San Francisco. We actually came here for what I thought would be six months to a year to get the experience I would need to become a colorcaster. You couldn't blast me out of here now; I just love it.

BK: Yakima was a Seals farm club way back.

BD: Yeah. When I finally started hearing about Yakima, Nini Tornay and Will Tiesera both played up here. You've heard of Hub Kittle? Hub lives up here and is *still* active. He's gotta be mid 80s, at least.

Now my son has taken over the advertising agency. That's always been one of the saddest things. He could've made it. He was a *very* good left-handed pitcher, had good years with Stanford and went up to Alaska, pitched in that Alaskan league two summers. The second summer he hurt his elbow and was drafted with the number one draft choice of Pittsburgh in the fall draft and went to Pittsburgh and pitched one inning and walked off the mound and never walked back. I've often wondered if they couldn't have done that Tommy John surgery on him. They did operate on him, but it just didn't work.

ROBERT LOUIS PAUL DIPIETRO
Born September 1, 1927, San Francisco, CA
Ht. 5'11" Wt. 185 Batted and Threw Right
First baseman, Outfielder

Year	Team, Lg	G	AB	R	H	2B	3B	HR	RBI	BA
1947	SanJose, Cal	140	471	131	148	24	6	21	111	.312
1948	Scranton, EL	137	463	77	128	17	8	10	90	.279
1949		134	435	89	131	31	6	8	82	.301
1950	Birm., SA	89	307	53	92	23	4	5	46	.300
1951	Boston, AL	4	11	0	1	0	0	0	0	.091
	Lvl, AA	2	1	1	1	0	0	0	0	1.000
	Scranton, EL	132	468	92	143	26	6	10	77	.306
1952	Lvl, AA	85	260	35	71	4	2	4	39	.273
	Birm., SA	14	43	5	9	0	0	2	9	.209
	SanAntn., Tx							1	8	.207
1953	Lvl, AA	98	268	38	53	10	1	5	35	.205
1954	SF, PCL	109	331	54	89	22	3	7	49	.269
1955		64	221	36	82	18	2	6	39	.371
1956		126	365	46	98	19	3	11	60	.268
1957	SF/SD, PCL	81	208	28	57	9	0	5	21	.274
1958	Port., PCL	149	539	65	151	32	5	14	72	.280
1959		107	344	50	79	17	6	11	36	.230

DON LENHARDT

Seals 1956

After a five-year major league career, in 1954 Don Lenhardt found himself property of the Boston Red Sox for the second time. Boston sent him to Louisville in the American Association for the 1955 season, then in 1956, when the Sox became the parent club of the Seals, he was sent to San Francisco.

The 1956 Seals were a blend of promise and past performance. On their way up were such players as Frank Malzone, Ken Aspromonte, and

Don Lenhardt (courtesy Richard T. Dobbins collection).

Albie Pearson and at the end of the line were fellows like Bob DiPietro, Sal Taormina, and Lenhardt, who had all been good ballplayers but time was running out.

And it ran out for Lenhardt after that season. Two-thirds of the way through the season, he broke an ankle, the second such injury of his career. At the time of the injury he was leading the team in home runs and was on a pace to break Joe DiMaggio's 1935 Seals Stadium home run record. And he was second or third in the other major offensive categories. Even with missing the last third of the year, his 16 home runs remained the team's best.

Rather than try to come back from the injury, Lenhardt retired after that year, but he remained in baseball as a Red Sox employee for another four decades as a scout and a coach.

Lenhardt originally came to the majors in 1950 with the St. Louis Browns and broke in with great numbers: 22 HR, 81 RBI, .273. In many years that would have put him in the running for Rookie of the Year, but 1950 was also the rookie seasons for Walt Dropo, who had one of the greatest first years in history, Whitey Ford, Irv Noren, and Chico Carrasquel.

BK: When you began playing professionally in 1946, you were 23. Had you been in the service?

DON LENHARDT: I had been in the service, yes.

BK: How were you signed?

DL: I had actually been scouted before I went into service. I was playing ball in Alton, Illinois, on Sundays and I was playing a lot of softball. One of the scouts saw me play baseball and liked me and wanted me to sign and I said, "No, I'm going to college," so I went to Illinois U.

I thought I was going to eliminate all the lower leagues by doing this, but while I was at Illinois the war came along and that was the end of that. I lost about four or five summers in service.

BK: Did you finish college?

DL: I did not. I went back to Washington University [in St. Louis] for one semester during the off-season and that's as far as I went.

BK: You walked a lot. You had a pretty good eye.

DL: I think that was my best tool. I did have a little power and I think that's what kept me in the big leagues five years.

BK: You always had a good RBI percentage.

DL: I loved to hit with men on base.

BK: You joined the Seals in 1956 and led the team in home runs even though you were hurt.

DL: I broke an ankle. I broke an ankle my first year in pro ball, so I had two broken ankles — each one.

BK: Did the second break end your career?

DL: Yes. But whenever you go down you think, "Oh, boy, I've still got a chance to get back up," but at my age at that time I almost could feel that it was not going to happen. The doctor that fixed my ankle said I should go pursue something else, so that's what I did. [Laughs]

BK: At one time or another, you played first base, third base, and the outfield. What was your best position?

DL: I think left field was my best position. My arm was very average.

BK: Your nickname was "Footsie." Why?

DL: [Laughs] Buddy Blattner gave me that nickname when I was with the Browns. We used to have our shoes made. I *had* to have mine made because I have a *very* narrow foot even though I wore size 12. You were constantly having problems with your shoes and even though you'd have 'em special-made it didn't mean that they were all going to fit the same.

I wasn't that fast, but that wasn't the reason for the nickname. [Laughs]

BK: Is there one game that stands out in your career?

DL: I don't know. I know I had one series in Philadelphia; I used to love to hit in Philadelphia. That was old Connie Mack Stadium. I think I hit five home runs in that one series.

I had a couple of other good parks. I loved Boston; that's probably why I was with 'em twice.

BK: The first time you were with Boston, you were hitting nearly .300 when you were traded.

DL: I hit a grand slam the day I was traded and won the ballgame. The deal had already been made before that, I'm sure.

That was a big trade: [Johnny] Pesky and [Walt] Dropo and me and

[Fred] Hatfield and [Bill] Wight for [Hoot] Evers and [Dizzy] Trout and [George] Kell and somebody else [Johnny Lipon]. They [Boston] wanted Kell; they thought he was going to win the pennant for 'em.

BK: Who was the best player you saw?

DL: The best hitter was Ted Williams; the best player was Joe DiMaggio. Definitely.

BK: Who was the toughest pitcher for you?

DL: Hey, I had a lot of 'em! At that time, there were some real tough pitchers. Like at Cleveland, you faced the same four every time you went in there: [Early] Wynn, [Mike] Garcia, [Bob] Lemon, and [Bob] Feller, and they never missed a turn. In those days they pitched every fourth day.

The Yankees had [Vic] Raschi, they had [Allie] Reynolds. Even Detroit had some tough guys, like Virgil Trucks. There was really some good pitching at that time. They were mean pitchers, also, who would knock you down right now. The pitchers won't throw inside now and it makes hitting much easier.

You know, you could hit anybody you wanted now because nobody's ever looking to be hit. The batters are all going the other way; they're standing way back with a very, very closed stance. It's much different than it used to be.

BK: What's the biggest change in the game?

DL: I think the biggest change has been the Astroturf. I really do. I think it's changed the game entirely. It's played so much differently now than it was then because of the Astroturf. There's a lot more hits that go through the infield; there's more extra base hits. You just bunch everybody — hold 'em to doubles and try to stop triples going in between the outfielders.

I can't comment on the players because I don't know. I'm sure they're as good athletes now, maybe better than we were.

BK: Today the players can stay fit year around. You guys had to work in the off-season to support your families.

DL: *Every* winter. Fortunately, I married a very nice girl; she loves to work and she's been working ever since we've been married. That let me stay in baseball. It was tough at times.

The minimum when I started was $5,000. My first year I hit 22 home runs, drove in 80-some runs, and hit .270-something and I couldn't get a $2500 raise. I was afraid if I didn't sign, somebody would take my place. That's the way it was then.

You know, at one time the Cardinals had 33 minor league clubs, so you can imagine if you were a shortstop there were 32 other ones out there somewhere.

BK: Today the ballplayers have the upper hand.

DL: They do. They're controlling the whole thing. As long as the owners are going to give it [money] to 'em, they've got to take it.

It may be slowly coming to an end. I think they over-extended themselves. As soon as the TV money slows, they're going to run into more trouble with the salaries because, basically, that's where all the money's coming from.

They keep raising ticket prices and every year people say, "I'm not going to go," yet every year baseball sets new attendance records. I think someday they'll price themselves out.

BK: After the '56 season with the Seals you became a scout with the Red Sox.

DL: I did. I coached for four years when Eddie Kasko was the manager. I went back to scouting after that.

BK: Are there any players that you scouted that we'd know?

DL: Probably the best one would be Al Nipper. Then there was a kid who I thought would make it. His name's Scott Cooper.

BK: Did you enjoy scouting?

DL: Oh, yes. I've enjoyed baseball. It's the one thing that I was able to do, fortunately, for my whole life.

BK: Did you save souvenirs from your career?

DL: I did not save any. [Laughs] It sounds ridiculous, doesn't it? I wish I had uniforms and a number of things. I've got some bats of my own I kept, which I'm going to keep. Probably my grandson will get 'em. Other than that I have very little.

I had a very good friend who was the scouting director. When he died, his wife gave us a bunch of those press pins, which are very valuable. I'm going to hang on to those.

BK: Do you still receive fan mail?

DL: I get probably two or three autograph requests a week. I don't mind signing at all; if somebody wants my autograph, they got it!

I'm not sure about those card shows. I've been to a couple of 'em here. I tell you what really bothers me. The first thing they do is charge the people to get in. The next thing, if you don't have anything to get signed they'll sell you a picture. Then if you want the picture autographed you get in line and pay for the autograph. It's really a rip-off. I'm sure some of the players make a lot of money doing that.

I get letters from people who say they saw me play and from kids who get my name out of the book and they collect cards. They're usually going to keep these things and I always sign.

BK: Do you think you'd have made it to the major leagues sooner without the service?

DL: I never look back like that. Everybody you see says, "Boy, if you were playing now you'd be making a million dollars!" I may not even be playing now; I don't know these things.

I'm just happy I was able to pursue my career for all my life so far. I've been at it for a long time and I work for a very good organization.

BK: Any regrets?

DL: None. I'd do it all again.

DONALD EUGENE "FOOTSIE" LENHARDT
Born October 4, 1922, Alton, IL
Ht. 6'3" Wt. 190 Batted and Threw Right
Outfielder

Year	Team, Lg	G	AB	R	H	2B	3B	HR	RBI	BA
1946	Ptsbrg, KOM	63	250	45	92	13	8	7	58	.268
	Aberd'n, No	39	136	28	35	5	2	1	22	.265
1947	Aberd'n, No	62	244	45	74	16	7	5	62	.303
1948	Sprngfld, Ill	107	390	64	119	22	5	22	73	.305
	SanAntno, Tx	4	11	1	5	1	0	0	1	.455
1949	SanAntno, Tx	131	434	65	112	23	2	26	78	.258
1950	StL, AL	139	480	75	131	22	6	22	81	.273
1951	StL/Chi, AL	95	302	32	80	12	1	15	63	.265
1952	Bos/Det/StL,AL	93	297	41	71	10	2	11	42	.239
1953	StL, AL	97	303	37	96	15	0	10	35	.317
1954	Bal/Bos, AL	57	99	7	23	5	0	3	18	.232
1955	Lvl, AA	104	336	40	89	19	1	12	55	.265
1956	SF, PCL	91	294	46	88	11	1	16	49	.299

♦ CHAPTER 13 ♦

1957:
Going Out a Winner

First place: W 101 L 67 .601 3½ games ahead

During the winter of 1956–57 rumors persisted that major league baseball would be brought to the West Coast in 1958. And the rumors said it would be the National League, not the American League that the Red Sox were holding San Francisco for.

By early in the season, it was obvious that the Brooklyn Dodgers would forsake Flatbush for Los Angeles. Walter O'Malley, the owner of the Dodgers, was working on Horace Stoneham, the owner of the New York Giants, trying to convince him to come west, too, to San Francisco.

Meetings were held between the city of San Francisco and Giants officials and by mid August it was a done deal. The New York Giants would become the San Francisco Giants in 1958. Also, the Brooklyn Dodgers would become the Los Angeles Dodgers.

This required some relocations and some payments to leagues and teams. Boston was given the Giants' Minneapolis territory in exchange for San Francisco. The San Francisco franchise was moved to Phoenix as a Giants' farm team. The Los Angeles Angels moved to Spokane, Washington, to become a Dodgers' farm. And the Hollywood Stars moved to Salt Lake City. Phoenix, Spokane, and Salt Lake City became members of the Pacific Coast League.

But all of that was after the 1957 season ended. As the season opened it was all still rumor.

Joe Gordon was back as the Seals' manager and, again, it was a reworked team that took the field in 1957. The same three old familiar

239

SAN FRANCISCO (SEALS) BAY AREA BASEBALL CLUB

Bottom Row: L to R—TOM HURD, P; SAL TAORMINA, O F; BILL ABERNATHIE, P; JOE GORDON, Mgr.; GLENN WRIGHT, Coach; NINI TORNAY, C; HARRY DORISH, P; KEN ASPROMONTE, 2nd B.

2nd Row: L to R—LEO HUGHES, Trainer; BILL PROUT, P; JACK SPRING, P; LEO KIELY, P; FRANK KELLERT, 1st B; HAYWOOD

SULLIVAN, C; BILL RENNA, O F; ED SADOWSKI, C; ALBIE PIERSON, O F.

Top Row: L to R—GRADY HATTON, 3rd B; R. W. SMITH, P; BERT THIEL, P; JACK PHILLIPS, Inf; MARTY KEOUGH, O F; TOM UMPHLETT, O F; ROBERT CHAKALES, P; HARRY MALMBERG, S S.

Join **CHRISTOPHER MILK JR. SEALS BASEBALL CLUB** *At Your Grocer*

1957 PCL champion San Francisco Seals (courtesy Richard T. Dobbins collection).

faces were still there on Opening Day, but Bob DiPietro was traded to San Diego early in the season, leaving only Nini Tornay and Sal Taormina.

Among the players from 1956, Ken Aspromonte was back; he led the PCL in batting with a .334 average and was recalled by Boston before the season ended. Marty Keough also returned and had a good year (13-53-.285) in center field. He spent the next nine years in the major leagues. Eddie Sadowski (7-38-.245), Haywood Sullivan (6-33-.293), and Tornay (0-9-.241) were back as the receivers, and Tornay played three times as much as he did in '56.

On the pitching staff, only Riverboat Smith returned, but he made his presence known. He was the leading starter on the team with 13 wins (against 10 losses), and his ERA was down more than a run to 3.35. He led the league with six shutouts, was among the leaders in strikeouts, and even hit a home run, not something he was accustomed to doing.

The rest of the team was made up mostly of veterans. One of the most important acquisitions was first baseman Frank Kellert (22-107-.308), traded from L. A. for Bill Henry and cash. Another top hitter and run

Left: First baseman Frank Kellert, who led the Seals in RBIs. *Right:* Outfielder Bill Renna, the Seals home run leader in 1957 (photographs by the author).

producer was Bill Renna, whom the Red Sox got from the Yankees for Eli Grba, Gordie Windhorn, and $10,000. Renna (29-105-.281) used the '56 season with the Seals to earn a return trip to the major leagues.

Veteran free agents were signed. Grady Hatton (3-63-.317) did well at third base, platooned with another veteran, Jack Phillips (9-38-.274). Frank Malzone, 1956's third baseman, was beginning a productive big league career.

Pitchers were the main free agent signings. Harry Dorish, Jim Konstanty, Walter Masterson, and Duane Pillette — all major league fixtures within the previous few years— were added to the staff. Dorish (9-12, 3.32) joined the rotation. Masterson and Konstanty met with little success and were gone soon.

Pillette was pitching very well. He began 4–1, 2.91 and at that point was the best pitcher on the team. He explains what happened. "The Seals at that time had a very strong working agreement with the Boston Red Sox. They wanted to send down young pitchers and the Seals had a number of older pitchers.... They were very nice. They gave me my choice. Do you want to be traded or do you want to go out on your own and maybe get a couple dollars to sign 'cause you're obviously playing quite well, etc? So I said, 'I'll take my chances.' I called Lefty [O'Doul, now managing Seattle] and he said, 'Sure.' I got a few dollars to sign and I went with a ballclub that I really appreciated being with. I wasn't happy about leaving [the Seals] because I was living at home [in San Jose]."

Pillette won 12 and lost 7 at Seattle. For the year he was 16–8, 3.15.

The Red Sox did send young pitchers to the Seals. Jack Spring, a southpaw who began the year in Boston, came west in May. He went 11–9, 3.18 the rest of the way to have the second most wins of the club's starters. Tommy Hurd (8–6, 3.36) also did well.

But the pitcher who did better than anyone began the season as a starter, went an uninspired 1–2, and was sent to the bullpen. In that role, lefthander Leo Kiely won 20 and lost 4 with a 2.09 ERA. His numbers for the season were 21–6, 2.22. He became the first and, so far, only pitcher to win 20 games in relief at any level. Only another inhuman effort by the Angels' Steve Bilko (56–140–.300) prevented Kiely from being the MVP. Bilko won the award for the third straight year.

Southpaw reliever Leo Kiely, the only relief pitcher ever to win 20 games (photograph by the author).

If ever there was a team built around the bullpen, this was it. Bill Abernathie (13–2, 4.23), Bert Thiel (5–4, 2.79), and Bill Prout (6–6, 4.20) joined Kiely in one of baseball's greatest relief groups.

Rounding out the team was 5'5" Albie Pearson (5-50-.297) in right field. Batting leadoff, he scored 99 runs. After the season he was traded to the Washington Senators, where he was named American League Rookie of the Year in 1958.

Tommy Umphlett (4-35-.233) and Taormina (3-37-.296) were back in the outfield. The shortstop from 1956, Jim Mahoney, had been drafted into the military, so Harry Malmberg, a long-time minor league infielder, was signed. He had the best season of his career (4-54-.277).

On Friday evening, September 13, 1957, the Seals held a three-game lead with four games remaining over the second-place Vancouver Mounties. The Seals were playing Sacramento and the Mounties were playing the Seattle Rainiers.

Riverboat Smith, San Francisco's leading starter, took the mound against the Solons' Earl Harrist, who was his team's ERA leader. Riverboat tossed a four-hitter for his league-leading sixth shutout and downed the visitors, 3–0. He even drove in a run with a sixth-inning single.

Vancouver lost to Seattle, so the Seals' final PCL championship was aided by two former Seals managers. Seattle was managed by Lefty O'Doul and Sacramento was managed by Tommy Heath.

Reliever Bill Abernathie, who set the Seals all-time winning percentage record in 1957 (photograph by the author).

San Francisco took the league lead on June 11, in the 61st game of the year, and held it the rest of the way with the help of some great hitting, an outstanding bullpen, and some pretty solid starting pitching. The clincher was slow to be realized, though, as the Seals game was over for quite a while before the result of the Mounties-Rainiers game was learned. When the call came to the clubhouse phone, winning pitcher Smith was doused with beer by teammates Frank Kellert, Bill Renna, Grady Hatton, Marty Keough, Eddie Sadowski, Haywood Sullivan, and Sal Taormina.

The next day the *Look Magazine* all–PCL team was announced. It included Keough, Leo Kiely, and Ken Aspromonte. The parent Boston Red Sox rewarded the team with a victory banquet at DiMaggio's.

Sac	AB	R	H	RBI	*SF*	AB	R	H	RBI
Agosta, 2b	4	0	2	0	Sadowski, 2b	5	1	2	1
Heron, 3b	3	0	0	0	Keough, cf	4	0	2	0
Westlake, 1b	3	0	1	0	Pearson, rf	3	0	1	0
Greengrass, rf	4	0	0	0	Kellert, 1b	3	0	2	0
Heist, cf	3	0	0	0	Hatton, 3b	4	0	1	0
Rushing, lf	4	0	0	0	Renna, lf	4	0	0	0
Righetti, ss	3	0	1	0	Sullivan, c	4	0	1	0
Barragan, c	3	0	0	0	Green, ss	4	2	2	0
Harrist, p	1	0	0	0	Smith, p	3	0	1	1
Bridges, ph	1	0	0	0					
Candini, p	0	0	0	0					
	29	0	4	0		34	3	12	2

Pitching	IP	H	R	ER	SO	BB
Harrist (L, 5–13)	7	11	3	3	1	1
Candini	1	1	0	0	0	0
Smith (W, 13–10)	9	4	0	0	7	4

Sac	000	000	000	0	4	1
SF	110	001	00x	3	12	0

E: Agosta. LOB: Sac 7, SF 10. 2B: Sadowski, Green, Keough. SB: Green. Sac: Kellert, Smith. Double Plays: Sadowski to Kellert, Kellert unassisted. Umpires: Pelekoudas, Mutart, and Orr. Time: 2:00. Att: 4,438.

The pennant was clinched with a win on Friday, September 13, and then they won again on Saturday, but on the final day of baseball for the San Francisco Seals, Sunday, September 15, 1957, they lost a double header to Sacramento. Attendance on that final day was excellent; 15,484 fans turned out. Everyone knew at this point that there would be no more Seals.

The opener was played seriously, but the seven-inning nightcap was far from it.

Gordon's starting lineup for the second game had Pearson pitching, Gordon himself at second base, Sadowski at shortstop, Sullivan in center field, and Umphlett at third base. When Gordon led off the Seals' first inning, Heath had his entire infield sit down. Gordon lined a shot that would have been a hit even if the fielders had been standing. As the game went on, Pearson, who pitched only the first inning and was the loser (allowing four runs), played all the infield positions. Taormina took over for Kellert at first base, Lou Stringer came in for Umphlett at third, and Hatton and Gordon pitched. Late in the game with Gordon on base, Solons manager Tommy Heath inserted himself as a pinch runner for the Seals' manager.

When Gordon took the mound in the sixth, facing former Seal Jim Westlake, plate umpire Chris Pelekoudas called a ball. An "argument" ensued and Pelekoudas said, "Maybe you think you can do better." With that, he took off his umpire's jacket and took Gordon's cap. He threw one pitch and they traded places again. With Gordon back on the mound, Westlake singled.

Infielder Grady Hatton pitched the final two innings, The ball used for the final out was sent to the Hall of Fame in Cooperstown, New York.

The final score was Sacramento 14, San Francisco 7. Solons' Reeve Watkins went the distance, tossing a 17-hit-

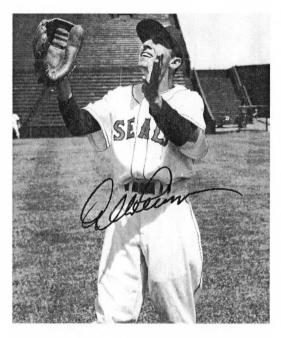

Outfielder Albie Pearson, who became the American League Rookie of the Year with the Washington Senators in 1958 (author's collection).

ter. His teammates got only 16 hits, but received eight walks. It was a game the fans would never forget.

FINAL GAME BOX SCORE*

Sac	AB	R	H	RBI	SF	AB	R	H	RBI
Agosta, 2b	4	3	2	0	Gordon, 2-p-s	3	0	1	0
Bright, 3b	5	2	3	2	Malmberg, 2b	0	1	0	0
Westlake, 1b	4	3	3	1	Sadowski, ss	5	2	3	1
Gr'ngrass, rf	3	3	2	3	Green, rf	4	1	3	2
Heist, cf	5	0	2	2	Pearson, p-if	4	1	2	0
Rushing, lf	3	0	2	1	Kellert, 1b	0	0	0	0
Righetti, ss	2	1	0	0	Taormina,1b	4	0	2	2
Neal, c	4	1	0	4	Renna, lf	3	0	0	0

*The above box score does not quite add up. It was taken from two different sources, so whatever mistakes were made are not correctable now.

Sac	AB	R	H	RBI	SF	AB	R	H	RBI
Watkins, p	4	0	0	0	Sullivan, cf	2	1	2	0
					Umphlett, 3b	0	0	0	0
					Stringer, 3b	3	0	1	0
					Tornay, c	3	0	1	0
					Prout, p	2	1	2	0
					Hatton, p	0	0	0	0
	34	14	16	13		33	7	17	5

Pitching	IP	H	R	ER	SO	BB
Watkins (W, 8–10)	7	17	7	6	1	1
Pearson (L, 0–1)	1	2	4	4	0	4
Prout	4	10	9	9	2	4
Gordon	0	1	0	0	0	0
Hatton	2	3	1	1	0	0

Gordon pitched to one batter in the 6th.

Sac	430	151	0	14	17	1
SF	201	129	1	7	17	1

E: Bright, Sadowksi. LOB: Sac 8, SF 5. 2B: Greengrass, Prout, Heist, Pearson, Taormina, Tornay, Agosta, Sullivan. 3B: Prout. HR: Greengrass (20), Bright (6). SB: Agosta. Double Plays: Umphlett to Gordon to Kellert, Bright to Agosta to Westlake, Stringer to Tornay to Taormina. Umpires: Pelekoudas, Mutart, Orr, and Gordon. Time: 1:50. Att: 15,484.

The Seals led the league in batting (.278) and finished 3½ games ahead of the greatly improved Vancouver Mounties, who were led by first baseman Jim Marshall (30-102-.284). Third place Hollywood was 7 games back. Their offense was led by $100,000 bonus baby pitcher Paul Pettit (20-102-.284), who had been switched to the outfield. San Diego was 12 back; Seattle, now managed by Lefty O'Doul, 13½ out; and L. A., Sacramento, and Portland trailed.

Former Seals were getting fewer around the PCL, but Larry Jansen and O'Doul were teamed once again in Seattle. In a game in San Francisco, Jansen belted a colossal home run over the center field scoreboard. It was only the third of his career. As he rounded third base, O'Doul pretended to faint in the coach's box. He fell flat on his back. The Seals' fans loved him, as always.

The season and the Seals were over. Attendance for the final season was nearly 300,000. The players each received $400 for winning the pennant. Everybody but the Seals' fans profited.

And what became of the last three "real" Seals? DiPietro left San Francisco in 1957 and played the rest of that season in San Diego, then played in Portland in '58 and '59. He eventually opened an advertising agency in Yakima, Washington.

Tornay went to Portland in 1958 and '59, where he had the best years of his career offensively, then he spent part of 1960 with Columbus in the International League. Later he had a sporting goods store.

Taormina signed with the Giants and played in Phoenix in 1958 and '59. He had a good spring training in '58 and there was hope he would make the Giants' roster, but he didn't. He played in Tacoma (PCL) in 1960 and when he left professional baseball he coached Santa Clara University's baseball team. He was eventually named to the College Baseball Coach's Hall of Fame. He passed away from a heart attack after jogging in the 1970s.

RIVERBOAT SMITH

Seals 1956–1957

"Bob Smith" is not an uncommon name and back in the mid 1950s the Boston Red Sox had two of them in their farm system. To make matters more confusing, they were both pitchers. Still even more confusing, they were both southpaws. And in 1956, they were both assigned to the Seals.

So they became known by their initials. Robert Gilchrist Smith was R. G., Robert Walkup Smith was R. W. And this was how they were presented in the box scores. Finally they became differentiated further. Bob Stevens, a wonderful sports columnist for the *San Francisco Chronicle*, compared R. W.'s demeanor in pitching to that of a Mississippi riverboat gambler and "Riverboat" stuck. It was fitting; Riverboat hails from Missouri, on the banks of the Mississippi.

In 1957, Riverboat Smith led the Seals' starters in victories (13), innings, and strikeouts, and led the PCL in shutouts (6).

RIVERBOAT SMITH: I was on so dag-gone many ballclubs. I was

R. W. "Riverboat" Smith (photograph by the author).

in all three Triple-A leagues and both major leagues for a little bit. I've done a gob of traveling. I went to South America for two winters.

BK: How were you originally signed?

RS: I almost signed with Brooklyn out of college and I didn't. I went back to school another year. University of Missouri. I played summer ball — semipro — in the Iowa State League. It was a gob of college ballplayers. I was up there two summers and that's where I really signed from. I signed with Boston. The scout was Chuck Stevens. They had to fly him to meet me in Chicago and I signed while I was in Chicago. Actually, John Murphy, who was the minor league farm team manager, was the one that actually signed me, but as far as the paperwork, it was Chuck Stevens.

I had a guy — John Hyde Simmons — who was the [college] coach. He was a funny man and he really liked me.

My wife would love to tell you the story 'bout how I started playing. I'll try to say it like she does. I had a friend that lived right here in the hometown, went to school at the same time as I did. He wanted to go out to the ballfield. I said, "Hell, I don't want to go out there. I can't play." You know, during the war there wasn't anybody here to play ball. Little ol' country town.

Anyway, we went out. I said, "I'll be cut right away." He said, "Go out as a pitcher. They cut them last. By the time you get cut, I'll know everybody." [Laughs] He got cut the first trip around, so I quit. They come and hunted me up; John said that I might be able to be a good pitcher. That's how I got started.

BK: You spent very little time in the lower minors, playing mostly for Triple-A Louisville. They must have thought pretty highly of you.

RS: I was going to Boston after one year. When Frank Malzone, Sammy White, Ike Delock, and all them went up, I was going, too. I went to what they called that Kiddie Corps school in January — that's one of the first years they ever had it — and I went down there and tried to show too much too quick and hurt my arm.

I signed a Louisville contract after Scranton. Scranton was my first year and I was 15-and-5. Like I said, I could throw and I was gonna go up with Boston, but when I hurt my arm and I couldn't throw very good I went to Louisville. Louisville sent me down. I went to Albany and I went to Roanoke. That was a bad summer for me; we was travelin' all the time. I kept goin' down-down-down where it was warmer. I pitched a no-hitter there at Newport News and I came back to Louisville at the end of the season. Then I was in Louisville the next two or three years.

BK: When the Red Sox acquired the Seals, they sent a lot of you fellows who were high on their prospect list there.

RS: I enjoyed it out there. In fact, we enjoyed it better than either major league. You played Tuesday through Sunday, had Mondays off. You stayed in town a week.

We really enjoyed San Francisco and enjoyed the league. You never saw such weather in a whole league; from Vancouver down to San Diego it was just optimum. You'd come in to San Francisco and *freeze* in July. [Laughs] My wife used to take blankets. And then we'd go in Sacramento where it was about 110 in the shade. [Laughs] We thoroughly enjoyed it.

I lived in South City [South San Francisco] the first year and then San Mateo the second.

I played winter ball in '54 and then again in '57 down in Venezuela. I enjoyed that. And we enjoyed Toronto. Vancouver was one of the cleanest towns I was ever in. Seattle was always raining; they needed a dome.

I set a Seals record for shutouts in '57 before I came up. I made the all-star team in '56 and led the league in strikeouts *and* walks.

BK: How many years did you spend with R. G. Smith?

RS: Two different hitches. No more than two years. It was very confusing. That no-hitter I pitched, they came out with his picture in the paper. [Laughs]

I got the name "Riverboat" because of him. They were trying to distinguish between R. G. and R. W. I pitched a ballgame in San Francisco one night and Bob Stevens of the *Chronicle* wrote that I pitched with the finesse and the ease of a Mississippi riverboat gambler. I was from Missouri. That's how I got the nickname. I called him "Tugboat"; he was a little short, stocky guy and he wound up being called Tugboat a lot. He wrote for the *San Francisco Chronicle*.

BK: You went to Boston after the '57 season.

RS: I enjoyed gettin' to go and I thought that I could've made the ballclub. If I'd've had really a decent shot I could've made it and stayed there, but [manager Pinky] Higgins and I didn't get along. Another reason, I was a lefthanded pitcher and the Green Monster was there and they just didn't believe in pitchin' lefthanders.

But I enjoyed people tryin' to pull me. Like Mantle and Maris; I pitched against the Yankees more than any other ballclub probably. Because they tried to pull, I bet Mantle and Maris didn't hit .200. I don't really know, but the spray hitters— Tony Kubek, Elston Howard, Bobby Richardson — those spray hitters hurt me worse than anybody.

BK: You went to Minneapolis and pitched well.

RS: We were in the Junior World Series and won it. I was in three of them, with Louisville, Minneapolis, and Toronto.

BK: You had your best years in Toronto.

RS: Yeah. I enjoyed it up there. We really liked Toronto and kind of wanted to go back up there and live. We had a lot of good friends up there and we had a heck of a ballclub.

BK: Your record at Toronto would indicate that some major league team should look at you.

RS: I went to spring training with Philadelphia, but I didn't look very good. I'll admit I didn't. I should've made it. Gene Mauch was manager and he was one of my managers at Minneapolis when we won it. I just didn't show good and they sent me to Little Rock.

BK: What pitches did you throw?

RS: I had a good fastball and until I hurt my arm I had a heck of a curveball. I got to where I had a pretty good slider. The thing that I never did master real good was the changeup until the last couple of years.

I wish they'd've had a gun. I'd say I was middle 90s. I could throw. I was probably as fast at the time as Herb Score. I could throw as hard as he could.

BK: Would you be a ballplayer again?

RS: Yes, sir. I enjoyed it. I got married while we were in school and lived right behind the ballpark in a dorm, kind of a Quonset hut.

BK: Talk about some of your teammates with the Seals. Frank Kellert.

RS: He was just a pretty darn good ballplayer. He hit 20-some home runs. He was a nice fella, had a nice family.

BK: Ken Aspromonte.

RS: He was an average ballplayer, kind of a sullen ballplayer. If he screwed up, he kinda sulked a little bit. He led the league in hitting in '57.

BK: Jim Mahoney.

RS: Mahoney was a smooth fielding shortstop with a shotgun arm. Quiet. He was good. He couldn't hit very good, but he was a very good defensive player. He wasn't as good as Billy Moran, defensively. We called him [Moran] "the human vacuum cleaner." Mahoney's arm might've been a little better.

BK: Bob DiPietro.

RS: [Laughs] He was a dandy. Bob was a hustler, a clubhouse comic. He was just an average ballplayer, but he always tried. Everybody liked him, very popular.

BK: Albie Pearson.

RS: Little Albie. I don't know how he done it, but he sure did. [Laughs] He was just not too bad. He could hit pretty decent. He was an above average outfielder. He made the most of his size.

BK: Marty Keough.

RS: Marty Keough was a good outfielder, a good hitter. I thought he'd do a little bit better in the big leagues than what he did.

BK: Tommy Umphlett.

RS: One of the better center fielders that's ever been out there. I thought he'd do better in the majors but he just didn't hit enough. He was a loosey-goosey guy; when he ran it looked like he was gonna fall apart, but he could go get that ball. Umphlett had 14 successive hits in '57.

BK: Haywood Sullivan.

RS: A good catcher. I didn't care to throw to him as well as I did some of the other boys, but he wasn't that bad. Sammy White I enjoyed throwin' to. An excellent receiver. He had a knack of just gettin' you to do it. Sullivan was an $80,000 bonus catcher.

BK: Eddie Sadowski.

RS: Eddie caught me quite a little bit. He'd make me mad 'cause he'd throw the ball back to me so hard. He'd try to rev me up by burning me out back on the mound and, boy, that made me mad. He kept on doin' it. We became friends; his wife came up here and stayed with my wife. They were from Pittsburgh. She used to make a rolled cabbage dish that I never will forget.

I pitched a game against the Mounties. It was the fifth game that I won in '56. He hit a triple and I squeezed him home.

BK: Nini Tornay.

RS: Nini I liked. He was a happy-go-lucky guy and an excellent receiver and an average hitter. He was another one that I kinda liked to throw to. He gave you a good target. That expression of his that he put out kinda made you feel good. He had been there for a while.

BK: Sal Taormina.

RS: Sal wasn't the best outfielder, but he was a good hitter and a team player. Short and stocky. Very popular. I enjoyed playing with Sal. He worked real hard.

BK: Leo Kiely and Bill Abernathie.

RS: Leo won 21 game sin '57. There was a headline — August 27, 1957: "Kiely and Abernathie can clinch the flag." They did it.

BK: Jack Spring.

RS: Jack had possibilities, but, I don't know, it just never did work out. He was a decent minor league ballplayer like me, but he couldn't throw near as hard as I could, but he wasn't quite as wild, either. [Laughs]

BK: Bill Renna.

RS: Bill was a hustler. He was big; he really had to work to keep his weight down. He was a pretty good slugger.

BK: Gordie Windhorn.

RS: I'm not runnin' him down, I just never did really care for Gordie as a real good ballplayer. He was a decent outfielder, but for some reason he just didn't cut the mustard.

BK: Don Lenhardt.

RS: Ol' Footsie. [Laughs] Don was a very, very likable person and he was a good ballplayer. He was on his way down then. He broke an ankle that season [1956]. He lives in St. Louis; he's scouting.

BK: Larry DiPippo.

RS: Pretty good power. He had a real heavy swing. He never did hit for a high average, but he hit the long ball occasionally. He was a well-liked person. He was there in '56.

Grady Hatton; I liked Grady. He was on his way down, too, but he was a good ballplayer. He had a good big league career.

Harry Dorish relieved and started a little. Max Surkont was a good reliever. I didn't know him real well and he wasn't there real long, I don't think.

BK: Jerry Casale.

RS: He had real, real good stuff, but he was pretty wild. He was about as wild as I was, or wilder. He was a good hitter. Big, strong boy from New York. He had pretty good stuff and couldn't control it. They had high hopes for him and it just didn't turn out.

Another guy that they got from the Phillies that was with us, on the sideline he could strike out anybody. Tom Casagrande. You remember him?

BK: The best player to come off those teams was Frank Malzone.

RS: Probably. Frank was real quiet at that time. He became to where he wasn't so quiet. He was just a real good, sound ballplayer. Very good common sense.

BK: The Seals went out as champions in 1957. Do you have any particular memory of that season?

RS: Yeah. I hit the only homerun I ever hit in my life. It was up in Portland and I wound up losing the ballgame. [Laughs] I don't remember who I hit it off of; I just remember being so excited about it. I got hits, but they were dribblers. I was sure a poor hitter.

ROBERT WALKUP "R.W.":"RIVERBOAT" SMITH
Born May 13, 1928, Clarence, MO
Ht. 6' Wt. 185 Batted and Threw Left

Year	Team, Lg	G	IP	W	L	Pct	SO	BB	H	ERA
1951	Scranton, EL	27	172	13	8	.619	134	76	160	3.30
1952	Lvl, AA	2	12	1	0	1.000	7	6	17	6.00

Year	Team, Lg	G	IP	W	L	Pct	SO	BB	H	ERA
	Albany, EL	5	17	1	2	.333	6	14	15	3.71
	Roanoke, Pd.	11	36	1	5	.167	35	37	35	6.00
1953	Lvl, AA	12	42	1	4	.200	23	17	45	3.86
1954		23	38	1	2	.333	28	27	34	3.79
1955		42	108	7	5	.583	91	59	112	4.25
1956	SF, PCL	33	174	9	10	.474	107	94	171	4.44
1957		36	191	13	10	.565	120	74	183	3.35
1958	Bos., AL	17	67	4	3	.571	43	45	61	3.76
	Mpls., AA	13	73	6	4	.600	61	29	69	2.47
1959	Chi., NL	1	1	0	0	—-	0	1	5	54.00
	Cle., AL	12	29	0	1	.000	17	12	31	5.27
	SD, PCL	11	71	4	4	.500	59	25	65	3.04
1960	Tor, IL	28	166	14	6	.700	142	114	143	3.04
1961		34	170	9	11	.450	167	115	132	3.65
1962	Col., AA	27	158	9	10	.474	121	87	140	4.61
1963	Ark/Atl, SA	35	121	5	11	.313	116	65	110	2.98

JACK SPRING
Seals 1957

I saw Jack Spring pitch twice for the Seals in 1957. He started both games. I don't remember how far he went — neither was a complete game — but he won them both. He was one of the team's better pitchers that year; his 11–9 record was the second best among the team's starters.

After that season, both he and I moved on. I went to southern California to live and he went further east to pitch, but he, too, ended up in southern California a few years later, with the Los Angeles Angels. Not the *real* ones, but the expansion major league Angels. And I saw him pitch again, several times, but not as a starter. I probably saw him five times in 1962, but never did I see him pitch a full inning. Frequently he faced only one batter.

Spring spent the better parts of ten seasons in the minor leagues, primarily as starter. He was good; he made all-star teams in three leagues. But in trials with the Phillies, Red Sox, and Senators, he could not stick as a major league starter.

With the Angels, however, manager Bill Rigney cast him in a different role. He made him into one of the very first *short* relievers, stressing the "short." Among the more productive hitters in the American League in the early 1960s were such lefthanded swingers as Roger Maris, Yogi Berra, Norm Cash, Jim Gentile, Carl Yastrzemski, Pete Runnels, Vic Wertz, and so on.

Jack Spring (courtesy Robert Zwissig).

Frequently this would be Spring's only job: to face one of these men. He did this job well, too. It was common to see in the box scores of the early '60s this line following his name: "⅓ — 0 — 0 — 0 — 0 — 0".

In the Angels' surprising third-place finish in 1962, only their second year of existence, Rigney credits Spring with playing a major role. In referring to that season, Rigney said, "I used him to get a lefthander out and he got just *every* one of them."

Because of this proficiency in getting lefty batters out, Spring had the lowest ratio of innings pitched to games (1.2:1) of anyone who ever played major league ball (minimum 150 games) until the late 1980s, when it became common to use pitchers in the manner in which Rigney used him.

BK: In 1963 you became the second pitcher in history to spend a full year with a team and have fewer innings than games. How did you feel being used that way?

JACK SPRING: At the time, I didn't even realize it until the season was nearly over that I was pitching that few innings in that many games. I've always wondered if it was a record.

I enjoyed it. I took it as a challenge and I felt like I did my job. I didn't have any problems with it. I never complained about innings. I thought Bill [Rigney] used me very appropriately.

BK: What did you think of Rigney as a manager?

JS: I thought he was outstanding, possibly because he gave me the greatest opportunity that I'd had in the major leagues and used me in the way that I was probably best suited, with the ability I had. I admired him. I thought he was a real people's person, I thought he was well liked by all the players, I thought he handled both the regulars and the guys that weren't playing so much and everybody knew their role. I thought he was one of the finest managers I played for.

BK: In the minors you had been a successful starter. How did the transition to the bullpen suit you at first?

JS: Looking back on it, I guess I wish that I would have made the transition sooner. Maybe I would have reached the major leagues sooner than I did and gotten in more years than I did.

I found out, kind of by accident, that I could pitch almost every day. A lot of guys can't; they pitch one day and they can't pitch for two or three. But I found that if I pitched no more than, say, two or three innings, I could pitch again the next day. I don't know the scientific reason, but I do know there are some guys that can pitch every day and there are some guys that just can't do it. They're stiff and sore for a day or two after they pitch. I never had that problem.

I liked relieving after I got into it better than I did starting. The reason I liked it was I liked the challenge and I liked the feeling that every day I came to the ballpark that I was probably going to be in the game. Even if I wasn't in the game, my head had to be in it because I had to have myself mentally prepared for it. That part of it I really liked and, looking back, I wish that I would have tried it sooner. I think I was suited to it, probably more so than as a starter, even though, as you say, I did have some success as a starter.

When I came to the Angels in '61 I started some games and won three or four games. I'm pretty sure all those were in starts.

BK: You had four starts that year and went 3-and-0 as a starter.

JS: I won my first major league game there. I beat Kansas City and then I beat Chicago. I remember those, but I don't remember who I beat in the other game.

I think it was the next spring that it was obvious if I was going to make that team, it was going to be in the bullpen. That's when I really found out that I could pitch a lot.

BK: What pitches did you throw?

JS: I was a pretty generic pitcher. I was sneaky fast, but I think my best asset was my control. Lefthanders, of course, are notoriously wild and I wasn't that wild. I threw a changeup and late in my career I started throwing a slider, but I didn't throw it a lot, and, of course, a curveball. The four generic pitches, but if I was gonna get you out it was gonna be a fastball to a spot.

BK: Historically, lefthanded pitchers are brought in to face lefthanded hitters, but you had *much* better luck than most.

JS: My control was pretty good; I could always pitch in and out. Nowadays, with computers and everything, they can tell what the batting averages were — lefthanders versus lefthanders and so on. I'd be interested to know what that was.

I just always felt comfortable against lefthanded hitters and had good luck against some pretty good ones.

BK: Who was the toughest batter for you?

JS: There were a lot of good hitters in the league in those days, but there's no question. The *toughest* out for me in the American League was Al Kaline.

One of the highlights of my career was facing Al Kaline with the bases loaded and one out. I can't remember why Rigney left me in there in that kind of spot. [Laughs] He [Kaline] hit a screaming line drive that the shortstop, Jim Fregosi, snagged and doubled a guy off second to end the inning. That's the only time, honest to God, that I can ever remember getting him out.

I faced him quite a bit. McAuliffe hit ahead of him and Cash behind him — two lefthanders — and I'd come in to face the first one and stay for Cash, so I got to face Kaline more than I did a lot of righthanders.

BK: Who was the best hitter you saw?

JS: That's an easy question. Ted Williams is the greatest hitter I ever saw. I was a teammate of his in spring training a couple of years and I did go north with the Red Sox in 1957, the year I got sent out to San Francisco. I got to observe him and watch him hit in a few games.

One that stands out — we went out west to Arizona and we played Cleveland. Herb Score was at his prime and he pitched against us — seven or eight innings. We had two hits off of him and Williams had both of 'em; one was a long home run and the other was a line drive single.

Just watching him in batting practice, you'd see the concentration he had. One of my most cherished personal possessions is a newspaper article written by a guy with the Sarasota newspaper. Ted Williams and myself and several other players that didn't travel to a spring training game away were there. I was pitching batting practice to him and Sammy White was catching and we were working on him; in other words, we were calling pitches. The writer put in a little bit of the dialogue. When I'd make a nice pitch, Williams would complement me. It's a real keepsake.

He's the best natural hitter, the best student of hitting, that I've ever been around.

BK: Who was the best pitcher?

JS: That's a very difficult question. I saw a lot of good pitchers.

As a teammate for a couple of years, Dean Chance with the Angels was an outstanding pitcher. He was especially tough on the Yankees.

Whitey Ford, he was an outstanding pitcher. I saw Herb Score a little bit; he was a great pitcher with great stuff. He probably had the best
arm that I saw. Those were a couple that come to mind.

There was another that was really, really tough and was consistently
a good pitcher: Jim Kaat when he was at Minnesota. He was a tough
pitcher, a great fielder, and a great hitter — just an all-around great player
for a pitcher. He could beat you more ways than one.

BK: A teammate of yours with the Angels occasionally looked as if
he was going to set the world on fire. Ken McBride.

JS: Yeah. He came to mind when you asked that question. Ken
McBride's problem was that he was a sinkerball pitcher — he had probably the best sinkerball that I've ever seen outside of Mel Stottlemyre —
but if his mechanics weren't just perfect he would lose his sinker, or it
wouldn't be as good some days. I think that prevented him from maybe
being as effective as he might have been. But he was a fine pitcher and,
ooh, when he had his sinker going, there wasn't anybody that could beat
him.

I remember he used to work very hard between starts to be very care-
ful when he was warming up or throwing on the side not to get out of
synch, to keep his rhythm and his same release. That sinkerball was his
bread-and-butter.

I remember one of the funniest things; it wasn't funny at the time,
but rather ironic. We were in Washington. They brought him out of the
game and put a relief pitcher in. It wasn't me. [Laughs] He had a one-run
lead, two men on, and two men out in the ninth.

There was a ground ball to the left side of the infield. The infielder
picked the ball up and threw to second for the force out — a simple play,
but he threw it into right field. The runner kept on going around third.
The outfielder picked the ball up in right field, threw it over third base
and the ball bounced into our dugout and landed in Ken McBride's lap
and both runs scored. [Laughs] So Kenny carries the ball away; you know,
it's usually in the hands of the winning pitcher.

BK: You mentioned Jim Kaat's hitting. You had three hits in your
major league career and you spaced them out pretty evenly.

JS: [Laughs] Yeah. They wouldn't let me bat much.

I remember one of 'em real well because it was off one of my idols—
Robin Roberts. I got a basehit by Brooks Robinson; he was playing so far
off the line, he knew I couldn't pull the ball. I hit the ball right by third
base down in the corner and I managed to keep it to a single.

When I was a rookie I came up with the Phillies and went north with
them in '55 and Robin Roberts was there. I probably should have included

him as one of the great pitchers. I went to spring training with him twice and he was a great pitcher.

My other favorite hit isn't in the book. I got a basehit off of Sandy Koufax in an exhibition game. He hung a curveball up over my hat and I swung where he was throwing and got a hit. [Laughs]

BK: Were you originally signed by the Phillies?

JS: Yes and no. I signed with the Spokane Indians, an independent club in my hometown. It was in the Class B Western International League. My second year that I was there, the Philadelphia Phillies came in with a working agreement with Spokane.

Looking back on it, I'm pretty sure I know why they did it. There was another fellow by the name of Ed Bouchee. He and I were high school buddies. We had a big impact on one another. He signed first and I signed about four days later.

Don Osborne signed me. He was pitching coach for Pittsburgh later. I kind of think that the Phillies kind of recognized that Ed and I were prospects, so they came in with the agreement probably to obtain our contracts. The end of that year they officially purchased my contract and I became property of the Phillies at the end of my second year.

BK: Bouchee could hit the ball a long way.

JS: A *great* natural hitter. Each step that he went up, whether it was Little League to American Legion to high school to college, he could really hit the ball. He remains one of my good friends. I see him about every other year; he lives in Chicago now.

BK: I seem to remember that he found the glove to be a little inconvenient.

JS: Yeah. He was a big boy, probably 220 to 230 pounds. He was no gazelle. [Laughs] But he could hit the ball.

BK: What were your feelings when the Angels drafted you? You had been up and down for several years at that point.

JS: I was realistic enough to realize I was a marginal major league player and, quite frankly, maybe I never would have had an opportunity if it wasn't for expansion. I worked hard and I wanted to play up there.

I had a couple of big disappointments. In 1957 with the Red Sox, it was my *biggest* disappointment. I pitched more games than any other pitcher in spring training. I was relieving and if that had worked out maybe I could have found out earlier I could be a reliever. I had an earned run average right at three; I didn't think I had the club made, but I thought I'd have to do something wrong to be sent out.

When the season opened, I pitched one inning and then was shipped to San Francisco. I pitched against Baltimore. I felt good about what I'd done and I was really shocked. But they had a lot of veterans on the pitching staff and, of course, in Fenway Park a lefthander was something they could do without. That was really disappointing.

I guess my other disappointment was in 1965 with Cleveland. That was my last major league stop. They sent me to Portland in late July or early August. We knew there was a player to go. I don't remember why we were a player over. Billy Moran, who was one of my close friends from the Angel years, had his bags packed the day that they were going to make the cut. [Laughs] He knew that he was leaving and they called me in and sent me to Portland.

BK: You weren't doing badly at all.

JS: No, I wasn't. Birdie Tebbetts was the manager. I said, "Birdie, what's the deal here?" He said, "You drew the short straw."

I didn't qualify for the pension in spite of all the years I've got in. I'm still about 60 days short.

I thought about my situation when I quit the game. I managed two years out here in the Northwest League, a rookie league, but the thought of starting all over again didn't appeal to me. At that time my kids were teenagers. Now, at this point, you wonder if you did the right thing. But I love what I'm doing now.

BK: You're a high school coach?

JS: I coached for about 16–17 years. I became a high school teacher and coach after I quit baseball, which I really have enjoyed.

I became the athletic director at this high school. That became a bigger and bigger job with the advent of girls' sports. Then I became the activity director, in charge of athletics and all activities. I had the fortitude to go to college in the off-season and get a degree so I could fall back on something else when I was not playing.

BK: Did you save souvenirs from your career?

JS: Unfortunately, no, other than autographed baseballs. I have a collection of autographed baseballs from many of the teams that I played for. The only one I have that I think might be of some value is the 1964 Cardinals. I was traded to the Cardinals with Lou Brock and I was only there for about a month when they sent me down. I refused to go and went home and ended up in Hawaii of the Pacific Coast League. The Cardinals were World Series champions that year. Stan Musial's on it [the ball], although he wasn't a player; he was a kind of unofficial coach.

BK: Would you do it all again?

JS: Oh, yes. God, yes! I didn't make a lot of money — my highest salary was about 22,000 — but I made a lot of friends and I had a lot of fun. My wife and I reminisce about this every once in a while and it's one of the things that makes me wonder if I should've stayed in it.

Absolutely no regrets. I heard a lot of guys say, "I hope it rains today," and I can honestly say that I never ever felt that way. I looked forward to every day. That's one of the things that disappointed me about some major leaguers; they never appreciated what was happening to them. But I did. I would do it again in a minute. No different.

JACK RUSSELL SPRING
Born March 11, 1933, Spokane, WA
Ht. 6'1" Wt. 175 Batted Right, Threw Left

Year	Team, Lg	G	I	W	L	Pct	SO	BB	H	ERA
1952	Spokane, WI	21	90	6	5	.545	84	60	88	3.20
1953		27	188	14	8	.636	157	94	173	4.02
1954	Syracuse, IL	28	118	3	10	.231	42	37	127	3.13
1955	Syracuse, IL	39	135	7	8	.467	55	44	145	4.00
	Phi., NL	2	3	0	1	.000	2	1	2	6.00
1956	Miami, IL	30	93	6	6	.500	47	38	105	4.06
1957	Boston, AL	1	1	0	0	—	2	0	0	0.00
	SF, PCL	28	169	11	8	.550	72	53	183	3.19
1958	Mnpls, AA	22	49	1	3	.250	21	25	50	4.41
	Wash., AL	3	7	0	0	—	1	7	16	14.14
	SD, PCL	9	48	2	1	.667	22	10	43	3.00
1959	Dallas, AA	39	238	15	13	.536	97	62	239	2.87
1960	Dal-FtW, AA	26	120	5	11	.313	60	31	160	4.50
1961	Dal-FtW, AA	24	128	8	7	.533	64	28	146	4.01
	LA, AL	18	38	3	0	1.000	27	15	35	4.26
1962	LA, AL	57	65	4	2	.667	31	30	66	4.02
1963		45	38	3	0	1.000	13	9	40	3.08
1964	LA, AL	6	3	1	0	1.000	0	3	3	3.00
	StL/Chi, NL	9	9	0	0	—	1	3	12	3.77
	Hawaii, PCL	30	47	3	3	.500	36	13	39	2.11
1965	Sea/Prt, PCL	33	55	5	3	.625	54	14	56	3.76
	Clev'land, AL	14	22	1	2	.333	9	10	21	3.68
1966	Portl'nd, PCL	59	88	4	1	.800	62	24	89	2.97
1967		69	92	10	5	.667	73	32	72	2.45
1968		43	71	2	5	.286	49	17	91	4.06
1969	Sp'k'ne, PCL	52	65	5	6	.455	32	21	85	4.29

BERT THIEL

Seals 1957

Unfortunately, the Seals went out as losers. The final double header of their history was lost to the Sacramento Solons on September 15, 1957, the final day of the season, but the pennant had been clinched on the previous Friday, when they won their 100th game of the year. The first game of the final day was decided on a ninth-inning, two-run home run by Solons' pinch hitter Lenny Neal off Jack Spring, who pitched the whole game for the Seals. The Solons won, 5–4.

The very last game really shouldn't count; it was played for fun and no one, on the Seals, at least, took it seriously. The announcement that the New York Giants were going to be the San Francisco Giants in 1958 had already been made, so the world knew that second game was it for the Seals.

Bert Thiel (courtesy Robert Zwissig).

On the day before, however, Saturday, September 14, 1957, there were still more games to play. With the pennant clinched, manager Joe Gordon gave the ball to a pitcher who had not started a game all year, but who had been a successful starter in the minor leagues for a decade. He was Bert Thiel, who just the year before had won 18 games with Dallas in the Texas League.

The Red Sox drafted him after that season and envisioned him as a reliever, so that was the role in which he was used in 1957. That is, until that Saturday. Thiel showed he was still capable of starting, hurling a 3–2 complete game victory over the Solons. He will always be the last pitcher to win a game for the Seals.

It was Thiel's only start of the season and it took 11 innings to down the Sacramento Solons, 3–2.

Bill Renna's sacrifice fly drove in Pumpsie Green in the first inning for the Seals and the Solons tied it in the fourth when Lenny Neal drove in Al Heist. Tied at 1-apiece after nine innings, Sacramento took the lead in the top of the 11th on Heist's 8th home run of the year.

In the bottom of the inning, pinch hitter Sal Taormina drove in Albie Pearson and moved Renna, who had singled, to third. Then, with two outs, Nini Tornay singled to right to score Renna for the win.

Sacramento

	AB	R	H	RBI
Agosta, 2b	4	0	0	0
Heron, 3b	4	0	0	0
Westlake, 1b	4	0	1	0
Greengrass, rf	4	0	0	0
Heist, cf	4	2	1	1
Rushing, lf	4	0	1	0
Righetti, ss	5	0	1	0
Neal, c	4	0	1	1
Stanka, p	4	0	1	0
	37	2	6	2

San Francisco

	AB	R	H	RBI
Sadowski, ss	5	0	0	0
Green, 2b	5	1	2	0
Pearson, cf	5	1	2	0
Kellert, 1b	1	0	0	0
Stringer, 1b	2	0	0	0
Renna, lf	4	1	1	1
Sullivan, rf	4	0	0	0
Taormina, ph	1	0	1	1
Umphlett, 3b	3	0	1	0
Tornay, c	5	0	2	1
Thiel, p	4	0	0	0
	40	3	9	3

Pitching	IP	H	R	ER	SO	BB
Stanka, (L, 10–14)	10.2	9	3	3	5	2
Thiel (W, 5–4)	11	6	2	2	6	3

Sac	000	100	000	01	2	6	1
SF	100	000	000	02	3	9	0

E: Heron. LOB: Sac 8, SF 9. 2B: Rushing, Stanka. HR: Heist (8). Sac: Heron, Greengrass. SF: Renna. Umpires: Muttart, Orr, and Pelekoudas. Time: 2:03. Att: 6,120.

Thiel was signed by the Boston Braves in 1947 after he left the service. He was a 20-game winner in 1948 and in other years he won 18, 16, 15, and 14, all as a starter. As he points out below, he had only one losing season in his career and that was when he had arm trouble. Even then, he won 9 and lost 10.

He was up with the Braves briefly in 1952, but never had another shot. One would think that a consistent winner would at least be given a long look somewhere along the line.

BK: Talk about that last year of the Seals.

BERT THIEL: We had a good team at that time. We had Joe Gordon as the manager and we had a lot of veterans. Grady Hatton and Dick Phillips, Tommy Hurd and Harry Dorish. We just had a terrific ballclub. A lot of those fellas are gone already. We had a fine pitching staff: Kiely and all of them. It was just a great season. That was a good league to play in.

[Laughs] That's kind of an odd thing. You know, I'd always been a starter, even before the Red Sox drafted me off of Dallas in '56 and when

I went to San Francisco after leaving Boston they put me in the bullpen. I thought, "That's kinda odd. I won 18 games as a starter and now they put me in the bullpen," which was a lot different. I was a short relief man.

I always said to Joe Gordon, "Man, I can't figure out why you put me in the bullpen when I've been a starter all the years I've been playing." He said, "Well, that's what Boston wants," so that's what he did.

So the last day of the season he handed me the ball and said, "Okay, go get 'em for nine." And I did. I think it was 3–2 against Sacramento. I went nine innings and that finished the Seals.

The game didn't amount to anything. We had already won the pennant. It was a game just to finish the season.

I went to Minneapolis in '58. That's when Gene Mauch was manager.

I'll tell you one thing about that Seals Stadium. I live in the north in Wisconsin and that's the coldest place I ever played in. In the bullpen we had these big hoods on and everything. [Laughs] It was unbelievable.

But it was a good town and I really enjoyed it. It was a good town for food and we had a veteran ballclub. They knew how to play. It was just fun playing with a group of fellas like that.

We had Kellert at first base. Little Albie Pearson. He went from Oklahoma City; I pitched against him in the Texas League and he went up there. He was a good little ballplayer for his size. Renna, I think he was with us. We had good bats, good power. Aspromonte, second base.

We had Abernathie, Leo Kiely. They both had good years in the bullpen. Tommy Hurd and Harry Dorish, they were mainstays, too. Sal Taormina was a hometown boy. He was a good man on the ballclub. They just all did their job.

And we had a good manager, Joe Gordon. I think we had a coach by the name of Wright.

BK: Where did you live in San Francisco?

BT: Harry Dorish and Tommy Hurd and I, we stayed at a little hotel. I think it was the Spalding. The Spalding Hotel. We rode the [cable] cars down to the park and all over.

BK: The Boston Braves signed you originally.

BT: Yeah. I started in 1947 at Eau Claire in the Northern League. Chuck Tanner and I both started there in '47. I just got out of the service. I think I turned 21 in May.

From there it was quite a long road. Jackson, Mississippi, the next year. I was very fortunate; I had a lot of good pitching coaches and managers. Willis Hudlin and Bucky Walters and Charlie Root. You learned a lot from those fellas.

From Jackson I went to Hartford and developed arm trouble, then they operated on my elbow and it came out real good. Then I had a good year the next year at Hartford and then I went up to Milwaukee in '51. We had a *fine* pitching staff. We just had a great ballclub. Charlie Grimm was our manager, and we had Ernie Johnson. We just had a *great* ballclub. George Crowe, Billy Reed, Johnny Logan, Billy Klaus.

And then I went to play ball in Puerto Rico and had a great year down there. I think I won 15, 7 shutouts. Then I came back and they — Boston — sent me out after about a month-and-a-half to Milwaukee.

You know, there's funny things in baseball you gotta put up with. You're always a starter and then somehow or other they say, well, we'll stick him in the bullpen. Boston had a pretty good bullpen at that time, so someone's gotta go. After I had arm trouble I could get rolling as a starter, but it took me a long time to be able to pitch every day or every other day.

Then in '56, Dallas bought me from Toledo. I won 16 games at Toledo in '54 for a seventh-place club and never even got to go to spring training with a major league club. I enjoyed every minute, but sometimes you wonder why. I never had a losing year except when I had arm trouble in Hartford. 9-and-10. I always had good records.

I pitched two no-hitters. One at Milwaukee, the last no-hitter pitched at Borchard Field [in Milwaukee] and a no-hitter at Hartford in the Eastern League in '49.

Then after my career ended, I happened to get associated with George Selkirk, who managed me a few years in Toledo. He more or less took care of me after that. He was general manager at Washington and he scouted and was a pitching coach and all that. That was another fine gentleman.

I stopped playing in '59. I went down and pitched for Mel Parnell in the Southern League for New Orleans in '59. They had an independent club and I was ready to give it up and that's when George Selkirk, who was player development man for Kansas City and happened to be in Shreveport where we played and he just offered me a job managing and I just took it.

BK: In '61 you pitched a little with Pocatello.

BT: I pitched a couple games. We had kind of a mixed ballclub there from the Giants and Kansas City. I was in good shape yet and sometimes you gotta emphasize a few things to younger pitchers. A lot of 'em say, "I'm a little hurt and I can't do this. I don't know if I can pitch tonight." So I grabbed the ball a couple times and went out there, just more or less to show 'em that a lot of mental things are in the way of their growing up. You gotta do that once in a while when you're managing, you know.

They had good ballplayers. They had Allen out there and a couple of good hitters on the Phillies. They were on their way up. I found out it's a lot easier to pitch the higher you go up than it is starting out. You got better defense, you know the hitters. It's a lot easier.

My last year managing was at Dubuque in the Midwest League in 1974. 28 years I was in baseball.

BK: What did you do when you finally left the game?

BT: I was always a logger in the wintertime. I hit the woods with my dad and logged. That's probably what kept me in pretty good shape. It almost took me a couple weeks in spring training to loosen all the tightened muscles from power saws and all that, but I give credit to that for keeping my legs and everything in good shape and I had good stamina. I did that every winter.

When I quit, I still did it. In fact, I still go out and start that power saw just to listen to it run. [Laughs]

But we had a big family. We had to keep going. We had nine children. I had a lefthander, Kevin. The Angels drafted him. He developed arm trouble in the elbow and they give him like a Tommy John surgery. He was a good pitcher, but we should've waited and sent him to a junior college until he filled out. He had good stuff, one of the best pickoff moves you'd want to see.

We had four boys and five girls, so that's a team in itself.

It's a lot different today. I think we had more fun in our day and I think more competitive. And we had to play hurt. I tell you, I just can't imagine players today and their manager saying, "Here. Give me five good innings. We've got someone to pick you up." I never heard of such a thing. If it was a close ballgame — 2-to-1 — and that manager came out in the eighth, ninth inning to take you out, he had to pull you out with a team of horses. [Laughs] But the relief pitchers get so much pay today, I suppose that's their job. But I know Maddox, he lost about four games after being ahead in the eighth or ninth inning.

BK: Would you do it again?

BT: Oh, hey, yeah. You got a contract? [Laughs] You bet I'd do it again. Money never was a problem in our day. We didn't even argue hardly. We were just glad to play. And you never let too many people know you were hurt because you were just afraid you were gonna get released. You played sometime when you shouldn't've been playing, but it all turned out for the best.

I had a lot of good teammates. Billy Reed, I hear from him once in a while. He's from a little town ten miles from me. Bill and I played together six years. He signed with Boston, good second baseman at Milwaukee.

But a lot of 'em are gone. I was surprised to hear that Harry Dorish was gone. He was a good pitching coach. Richards made him a pitching coach and Harry was a student of the game. He was a good teacher and he made that slip pitch famous.

And Tommy Hurd's gone. And Murray Wall, he died quite a few years ago. Man, him and I were teammates for quite a while.

I had a good teacher at Milwaukee, old Emil Kush, who was a pitcher for the Cubs. He was a short man for us, but if you just sat and listened to those guys and if you didn't learn pitching from them you'd never learn it.

MAYNARD BERT THIEL
Born May 4, 1926, Marion WI
Ht. 5'10" Wt. 185 Batted and Threw Right

Year	Team, Lg	G	IP	W	L	Pct	SO	BB	H	ERA
1947	EauClaire,No	30	150	10	10	.500	77	45	146	3.60
1948	Jackson, SE	42	262	20	12	.625	110	70	276	2.99
1949	Hartford, EL	24	131	9	10	.474	49	44	137	4.60
1950		30	222	15	7	.682	114	49	246	3.65
1951	Milw., AA	36	153	14	9	.609	62	34	155	3.71
1952	Boston, NL	4	7	1	1	.500	6	4	11	7.71
	Milw., AA	33	99	8	6	.571	63	31	109	4.36
1953	Toledo, AA	18	79	5	4	.556	44	28	84	3.76
1954		31	201	16	12	.571	100	35	225	4.52
1955		46	124	6	6	.500	59	22	153	4.57
1956	Dallas, Tx	34	249	18	11	.621	113	56	230	3.11
1957	SF, PCL	41	110	5	4	.556	40	23	124	2.79
1958	Mnpls., AA	32	134	6	6	.500	50	29	153	3.76
1959	N.O., SA	27	167	11	10	.524	83	52	203	4.63
	CrpsChrst,Tx	2		0	0	—				
1960		did not pitch								
1961	Pocatello,Pio	4		2	1	.667				

♦ CHAPTER 14 ♦

The Fans Are Still Here

The Seals have been gone for nearly a half-century now, but the fans live on. We are no longer kids, but we were when we were there at Seals Stadium. Fifty years dims a lot of things, but a good ballgame played by a good ball team is not one of them.

Jay Berman of Manhattan Beach, California, saw games at Seals Stadium in the mid 1950s.

> I saw the longest home run (or one of them) by Luke Easter of the Padres against the Seals in 1954. He was only in the league that one year. The home run was a long shot to right field. I was amazed at the distance. That was a year or two before the Angels got Steve Bilko, so I hadn't seen too many like it. I'm sure it was 400 feet or so.
>
> I remember the big glass screen behind home plate, instead of a wire screen. I remember Leo Righetti, the shortstop and father of Dave Righetti. A good fielder. I remember a reliever named Adrian Zabala because he was a complete sidearmer. I had never seen that kind of delivery. Absolutely came completely sidearm. I remember a guy named Reno Cheso making a great catch. I can remember how Lefty O'Doul always got a huge hand from the fans. I hadn't seen that kind of thing.
>
> I remember the big beer advertisement across the street — a big simulated glass. I think it was Rainier at one time, but it was Hamm's by that time. I remember I was impressed by the park. Very clean. Very nice. Much more permanent than today's minor league parks.
>
> The pitcher I remember best from the PCL in the 1950s was — I think — with Seattle longer than he was with San Francisco, but he was a Seal, as well. His name was Elmer Singleton. It just seemed as though he was the ultimate Angel killer. I don't know what his lifetime record was against them, but I thought he was better than Bob Lemon or Whitey Ford or any of his contemporaries in the majors.

Seals statue at ThreeCom Park (courtesy Irwin Herlihy).

Bob Berlo now lives in Livermore, California, but was born in San Francisco in 1941 and lived there until 1962.

Neither of my parents was in the least bit a sports fan, but one of my aunts, who was a teenager when I was a child, was. When I visited my grandparents, also in San Francisco, if there was a Seals game on the radio my aunt would be listening to it. Of course, in those days, the late '40s, the away games would be recreated broadcasts, done by one of San Francisco's most famous baseball announcers, Don Klein. I recall that my aunt was a fan of pitcher Elmer Singleton. She later entered the convent and became a Dominican nun, which she still is.

After this start from my aunt, I listened thereafter to Don Klein calling the Seals games. I also picked up Oakland Oaks broadcasts. I was only barely aware of major league baseball, but I did decide to become a Giants fan when Thomson hit his shot, so I was delighted when the Giants moved to the city. I lived from 1942 to 1962 in the Little Hollywood district by Candlestick Cove, within walking distance of Candlestick Park. Having played baseball in the area as a kid, I could have told them about the swirling winds and how to track pop flies.

Sometime in the early 1950s, dairy owner George Christopher, later mayor of San Francisco, put on a special promotion in which, if a youngster sent in bottle tops from his milk bottles, he could get a pass that let him into the bleachers at Seals Stadium for nine cents. I did this, and thoroughly enjoyed going to Seals games. Using a San Francisco Municipal Railway school ticket, which cost 50 cents for ten rides, I could go to a Seas game for 19 cents—five cents each way on the bus and nine cents to get into the stadium. I did this any number of times. I still remember some of the players' names from those days: pitcher

Al "Inky" Lien, first basemen Mickey Rocco and George Vico, catcher Roy Partee, and, of course, the eternal manager, Lefty O'Doul. I never spent a cent on keepsakes, so I have only memories.

Jim Price is in the sports department of the *Spokesman Review* in Spokane, Washington, now, but back then he was in San Francisco.

> I remember two things about the Seals, both, as I recall, in 1951. One Saturday afternoon, about midseason, Chuck Connors—yes, that Chuck Connors—of the L. A. Angels homered into the park across the street from the right field fence, a seriously mighty poke.
>
> That spring, the Red Sox played a preseason exhibition in Seals Stadium against the Cleveland Indians, who still trained in Tucson. Satchel Paige pitched in relief, and well, and as I recall, Ted Williams had a single against the Williams shift.

Jim Healey grew up down the peninsula from San Francisco, in San Jose. He now lives in Aptos, California.

> As a San Jose resident I always rooted for the Seals. I loved going to Seals Stadium where you could watch the Hamm's Beer glass fill up behind the right field wall and the vendors dispensed soup on the cold nights. And after a win, you threw your rented seat cushion up in the air.

Irwin Herlihy grew up in San Francisco.

> My early interest of the Seals came from the radio or more accurately through the earphones of my crystal set. The first broadcasters were Ernie Smith and "The Old Walnut Farmer" Jack McDonald. I can still remember McDonald describe a home run as "out Aunt Fannie's window." Since most games were after bedtime, those earphones sure came in handy. I used to laugh at the recreated out-of-town games when I heard the same vendor voices and between-inning music at all the ballparks.
>
> Ballplayers came and went, either through promotion to the majors, retirement, or change in major league working agreement. No sooner had I developed a favorite but they were gone. Some favorites were Bruce Ogrodowski with his victory garden and bullpen rabbits, Pard Ballou, Don "Jeep" Trower, Dino Restelli, Jim Moran, Ray "Little Buffalo" Perry, Frenchy Uhalt, Brooks Holder, and Dario Lodigiani.
>
> Through it all there was really only one hero for me, that is until 1951. Lefty O'Doul was Mr. San Francisco Baseball. To a young fan he was everything you would ever want in a hero.

Always time to talk to a fan, give an autograph, or answer a question about baseball. How could they call my hero "Old Marblehead"? He was famous for waving his hankie to rattle the opposition. Actually it was a red bandana and I still use one in my jeans. Each year they had Lefty O'Doul Day. Kids had a chance to catch a baseball thrown in the stands. I never got a ball, but I still have the Lefty O'Doul miniature bat that they gave me.

And who could forget the years 1946, '47, and '48? San Francisco was always "The City" and Oakland was "The Place Across the Bay." Both cities had great teams and colorful managers: O'Doul and Casey Stengel. The rosters were stocked with great veteran players that had returned from the service. It was a boom time for the game and the crowds were record-breaking. When the Seals and the Oaks played each other they had a morning game in one city on Sunday and an afternoon game in the other city. Real fans would take the ferryboat across the bay. This enabled me to do something my father had done years before and had told me about many times.

The years 1949 and '50 were a disappointment and Old Marblehead was gone in 1951. I was crushed.

During the last five years of the Seals I grew up and joined

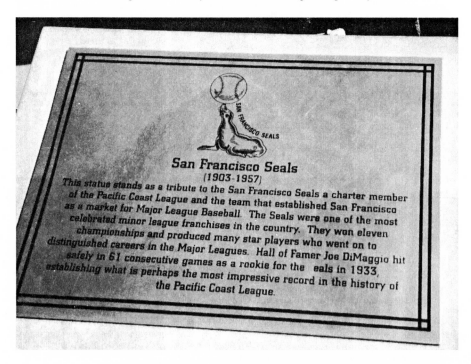

Plaque on statue (courtesy Irwin Herlihy).

the working world. No longer were my favorite players the Pards, Jeeps, and Little Buffaloes, but the Seals that I had played against in high school and American Legion. Now my heroes were Mike Baxes, Reno Cheso, Nini Tornay, Lowell Creighton, and Ed Cereghino.

Since 1958 I've been a season ticket plan holder (currently the entire season). Games at Seals Stadium, Candlestick Park, and now PacBell Park haven't allowed me to lose my feeling for the Seals and the old Coast League. I now hear "Bye-bye Baby" after a home run, but I still remember "out Aunt Fannie's window" and long for my Seals.

ROBERT ZWISSIG

Robert Zwissig is a native San Franciscan who still lives there. He has attended every San Francisco Opening Day since 1948 and even quit a job once when his employer was reluctant to give him that day off. His Seals memories pretty much cover the same period covered in this book, so he gets his own subchapter.

ROBERT ZWISSIG: They played double headers on Sundays. Generally off Mondays, then play on Tuesday, Wednesday, Thursday, Friday, Saturday, then a double header on Sunday. A seven-game series. Every Sunday either the Oaks were home or the Seals were home as a general rule. I'd get on a streetcar and meet a friend and we'd either go to Emeryville, which was easy to get to on public transportation across the bridge, or Seals Stadium.

I don't recall too much about the 1946 season when they won the pennant, but I do recall 1947. The Seals and L. A. were in a one-game playoff for the championship. I think it was zero-zero going into the last of the eighth. They were playing in Los Angeles. Jack Brewer was pitching for the Seals and Clarence Maddern hit a grand slam home run, followed by another home run, making the score 5-to-nothing. I cried myself to sleep. [Laughs] I must've been eight or nine years old at the time.

The Seals were in the community. The players were there. The second baseman lived across the street from me. Another guy with Sacramento lived up the street. The second baseman's name was Joe Futernick and his claim to fame was he was the first guy to lead the Seals in batting with an under-.300 average. I think he hit about .299, .298 [.291 in 1944].

Another friend of mine was getting phone calls from his parents because Bob Joyce had had the phone number before and people would call to talk to Bob Joyce. They were easily accessible and besides that, they had other jobs because they played ball six months and then they'd have to work six months because you couldn't exist on a baseball player's salary.

And the stadium. There was the Hamm's Beer sign and the Kilpatrick's Bread factory. When you walked in and walked up they'd have cushions on the right — the cushion concession — and then you'd walk up to the seats. The box seats were actually chairs. Most places have seats that are affixed. Each box had like eight chairs in it and you could move 'em around.

I think it was 1948. Bill Werle pitched a nighttime double header. He got a win and a tie. Double headers were nine and seven [innings]. Bill Werle became my mother's favorite player.

They used to have those *Call-Bulletin* fathers-sons nights. Preseason. Those were a big thing. They'd have drawings and things. That was always fun.

Remember Del Courtney? That was a trivia question: Who played for the Seals and the 49ers? It was Del Courtney because he had the band. He played down the right field line down from the broadcast booth on a little elevated section.

In '49 Luke Easter came to town [with San Diego]. That was something big. At that time African-Americans were called Negroes and I had never seen so many Negroes attending a game. Generally it was white. He was a big guy —*big* presence — and he was a good player. I remember walking to the ballpark and there were a lot of Negroes there. It was quite exciting. He was a huge drawing card

In Oakland — in Emeryville — if you sat on third base between home and third you could look out in the right field bleachers and you could see a group of people. I always wondered why they were sitting way out there, all those people together. Then the same thing in Seals Stadium. Up in the grandstand up between the left field wall and third base was a group of people. Those were the gamblers. If you walked by there you could hear 'em betting dollars, two dollars, anything you want on a pitch. The first pitch will be a ball or strike, he'll get out. [Laughs] There were signs around, "No gambling allowed," but they were ignored by these people.

After the game you were allowed to walk across the field. We used to park down the street. We sat in the third base boxes because Lefty O'Doul coached third base and the Seals' dugout was there. We'd walk around home plate and down the right field line — not on the field itself — and out the gate at the right field corner.

Lefty O'Doul was coaching third base and if the Seals started to rally he'd wave his handkerchief to try and upset the opposing pitcher. That became a tradition. People tried to start it when the Giants were here in '58. It quickly dissipated. It never caught on.

I remember when Paul Fagan banned the peanuts. What a controversy that caused here! People would bring their own and finally he had to relent.

Fagan built Paul's Porch. Used to be 365 down the line. Hell of a hit, high fence. Then he put the bleachers out in left field.

Dino Restelli's from St. Louis but an Italian in San Francisco—baseball and Italian went hand-in-hand in those days. Restelli went to the Pirates in '49. He had seven home runs in his first 12 games and there'd be headlines—big, almost like war declared: "Restelli hits another home run." It was headline news. Then somebody threw him a curveball or something. [Laughs] I think he'd been in the Navy. He came back and played for the Seals in '48 and '49.

There was a clock on the light tower in left-center. I remember what it said. It didn't dawn in me for while when I was a kid. It had the name of a funeral parlor; I think it was Dauphine's or something like that—a word I couldn't pronounce at that age. The clock was round and across the top of the clock was the name of the funeral parlor and under the bottom of the clock it just said "Eventually." [Laughs]

Chet Johnson went 22-and-13 in 1950. Of course, the season was 8,000 games long or whatever. He was here in '50 and '51. A couple of things he'd do. He was quite a character. During a regular game he'd get in the batter's box lefthanded and kneel down and take his bat and smooth out the batter's box, then take a big practice swing and point where he's gonna hit his home run, and then he would strike out generally.

On the mound he would look at the catcher and exaggerate and shake off sign after sign, reach into his back pocket, pull out an imaginary coin, flip it in the air, put it on the back of his hand, look at it, and then say, "Okay, we'll go that way." [Laughs]

When the Seals used to get major leaguers, what a thrill it was to see them. You thought because they were big leaguers they'd come down and burn up the league. Joe Page was down in '51 and Ewell Blackwell came down I think in '55. He was very impressive. He was here for a cup of coffee as they say, but his arm was gone since '47. He still had the same windup and delivery. Bill Bevens was here in '52 from the almost no-hitter [in the 1947 World Series]. Arky Vaughan in '49. Eddie Lake came down from Detroit in '51. I remember he hit 27 home runs here. He hit a home run to beat Oakland one night.

I had a paper route in those days and I'd get up at 4:30 or 5:00 and the first thing I'd do is go out to the curb and get the papers and before I'd do anything I'd read the sports to see what happened the night before.

In 1951 the Yankees had a working agreement with the Seals. They came here for an exhibition game. DiMaggio and Mantle were both on the roster at the time. The Seals won the game. The score was something like 15-to-4. In '51 the Yankees went on to in the World Series and the Seals finished last in the Pacific Coast League.

The Seals lost their first 13 games in '51. In the second game of a double header this .500 pitcher — Manny Perez — finally won a game.

Damon Miller was secretary of the club and he saved it for San Francisco with the Little Corporation. I have a stock certificate. I pleaded with my folks and they bought me a share of stock.

In '52 I remember Bill Reeder. Opening Night — Tuesday night — he had a no-hitter going into about the seventh or eighth inning and he finally gave up a hit. I think he was 2-and-9 or something that year.

Tony Ponce burst on the scene in '53. He won the last two games in a double header.

After that I remember Aspromonte and Albie Pearson and Frank Kellert, Frank Malzone — guys who became good ballplayers. Leo Kiely winning 21 games in relief.

The last double header Joe Gordon, the manager, played. It was played for laughs. There was a good crowd.

On Sundays they would usually draw about ten [thousand]. You could sit in the bleachers for nine cents, but I was a big spender. I sat upstairs in the grandstand for 50 [cents], which was a good deal. And it cost a nickel or a dime on the trolley to get down there.

My favorite players were Steve Nagy, Bill Werle, Dino Restelli, Bob Chesnes, Con Dempsey. Those were probably my favorite players. Jackie Tobin made too many outs for my satisfaction. I liked Dario Lodigiani; he played here and Oakland.

A friend of mine was a big Oakland fan and we had big Seals-Oaks fights here. I'd go to St. Mary's camp over in Moraga — summer camp with the Jesuits — and my cousin lived over there. We'd have water fights and pillow fights between the Seals and Oaks fans.

I still have great animosity toward the A's. People say, "Why don't you like the A's?" When I was a kid it was like Brooklyn and New York out here, if you can believe that. Everything that had to do with Oakland I was against and it works that way to this day. That's the way things were. There were Seals and Oaks and there was no in between.

Mickey Rocco, the first baseman, was one of my favorites, and Nick Etten played first for the Oaks at the time Rocco was here. He used to smoke a cigar in the shower. This friend of mine, the Oaks fan, we used to bet who'd hit the most home runs, but unfortunately Rocco was playing in Seals Stadium and Etten was playing in the bandbox in Oakland where the right field [fence] was so close you could hit a home run easily. Nicely hit a home run over right field there. That made headlines.

Gene Woodling hit .385 in '48. I remember his batting stance. I liked him. I think I liked him more in retrospect when he went to the big leagues than I did when he was in the Coast League. I always followed him playing for the Yankees and Cleveland. He was a good player.

San Diego had a wonderful team. They had Rosen and Suitcase Simpson. Minnie Minoso. Max West, Luke Easter, Harvey Storey. They were powerful.

♦ CHAPTER 15 ♦

Postscript

The Seals players scattered, but Seals Stadium stayed right there at the corner of 16th and Bryant streets. The Giants— now the *San Francisco* Giants— moved in to call it home in 1958.

The stadium was officially opened on April 7, 1931, with a win, 8–0, over Portland. The Seals lost the last game they played there on September 15, 1957, a 14–7 loss to the Sacramento Solons. The new tenants, the Giants, also opened with a win, 9–0, over the Los Angeles Dodgers on April 15, 1958. The last game ever played there was on September 20, 1959, as the old ballpark was closed out as a loser for the home team. The Giants fell to the Dodgers, 8–2.

Seals Stadium coming down (courtesy Richard T. Dobbins collection).

The DiMaggio Brothers at an old-timers game at Candlestick Park. *Left to right:* **Vince, Joe, Dom (author's collection).**

Demolition began a short time later, but the park lived on in Cheney Stadium in Tacoma, Washington. The seats and light towers were moved there in 1960.

Former Seals players played on with varying amounts of success. The last two to play were pitchers Jack Spring and Eli Grba in 1969. Grba sat out the 1968 season, then came back and made a token appearance for Lodi in the California League, so that makes Spring the last Seal. He spent the 1969 season in his hometown of Spokane, which at that time was a member of the Pacific Coast League.

Come 1970, the ballpark had been gone a decade and the last player was gone. But there would always be Seals as long as there were Seals fans and there are still Seals fans. We're a dying breed with no hope of a future generation. It was fun.

◆ APPENDIX ◆

Team and Individual Records

TEAM RECORDS

	Highest		Lowest	
	No.	Year	No.	Year
Games	230	1905	103	1918*
Wins	132	1909	51	1918*
Losses	117	1904	51	1918*
Pct.	.643	1925	.420	1929
HR	193	1929	9	1918*
			14	1944
Runs	1250	1925	364	1918†
RBI	1136	1925	575	1943
SB	413	1913	24	1953
BA	.319	1925	.226	1910

* Shortened season due to World War I
† RBI records not kept until 1921

INDIVIDUAL RECORDS

Batting

Hits	Smead Jolley, 309, 1928
Runs	Gus Suhr, 196, 1929
2B	Paul Waner, 75*, 1925
3B	Brooks Holder, 24*, 1939

279

HR	Gus Suhr, 51, 1929 (Recreation Park)
	Joe DiMaggio, 34, 1935 (Seals Stadium)
RBI	Bert Ellison, 188, 1924
SB	James Johnston, 124*, 1913
Total Bases	Smead Jolley, 516, 1928
BA	Smead Jolley, .406, 1928
Cons. Games	Joe DiMaggio, 61*, 1933

PCL record

Pitching

Games	Jim Whalen, 65, 1904
Complete Games	Cack Henley, 48, 1910
Innings	E. B. Erickson, 444, 1917
Wins	Roy Hitt, 36†, 1906
	Cack Henley, 34, 1910
Losses	Oscar Jones, 24, 1908
Pct.	Bill Abernathie, .867*, 1957
SO	Harry Suter, 339, 1911
BB	E. B. Erickson, 153, 1917
Shutouts	Sam Gibson, 9, 1942
ERA	Larry Jansen, 1.57, 1946
Cons. Wins	Frank Browning, 16*, 1908

PCL record
† *Some record books credit Hitt with only 32 wins in 1906.*

Bibliography

Dobbins, Dick. *The Grand Minor League.* Emeryville, CA: Woodford Press, 1999.

_____, and Jon Twitchell. *Nuggets on the Diamond.* San Francisco: Woodford Press, 1994.

Kelley, Brent. *Baseball Stars of the 1950s.* Jefferson, NC: McFarland, 1993.

_____. *In the Shadow of the Babe.* Jefferson, NC: McFarland, 1995.

_____. *They Too Wore Pinstripes.* Jefferson, NC: McFarland, 1998.

O'Connor, Leslie M., ed. *Pacific Coast League Official Record Book, 1903–1955.* San Francisco: The Pacific Coast League of Professional Baseball Clubs, 1956.

O'Neal, Bill. *The Pacific Coast League, 1903–1988.* Austin, TX: Eakin Press, 1990.

San Francisco Giants Official 1985 Yearbook. *A History of Baseball in the San Francisco Bay Area.* San Francisco: Woodford, 1985.

Snelling, Ken. *The Pacific Coast League: A Statistical History, 1903–1957.* Jefferson, NC: McFarland, 1995.

Spalding, John E. *Pacific Coast League Stars: One Hundred of the Best, 1903 to 1957.* Manhattan, KS: Ag Press, 1994.

Stadler, Ken. *The Pacific Coast League: One Man's Memories, 1936–1957.* Los Angeles: Marbek, 1984.

___. Donald R. *The Race for the Governor's Cup: The Pacific Coast League* ___ *1936–1954.* Jefferson, NC: McFarland, 2000.

___ ___d Mark Medeiros. *Runs, Hits, and an Era.* Champaign, ___llinois Press, 1994.

___ *n Francisco Chronicle.*

Index

Page numbers in italics have photographs

283